Critical Human Geography

'Critical Human Geography' is an international series which provides a critical examination and extension of the concepts and consequences of work in human geography and the allied social sciences and humanities. The volumes are written by scholars currently engaged in substantive research, so that, wherever possible, the discussions are empirically grounded as well as theoretically informed. Existing studies and the traditions from which they derive are carefully described and located in their historically specific context, but the series at the same time introduces and explores new ideas and insights from the human sciences as a whole. The series is thus not intended as a collection of synthetic reviews, but rather as a cluster of considered arguments which are accessible enough to engage geographers at all levels in the development of geography. The series therefore reflects the continuing methodological and philosophical diversity of the subject, and its books are united only by their common commitment to the prosecution of a genuinely human geography.

Department of Geography　　　　MARK BILLINGE
University of Cambridge　　　　DEREK GREGORY
England　　　　RON MARTIN

Critical Human Geography

PUBLISHED

Recollections of a Revolution: Geography as Spatial Science
Mark Billinge, Derek Gregory and Ron Martin (*editors*)

The Arena of Capital
Michael Dunford and Diane Perrons

Regional Transformation and Industrial Revolution:
A Geography of the Yorkshire Woollen Industry
Derek Gregory

Geography and the State
R. J. Johnston

Conceptions of Space in Social Thought: A Geographic
Perspective
Robert David Sack

FORTHCOMING

A Cultural Geography of Industrialisation in Britain
Mark Billinge

Development Theory: A Critique of Essentialist Approaches
Stuart Corbridge and Steve Jones

Between Feudalism and Capitalism
Robert Dodgshon

Regions and the Philosophy of the Human Sciences
Nicholas Entrikin

Strategies for Geographical Enquiry
Derek Gregory and Ron Martin

Social Relations and Spatial Structures
Derek Gregory and John Urry (*editors*)

Spatial Divisions of Labour
Doreen Massey

The Urban Arena: Capital, State and Community in
Contemporary Britain
John R. Short

Recollections of a Revolution

Geography as Spatial Science

edited by

Mark Billinge, Derek Gregory and Ron Martin

MACMILLAN PRESS
LONDON

First published 1984 by
THE MACMILLAN PRESS LTD
London and Basingstoke
Companies and representatives throughout the world

ISBN 0 333 27148 3 (hard cover)
ISBN 0 333 27149 1 (paper cover)

Typeset in Hong Kong by
Setrite Typesetters

Printed in Hong Kong

Contents

One Man's Quantitative Geography: Frameworks, Evaluations,
Uses and Prospects

Preface

The Critical Human Geography series has as one of its central concerns the construction of a genuinely human geography, and this means (in part) recognising that its concepts are specifically human constructions, historically rooted in particular social formations, and capable of – demanding of – continuous examination and criticism. This volume of essays has therefore been conceived to illustrate the importance of human agency in scientific change: to provide materials which illuminate both the boundedness and the contingency of research traditions and transformations in geography. Although it is concerned with a major episode in the evolution of post-war geography, the so-called 'quantitative revolution' which began to convulse the discipline in the 1950s and 1960s, it is in no sense a manifesto. We have provided no detailed commentary on the achievements of spatial science, and although the critique of positivist and post-positivist philosophy and the emergence of a neo-quantitative movement are important moments for critical inquiry that debate is more usefully conducted elsewhere. But we believe that the accounts which follow vitiate any representation of 'progress in geography' as an autonomous, disembodied process with its own internal, inexorable 'logic'; it is, rather, a history in which we are all implicated, and for which we are all in some measure responsible. And it is for this reason as much as any other that we have chosen not to offer any arguments of our own. To do so would be to impose, however tacitly, a pre-formed structure on to the text, whereas we prefer to engage its readers in a much more open (and, we hope, a much more honest) dialogue with the historical constitution of contemporary geography. The debate is in no sense closed around a privileged circle of participants.

In Part I, 'Reconstructions', we provide some outline comments on the ways in which a history of geography might be written, and on the overall course of the 'quantitative revolution'. These are intended to act as a counterpoint to the essays gathered together in Part II, 'Recollections', where a number of writers record their own experiences of those busy decades. There is no great mystery about their selection, and we do not claim that our sample is in any way representative. But all of these contributors readily accepted our invitation to write a short, autobiographical essay – many more did not – and their willingness to submit these private accounts to public scrutiny displays a collective generosity without which academic exchange would be utterly impoverished. Finally, Part III, 'Reflections', allows two authors to assess the impact and implications of spatial science from radically opposing perspectives, and to underscore the various ways in which the histories recorded in these pages are not closed around past or present, but resonate into all our futures.

We are deeply grateful to all of these contributors for their co-operation.

University of Cambridge   MARK BILLINGE
July 1983   DEREK GREGORY
                                                      RON MARTIN

List of Contributors

Contributors' names appear in order of appearance.

Mark Billinge is Fellow of Magdalene College and Lecturer in the Department of Geography, University of Cambridge.

Derek Gregory is Fellow of Sidney Sussex College and Lecturer in the Department of Geography, University of Cambridge.

Ron Martin is Fellow of St Catharine's College and Lecturer in the Department of Geography, University of Cambridge.

Harold C. Brookfield is Professor in the Research School of Pacific Studies, Department of Human Geography, Australian National University.

R.J. Johnston is Professor in the Department of Geography, University of Sheffield.

Richard L. Morrill is Professor in the Department of Geography, University of Washington.

Gunnar Olsson is Professor in the Nordiska instituet för samhällsplanering, Skeppsholmen, Stockholm.

Allan Pred is Professor in the Department of Geography, University of California, Berkeley.

Brian T. Robson is Professor in the Department of Geography, University of Manchester.

David M. Smith is Professor in the Department of Geography, Queen Mary College, University of London.

William Warntz is Professor in the Department of Geography, University of Western Ontario.

David Mercer is Senior Lecturer in the Department of Geography, Monash University, Melbourne.

Alan G. Wilson is Professor in the School of Geography, University of Leeds.

Part I
Reconstructions

Reconstructions

MARK BILLINGE, DEREK GREGORY, RON MARTIN

> There are all sorts of reasons why there is no past era one knows so little about as the three to five decades that lie between one's own twentieth year and one's father's twentieth year.
>
> ROBERT MUSIL, *The Man Without Qualities*

The history of geography is often represented as an intellectual arc descending from the past to the present, and its path is illuminated by a series of progressions which, characteristically, conflate historical relations and logical dependencies. Hartshorne's *The Nature of Geography* is perhaps the most obvious example. Its descriptive journey 'from Kant through Humboldt and Ritter to Richthofen and Hettner' is also, as Stoddart recognises, unequivocally prescriptive: 'the actors in the history are readily characterised into those who followed the track (and who were therefore right) and those who blundered off (and were hence wrong)'.[1] Much the same point was made by Gouldner:

> The search for convergences with and in the past...seeks to reveal a tacit consensus of great minds and, by showing this, to lend credence to the conclusions that they are held to have converged upon unwittingly. Convergence thus becomes a rhetoric, a way of persuading men to accept certain views. The implication is that if these great men, tacitly or explicitly, agreed on a given view, it must have a *prima facie* cogency.[2]

We have no sympathy with these manoeuvres, and the recollections gathered together in the following pages should dispel any doubts about the variety – and the historical contingency – of developments within post-war geography. Even so, there is still some justification for regarding all exercises in historiography as irredeemably normative. One does not have to accept Lakatos's insistence on the primacy of 'rational reconstruction' in the history of science – on 'the most important problems of external history [being] defined by internal history' through a prior commitment to particular 'logics of scientific discovery'[3] – to realise that historical inquiry is always in some sense 'interested': that an 'innocent' reconstruction of the past is impossible. And this is not simply a matter of the historian's own purposes, selections and emphases, as some commentators have supposed, but also (and more significantly) one of the necessary engagement of one system of concepts with another. The interrogation of historical discourse does not require us somehow to overcome the distance between one frame of meaning in the past and another in the present, to 'set ourselves within the spirit of the age and think with its ideas and thoughts', but rather to see 'the distance in time' as providing what Gadamer called 'a positive and productive possibility of understanding'.[4] In other words, the separations between past and present geographies are the very conditions of critical intelligibility, and properly understood they allow us to make sense of our collective biographies.[5] Such a deliberately creative mediation clearly entails the careful explication and examination of our own interpretative frames, and the purpose of this essay is to set out some possible modes of representing scientific change and, more particularly, of situating the historical constitution of geography as 'spatial science'.

None of this condemns historical inquiry to a formless relativism, of course; one history is *not* as good as any other, and the protocols derived from one programme are *not* entirely incommensurable with those derived from another. Some sort of comparative evaluation is both possible and pertinent, therefore, but in our view it cannot be purely intra-discursive. Our objection to Lakatos – and to other writers who have proposed similarly rationalist procedures – is a considered rejection of partitions between supposedly 'internal' and 'external' histories, in so far as these confer a privileged autonomy upon the domain of science. What Lakatos terms a 'rational explanation of the growth of objective knowledge' cannot be closed around and conducted through the rival claims of (say) inductivism, conventionalism or falsificationism,[6] and neither can it be confined to the disclosure of intra-discursive structures of (say) coherence and connection.[7] To widen the circle of intelligibility, and to insist on the salience of the extra-discursive social structures in which scientific knowledges are embedded, is not to assume that the relations between discourses and their constitutive social formations are simple and direct, and we certainly do not suppose that there is an immediate correspondence between them. We want to say, rather, that the constitution of 'science' is not independent of the constitution of society. Although it is necessary to specify the epistemologies which provide the logical conditions for particular claims to knowledge, these cannot legislate between competing discourses. As Scott has reminded us:

> Discourse is not different from and separate from society as a whole but is indeed fully continuous with the totality of social phenomena. There can be no special dispensation for discourse as somehow lying outside of a specific field of historical action, no matter what (intra-discursive) claims discourse might make for itself as a spontaneously generated entity.[8]

Discourse is not a free floating grid of intellectual constructs, therefore; however much a history of geography might be reconstructed in terms congruent with a *philosophy of science* (and the gains are likely to be considerable), it will also have to depend upon a *social theory* which binds the production and reproduction of discourse into the production and reproduction of society.

In 1962 T. S. Kuhn published *The Structure of Scientific Revolutions*, in which he proposed a model of the history of science as a discontinuous series of coherent, 'puzzle solving' frameworks – *paradigms* – punctuated by spasmodic 'crises' which restructured pre-existing conventions. More formally, a paradigm was supposed to consist of the working assumptions, procedures and findings routinely accepted by a group of scholars, which together serve to define a stable pattern of scientific activity and which in turn defined the community which shared in it. Kuhn argued that 'normal science' proceeded uninterrupted through the cumulative sedimentation of theoretical systems and empirical materials, until it began to be disrupted by a cluster of 'anomalies' which could not be explained away or subsumed within the existing framework. The 'pressure' was temporarily accommodated by 'extraordinary research' which, if successful, eventually produced a 'revolution' – that is, a 'paradigm shift' – which inaugurated a new disciplinary matrix.[9]

Some five years later Kuhn's arguments were first introduced into geography by Haggett and Chorley in their preface to *Models in Geography*.[10] There they distinguished a traditional, 'largely classificatory', paradigm which was 'under severe stress' – that is, the regional school's commitment to the Hartshornian orthodoxy of areal differentiation – and prefigured the emergence of a new, 'model based' paradigm which would be capable of structuring the expanding data matrix in a coherent fashion and in such a way as to accommodate future expansions. In some measure their usage was only gestural, in that while the distinction between 'normal science' and 'extraordinary research' was clear enough – a number of commentators had already underscored the 'revolutionary' character of the Madingley Lectures at Cambridge which were the springboard for the volume – the 'anomalies' within the traditional paradigm which were central to Kuhn's thesis were never identified in any detail. To be sure, the traditional paradigm was supposed to have been 'weakened' by both 'the explosion of the data matrix' and by the incipient disintegration of 'conventional vector analysis' (in other words, by the difficulties of explaining regional configurations in purely regional terms and the translation of systematic geographies into the domain of the systematic sciences): but neither of these pressures was shown to be an 'anomaly' in the Kuhnian sense. Even so, the direction of their argument was unmistakable. Geography ought to break decisively from its traditional preoccupation with the description of absolute spaces (regions), perhaps even to construct a 'general theory of locational relativity', and to concern itself with the rigorous analysis of 'distinctive geometrical forms with particular mathematical properties', whose unrestricted purchase would establish geography as a properly 'nomothetic' science.

In one sense, of course, such an affirmation of the protocols of spatial science was little more than an endorsement of Schaefer's much earlier rejection of 'exceptionalism', and his hypostatisation of 'spatial relations' as 'the ones that matter in geography, and no others'.[11] But what was uniquely formative about Haggett and Chorley's essay was that its use of Kuhn's terminology effectively obscured a series of continuities between 'old' and 'new' geographies,[12] and so confirmed the 'radical transformation of spirit and purpose' which Burton had seen in the 'quantitative revolution' as a *deep-rooted redirection of the discipline*.[13] This division was aggravated still further by Harvey, who suggested that the entire history of geography (and not just the convulsions of spatial science) could be represented as a succession of paradigms. Some authors have since distinguished a whole sequence of 'geographic exemplars' revolving around particular primary texts,[14] but for Harvey the object of exercises of this sort was not especially historiographic: their focus was much narrower, and they were directed towards the *present*. Their purpose was partly 'to help us to understand why we now tend to reject as intractable many of the problems and questions posed by, say, Ratzel or Griffith Taylor' – in effect, to emphasise that geography had already moved far beyond its traditional designations; notice that here, too, the stress falls on the incommensurability of paradigms rather than on the anomalies which fracture them. Of much greater strategic importance, it was partly to expedite 'the search of many geographers for some new paradigm' which, he freely admitted, *Explanation in Geography* was 'designed to promote'.[15]

These materials should make it clear that the use of Kuhn's scheme to characterise the 'quantitative revolution' is not merely, or even primarily, a retrospective codification: these notions had an extraordinary *contemporary* resonance. This is scarcely surprising. Kuhn's early writings were coincident with the first formalisations of spatial science, and one might reasonably expect those most concerned with effecting the transition from a 'pre-scientific' to a 'scientific' geography to secure their arguments with appeals to the history and philosophy of science. But other commentators have suggested other reasons. Stoddart, who had at the time explored in patently Kuhnian terms 'the potential paradigmatic value of biological models' in reuniting geography with 'the mainstream of [natural] scientific progress',[16] has since argued that:

The concept of revolution bolsters the heroic self-image of those who see themselves as innovators and who use the term 'paradigm' in a polemical manner.... Kuhn's terminology supplies an apparently 'scientific' justification for the advocacy of change on social rather than strictly scientific grounds.[17]

Views like these are hardly disinterested either, of course, but the presumed importance of the structure of the scientific community (rather than the strictures of a scientific programme) is exaggerated to even more telling effect in Taylor's caricature of the course of the 'quantitative revolution' in British geography. He suggests that the triumph of spatial science was won through four stratagems which are central to the successful transformation of any discipline. These revolutionary maxims, called from Johnson's earlier study of the Keynesian revolution and the monetarist counterrevolution in economics,[18] are: 'attack the old orthodoxy at its very core'; 'attempt to keep as much as possible of the old' but camouflage the continuities by 'giving the different parts different names'; 'include an appropriate degree of difficulty to make it unlikely that the "old guard" will be able to master it'; and 'incorporate an appealing methodology to replace the existing approaches'. The formal lexicon of spatial analysis provided the weapons to achieve each of these objectives. But reinforcements were necessary, and here Taylor casts the Kuhnian model in a vital, propagandist role. To describe the 'quantitative revolution' as a paradigmatic change 'immediately provides prestige by association since Kuhn's re-volutions are nearly all from physics', and so covers the corpus of spatial science with the cloak of scientific status.[19]

These arguments taken from the sociology of science are import-ant, although they are overdrawn and often confuse consequences with intentions; but they are not confined to the advocates of spatial science. Harvey used similar propositions in *Social Justice and the City* to represent the quantitative movement in geography 'partly in terms of a challenging set of new ideas to be answered, partly as a rather shabby struggle for power and status within a disciplinary framework, and partly as a response to outside pressures to discover the means for manipulation and control in what may be broadly defined as "the planning field" '. The last clause is a significant extension of Kuhn's original scheme, as we shall show, but in seeking to dismantle much of the scaffold of con-ventional spatial science which he had so assiduously erected a few years earlier Harvey continued to work with essentially Kuhnian tools. His starting point was a simple question: 'How and why would we bring about a revolution in geographic thought?' His answer was twofold. First:

The quantitative revolution has run its course, and diminishing marginal returns are apparently setting in; yet another piece of factorial ecology, yet another attempt to measure the distance–decay effect, yet another attempt to identify the range of a good, serve to tell us less and less about anything of great relevance. In addition, there are younger geographers now, just as ambitious as the quantifiers were in the early sixties, a little hungry for recognition, and somewhat starved for interesting things to do. So there are murmurs of discontent within the social structure of the discipline as the quantifiers establish a firm grip on the production of graduate students and on the curricula of various departments. This sociological condition within the discipline is not sufficient to justify a revolution in thought (nor should it), but the condition is there.[20]

This restatement of the importance of the structure of the scientific community was later formalised in Johnston's 'generational-cum-institutional' model of scientific change in post-war human geography,[21] but in Harvey's writings it was tempered by a second, and much more important, consideration:

There is a clear disparity between the sophisticated theoretical and methodological framework which we are using and our ability to say anything really meaningful about events as they unfold around us. There are too many anomalies between what we purport to explain and manipulate and what actually happens. There is an ecological problem, an urban problem, an international trade problem, and yet we seem incapable of saying anything of depth or profundity about any of them. When we do say something, it appears trite and rather ludicrous. In short, our paradigm is not coping well. It is ripe for overthrow. The objective social conditions demand that we say something sensible or coherent or else forever (through lack of credibility or, even worse, through the deterioration of the objective conditions) remain silent. It is the emerging objective social conditions and our patent inability to cope with them which essentially explains the necessity for a revolution in geographic thought.[22]

What is striking about this in Kuhnian terms is the clear (and unprecedented) admission of *anomalies* within an 'old paradigm', and the consequent identification of the 'immediate task' for geography as 'nothing more nor less than the self-conscious and aware construction of a new paradigm'. According to Harvey, this was to be accomplished 'by marshalling concepts and ideas, categories and relationships into such a superior system of thought when judged against the realities which require explanation that we succeed in making all opposition to that system of thought look ludicrous'.[23] The details of Harvey's own programme need not detain us here;

the critique of spatial science is now extensive, and it has had a considerable impact not only on non-quantitative research but also on the rise of a 'neo-quantitative' movement much more sensitive to post-positivist epistemology.[24] But rather more important for our present purposes is that Harvey, like his predecessors, uses Kuhn's scheme to argue for the supercession of one paradigm by another – and to buttress the transition from one kind of *absolutism* to another.

It is this more than anything else which has prompted a re-evaluation of the utility of Kuhn's writings. It is now a commonplace of historians of geography that its progressions – whether 'evolutionary' or 'revolutionary'[25] – were much more heterogeneous than these accounts allow. Johnston dismisses the Kuhnian model as 'irrelevant' because he can find 'little evidence of large-scale disciplinary consensus for any length of time about the merits of a particular approach, or of any revolutions that have been entirely consummated'.[26] Yet he seems to make some sort of exception of the 'quantitative revolution'. He draws on Kuhn's later writings, and in particular his key distinction between a *disciplinary matrix* (a general set of inter-subjectively negotiated means and ends endorsed by members of a scientific community) and an *exemplar* (an accepted 'model' application of the matrix to the solution of a specific problem), to suggest that the 'quantitative revolution' emerged from within the disciplinary matrix of traditional regional geography, only to develop its own distinctive exemplars which then successfully established a new and 'apparently' paradigmatic spatial science:

> A disciplinary matrix was assembled, and eventually codified by Harvey [in his *Explanation in Geography*], while early texts, such as Haggett's [*Locational Analysis in Human Geography*] provided major exemplars – as did the papers of Garrison, Berry, McCarty and others. The usual processes of normal science then operated, with the range of applications and the arsenal of tools being extended, thereby providing new exemplars. Comparison of the first and second editions of *Locational Analysis in Human Geography* indicates the extent of this normal scientific activity and illustrates the nature of progress within the paradigm.[27]

The historical and logical relations between 'matrices' and 'exemplars' are far from clear in this reconstruction, but in any event Johnston regards these sort of characterisations as inadequate, largely because they fail to account for the *plurality* of research traditions. His 'generational cum institutional' model is an attempt to resolve this by proposing not 'a major conversion of scientists from one paradigm to another at the moment of revolution' but instead a prolonged *stasis*, in which 'most scientists continue to work in the paradigm to which they were socialised academically.[28] In this view, 'conversion from one paradigm to another is comparatively rare' and 'a revolution only occurs within a discipline when a new generation of scientists, with its own philosophy and methodology, becomes numerically dominant'.[29] Whatever the merits of these arguments – and substantial objections can be registered against them, not least because they systematically misrepresent Kuhn's 'normal science' as a routinised and rigid *closure* and as such fail to explicate the intellectual trajectories of (to cite just a handful of examples) Kevin Cox, Peter Gould, David Harvey, Gunnar Olsson, Allen Scott and David Smith, all of whose writings disclose major progressions and transitions – their cumulative weight presses Johnston to reject the Kuhnian model as being at best of 'superficial' relevance to human geography:

Human geography has no single disciplinary matrix at the present time, therefore, and has not had one during the period since the Second World War. Rather there have been several competing for a stable position, if not dominance, both within the discipline and beyond. Each matrix has its own branches with their particular exemplars and their leaders who chart progress and seek influence over the whole discipline. At times the number of branches and their lack of cohesion, especially in the teaching sphere, may suggest anarchy. In a science about the complexity of people, and organized by complex people, perhaps the existence of such an anarchic situation (or at least the tendency towards it) is all that can be expected. There are schools of thought which wax and wane, some linked to others, some independent; but there is no consensus, no paradigm-dominance, only a series of mutual accommodations.[30]

This would perhaps be a remarkable reversal if Kuhn himself had not anticipated these same conclusions. Giddens has reminded us that claims of this sort, to the effect that social science has no 'single, universally accepted paradigm', are 'hardly illuminating', since one of the things which lead Kuhn to formulate the notion of paradigm in the first place, and to apply it to the development of the natural sciences, was his perception of deep-rooted disagreements about basic premises that seemed to him to characterise *social science, but not natural science – except in certain phases of transformation* [our emphasis].[31] There is surely no alternative, then, but to uphold Langton's summary verdict on Johnston's extended trial of the Kuhnian model: 'it is not surprising that disorder is apparent when the ordering principle turns out to be spurious'.[32]

This is not to exempt Kuhn from criticism, of course, and Stoddart's objections are of a different order: partly because he writes as a physical geographer committed to the philosophy and methodology of the natural sciences, but more particularly because he fastens on the debate between Kuhn and Popper as fundamental to an exploration of the limitations of models of paradigm change. He summarises their exchanges over the criteria for paradigm rejection as follows:

Essentially Popper emphasises the importance of methodological procedures, especially leading to the rejection of predictions rather than their confirmation, as the only sound criterion in science; whereas Kuhn's argument is concerned more with the changing attitudes and values of groups of paradigm adherents, not necessarily resulting from any demonstration of error in scientific terms. The problem is particularly intractable even in the more 'scientific' kinds of geographical work, such as quantitative human geography, where low-level predictions (called 'forecasts') are rarely used to test theory, and where the relationship between theory and reality often differs in fundamental respects from that in the physical sciences. . . . In its simplest formulation, the paradigm idea suggests the replacement rather than the testing of ideas, and by extension the replacement of practitioners also: in this lies the heart of Popper's criticism of Kuhn's thesis.[33]

Popper's critique was radically extended by Lakatos, who argued that 'mature' scientific progress, unlike the 'pedestrian' meanderings of 'immature' trial and error, was effected through competing 'research programmes' which could be adjudicated on the basis of the directed 'problem shifts' which they inaugurated. A series of scientific theories was to be counted as *theoretically* progressive 'if each new theory has some excess empirical content over its predecessor, that is, if it predicts some novel, hitherto unexpected fact', and as *empirically* progressive 'if some of this excess empirical content is also corroborated, that is, if each new theory leads us to the actual discovery of some new fact'. Unless a 'problem shift' satisfied *both* of these conditions it would be 'degenerating' rather than progressive: that is to say, it would be irrational and as such non-scientific.[34]

But these extensions, and others like them, change the very nature of historical inquiry. Their authors share a normative commitment to 'science' and its demarcation from 'non-science' which makes them immensely suspicious of standard narrative histories and, connected to this, of the admission of extra-scientific protocols into nominally scientific procedures. Their readings of Kuhn are in an important sense, therefore, avowedly stipulative: 'science' is defined by criteria derived from a (rationalist) *epistemology* rather than by canons disclosed through (convention-al) scientific *practice*. The two may, of course, be coincident, but in all cases epistemology provides the primary – and hence privileged – basis for what Lakatos, following Popper, regarded as 'the changing logic of scientific discovery'.[35] In effect, then, and as Barnes notes in an exemplary commentary, these writers:

> moralise with the term 'science' and about science. Accordingly, they tend to read Kuhn as a moralist also, and they dislike what they read. Kuhn does not make a satisfactory demarcation be-tween science and non-science; indeed, his work undermines any such demarcation, and consequently frustrates the grand under-taking of separating 'reason' from 'unreason'. If there are scientific revolutions, Lakatos points out, then the growth of knowledge is insufficiently determined by 'rules of reason'; it is then open to 'religious maniacs' to justify their irrationalism by pointing to its existence in science itself. Similarly, if normal science exists, then it is well nigh impossible to demarcate scientific from customary activity. Therefore, normal science must not exist.[36]

And it is substantially for these same reasons, we suggest, that Stoddart treats the Kuhnian model 'as itself an object of study, rather than a means of understanding the complexities of change', inasmuch as it 'supplies an apparently "scientific" justification for the advocacy of change on social rather than strictly scientific grounds':

> In this sense there is room for sociological inquiry into the extent to which the concept [of a paradigm] has been used in recent years as a slogan in interactions between different age-groups, schools of thought, and centres of learning, rather than a useful heuristic model of how and in what manner science is structured and change occurs. We might usefully analyse why some geographers choose to identify themselves as paradigm-changers at the present day, and whether, by their actions since 1960, they have so simplified our perceptions of the process of change that the paradigm idea comes to appear analytically useful. In other words, those who have propounded the Kuhnian interpretation have done so in ways which tend to make it self-fulfilling.[37]

There is indeed space for such a study, but Barnes insists that Popper and Lakatos are quite unable to furnish it: 'Popperian epistemology has fundamentally the character of a moral code; it has no sociological interest as an [empirical] account of science'. Lakatos's 'theory of scientific growth', for example, is *philosophical* and *prescriptive*, and a failure to recognise the significance of this is, Barnes contends, a serious category mistake:

> Historians have sometimes mistaken this for an empirical theory, and have attempted to test it against concrete historical materials, or to compare it with supposedly competing accounts like Kuhn's. What it actually involves, however, is the transposition of an empirical description – that of Kuhn – so that it no longer refers to the empirical realm. To quote Lakatos: 'my concept of a "research programme" may be construed as an objective, "third world" reconstruction of Kuhn's socio-pschological concept of paradigm'. Theories of the 'third world' apply to an independent realm of ideas, 'Plato's and Popper's "third world" ', wherein there occurs, not the growth of actual science, but the growth of a 'rationally-reconstructed' science.

Lakatos's 'theory of scientific growth' applies to a 'rationally-reconstructed' history of science. How, then, is this produced? The answer completes a circle: history must be rewritten so that it accords with Lakatos's theory – no matter that this involves writing false history, since the falsehoods will be the history of science as it should have been. Given this, it is scarcely to be wondered at that Lakatos's theory applies in the 'third world', since this 'third world' is actually designed to be in accord with the theory. It is a Platonic realm conjured into existence precisely to give Popperian epistemology something to refer to.[38]

In this sense, therefore, these 'rational reconstructions' are every bit as 'polemical' as Kuhn's: they are what Hacking calls *applied histories*, that is, 'the past applied to the solution of a philosophical problem'.[39]

It does not follow, however, as Barnes seems to think, that histories of science can be wholly indifferent to epistemology. Hesse maintains, quite properly, that it is pure idealism to 'abstain from evaluations of past science altogether and to attempt to understand it in terms of its own internal criteria and interrelations with the thought-forms of its age'. To do so would be profoundly 'unhistorical', she argues, since, as we have already indicated, 'the writing of history is a relation between two periods – that written about and that written from', so that 'historians of science need to recognise and to explicate various sorts of *rules of scientific inference* as these were consciously and unconsciously adopted *both in past and present* [emphasis added]'.[40] Central to Popper's discussion, for example, and hence to Stoddart's remarks about 'low-level predictions' in space–time forecasting models, is a particular view of the relation between theoretical statements and empirical observations: their whole conception of the hypothetico-deductive method and hypothesis 'testing' rests on a *non*-conventionalist, *non*-relativist epistemology. Kuhn's discussions, by contrast, are predicated on a different set of protocols, which are conformable with conventionalism and relativism.

But neither of these epistemologies can function as abstract and autonomous legislatures. Lakatos, for example, claims that:

Each rational reconstruction produces some characteristic pattern of rational growth of scientific knowledge. But all of these normative reconstructions have to be supplemented by empirical external theories to explain the residual non-rational factors. The history of science is always richer than its rational reconstruction. But rational reconstruction or internal history is primary, external history only secondary, since the most important problems of external history are defined by internal history... [that is] by one's logic of scientific discovery.[41]

This is a deliberate provocation of historians, of course, and those who have irritably championed 'historical logic' against 'scientific logic' no doubt deserve to have their noses tweaked in this way.[42] But the root problem is that, like other formalist procedures (including those which disclose the 'characteristic patterns' of spatial science itself), Lakatos's programme fails to disclose – to explicate and evaluate – its *own* logic. Now, as Hesse points out, one can accept without much difficulty the possibility of distinguishing between (say) 'the various kinds of rational rules adopted in a society on the one hand, and their conventions on the other. There may be hierarchies of rules and conventions, in which some conventions may be justified by argument in terms of some rational rules, and some subsets of those rules in terms of others'. All of this may be so; but 'none of these possibilities imply that rational rules go beyond social and biological norms to some realm of transcendent rationality'.[43] This is *not* to argue for a surreptitious determinism – what Hesse dismisses as a 'privileged direction of causality from substructure to superstructure'[44] – but it is to insist that the so called 'presuppositional approach' which some writers have proposed for human geography cannot be closed around a philosophy of science.[45] indeed, Barnes considers that the image of 'a ship of reason powering its own one way through a silent sea of social contingencies serves merely to discourage the study of scientific knowledge and judgement' for – and this is the heart of the matter – 'inferences and judgements in science are always structured by contingent features of the settings wherein they occur'.[46]

These 'settings' provide the fulcrum for the transformations of the Kuhnian model, although they are conceived in unduly restrictive terms: Kuhn does not say very much about social relations beyond the conventional boundaries of a scientific 'sub-culture', and so fails to clarify the social constitution of the sub-culture itself. What he does show, however, is that the paradigms which operate within it are constitutive of science – or 'give form to the scientific life' – in both a cognitive and a normative sense. They function:

by telling the scientist about the entities that nature does and does not contain and about the ways in which those entities behave. That information provides a map whose details are elucidated by mature scientific research. And since nature is too complex and varied to be explored at random, that map is as essential as observation and experiment to science's continuing development. Through the theories they embody, paradigms prove to be constitutive of the research activity. They are also, however, constitutive of science in other respects.... In particular... paradigms provide scientists not only with a map but also with some of the directions essential for map-making. In learning a paradigm the scientist acquires theory, methods and standards together, usually in an inextricable mixture. Therefore, when paradigms change, there are usually significant shifts in the criteria determining the legitimacy both of problems and of proposed solutions.[47]

This dual function means that the heterogeneous 'settings' of science provide different rules and resources for the constitution of different paradigms, so that they are *incommensurable*: that is, 'the proponents of competing paradigms must fail to make complete contact with each other's viewpoints' so that translation from one to the other is necessarily compromised.[48] This is *not* to say that translation is impossible, of course, as Kuhn makes perfectly clear; but he also makes it plain that 'languages cut up the world in different ways, and we have no access to a neutral sub-linguistic means of reporting', so that the evaluation of different 'language-games', and hence the switch from one paradigm to another, cannot be explained by what Barnes calls an autonomous, unconditioned 'reason'.[49] We use the term 'language-game' deliberately here. It comes from Wittgenstein's later writings, and particularly the *Philosophical Investigations*, where it is intended 'to bring into prominence the fact that the *speaking* of language is part of an activity, or of a form of life'. Early analytical philosophy had made the significance of a proposition dependent upon its logical form alone, and in the *Tractatus* Wittgenstein had argued that all languages have a uniform logical structure whose differences were simply 'superficial variations on a single theme', whereas ordinary language philosophy regarded the utterance of a meaningful expression as a conventional or rule governed activity which is irreducible to and refractory of any such essentialism. 'Nothing is more wrong-headed than calling meaning a mental activity', therefore, because meanings are embedded in and recoverable through the dynamics of 'language-games'.[50] These distinctions are rough and ready ones, but Kuhn's thesis is especially sensitive to them:

> The point-by-point discussion of two successive theories demands a language into which at least the empirical consequences of both can be translated without loss or change. That such a language lies readily to hand has been widely assumed since at least the seventeenth century when philosophers took the neutrality of pure sensation-reports for granted and sought a 'universal character' which would display all languages for expressing them as one. Ideally the primitive vocabulary of such a language would consist of pure sense-datum terms plus syntactic connectives. Philosophers have now abandoned hope of achieving any such ideal, but many of them continue to assume that theories can be compared by recourse to a basic vocabulary consisting entirely of words which are attached to nature in ways that are unproblematical and, to the extent necessary, independent of theory. That is the vocabulary in which Sir Karl [Popper]'s basic statements are framed. He requires it in order to compare the verisimilitude of alternate theories or to show that one is 'roomier' than (or includes) its predecessor. Feyerabend and I have argued at length that no such vocabulary is available. In the transition from one theory to the next words change their meanings or conditions of applicability in subtle ways.[51]

This much is agreed by most post-empiricist philosophies of science, and such a resounding rejection of empiricism (the corner stone of positivism) makes the employment of Kuhn to ring in the 'new paradigm' of spatial science all the more astonishing. There is far less consensus over the implications of these claims, but we want to argue that they need *not* underwrite a radical conventionalism. Rather, in Kuhn's own terms, the historical transition from empiricism to post-empiricism entails a redefinition of the meaning of 'objectivity'.

This is a complex issue, and we can do little more than summarise some of its main features. But the central point is this. Even if, as Bleicher shows, 'the normative function of paradigms precludes the possibility of judging their relative superiority from the outside, since that would constitute the unwarranted applicated of external standards originating in a different language-game',[52] this does not reduce science and its critique to an autism: to Scheffler's nightmare prison in which the practitioners of different paradigms are locked in separate cells, tapping their solitary messages on the bars in a babble of mutually incomprehensible codes. In this 'prison-house of language' a convict cannot be released from one sentence without being consigned to another.[53] But, as Bleicher recognises, science – like any other form of life – proceeds through the *articulation* of these sentences and the *mediation* of these language-games. They are not discrete and disconnected, because 'the process of learning a paradigm or language-game as the expression of a form of life is also a process of learning what that paradigm is not: that is to say, learning to mediate it with other rejected alternatives by contrast to which the claims of the paradigm in question are clarified'.[54] Thus Hesse, drawing in part on the writings of Gadamer and Habermas, represents science as a 'learning device' in which these 'dialogues' are themselves the conditions of objectivity; hence the:

> History of science, like all history, is in principle written anew in every generation. Historical interpretations are irreducibly relative to the historian and his time, but it does not follow that they are relativ*ist*, if by this is meant that there are *no* external criteria for the evaluation of past science. On the contrary, there are our criteria as they have emerged in the course of history. In our study of the science of the past we may not irresponsibly neglect them, for they constitute our side of an objective dialogue.[55]

This is clearly not what the empiricist means by 'objectivity': it provides no special dispensation for science. But neither does it privilege any other discursive space. If Kuhn wishes to claim that disputes between one paradigm and another 'are inexplicable by the logic of science, since they are precisely disputes about the content of that logic', and that for this reason they can be made 'intelligible' only by 'extra-scientific causation', then he must also accept that any such model of intelligibility and its representation of 'extra-scientific causation' will of necessity be implicated in these same historical reciprocations.[56] In short, these comments must apply both to the reconstruction of 'science' and to the conjoint reconstruction of its 'settings'.

Taken together, these materials suggest that the rules and resources which constitute divergent frames of meaning have to be grasped *contextually*; that science and its critique are *hermeneutic* tasks; and that in this sense they are indistinguishable from other social practices. In the language of polyhedral dynamics, the discursive fabric might perhaps be represented as a 'backcloth' over which nominally scientific propositions flow as 'traffic'. The routine transformations (normal science) and the spasmodic dis- placements (revolutions) of scientific practice are then moments in the production and reproduction of successive 'interaction structures' (paradigms), which are mediated by the continuous actions and interactions of knowledgeable human subjects within them and by what Layder calls the 'contextual structures' around them, which are indeed 'fully continuous' with the production and reproduction of social life.[57] If this is so, then it becomes possible to understand the fundamental opposition between Popper (and Lakatos) and Kuhn which, as Hesse notes, transcends the usual contest between rationalism and relativism.

> Those who ground their faith in universal rationality on a contingent belief that our language and science are somehow the high points of the historical evolution of ideas, are in effect progressive evolutionists with regard to ideas, while those who believe that social and historical analysis can provide a valid critique of even our own presuppositions, are nearer to the tradition of hermeneutics. And hermeneutics depends neither on uncritical analysis of our language as if it were language as such, nor on the incommensurable relativity of languages and forms of life, but on the assumption that cross-cultural understanding and self-reflexive critique are both possible and illuminating.[58]

These twin assumptions are deeply imbricated in the history of geography: as Tuan reminds us, 'to know the world is to know one's self'.[59] As we said at the very start, the separations between past and present geographies are thus the very conditions of critical intelligibility; they allow us to make sense of our collective biographies. If this is to restate Wright Mills's celebrated case for the 'sociological imagination', however, we would do well to remember that Harvey once called for the parallel exercise of a 'geographical imagination'.[60]

Notes and References

1. D.R. Stoddart, 'Ideas and interpretation in the history of geography', in D.R. Stoddart (ed.), *Geography, Ideology and Social Concern* (Oxford: Blackwell, 1981) pp. 1–7.

2. A. Gouldner, *The Coming Crisis of Western Sociology* (London: Heinemann, 1971) p. 17.

3. I. Lakatos, 'History of science and its rational reconstructions', in R.C. Buck and R.S. Cohen (eds), *Boston Studies in the Philosophy of Science*, vol. 8 (1970), reprinted in I. Hacking (ed.), *Scientific Revolutions* (Oxford University Press, 1981) pp. 107–27.

4. D. Gregory, 'The discourse of the past: phenomenology, structuralism and historical geography', *Journal of Historical Geography*, vol. 4 (1978) pp. 161–73; Hans-Georg Gadamer, 'The historicity of understanding', in P. Connecton (ed.), *Critical Sociology* (Harmondsworth: Penguin, 1978) p. 123.

5. For discussion of the potential of biographical approaches, see A. Buttimer, 'On people, paradigms and "progress" ', in D.R. Stoddart (ed.), *Geography, Ideology and Social Concern*; D.R. Stoddart, 'Ideas and interpretation'; for actual biographical materials see, for example, the 75th anniversary edition of the Association of American Geographers, *Annals of the Association of American Geographers*, vol. 69 (1979).

6. I. Lakatos, 'History of science'.

7. See, for example, B. Hindess, *Philosophy and Methodology in the Social Sciences* (Brighton: Harvester, 1977).

8. A.J. Scott, 'The meaning and social origins of discourse on the spatial foundations of society', in P. Gould and G. Olsson (eds), *In Search of Common Ground* (London, 1982) pp. 141–56.

9. T.S. Kuhn, *The Structure of Scientific Revolutions*, 2nd edn (Chicago: University of Chicago Press, 1970). See also his *The Essential Tension: Selected Studies in Scientific Tradition* (Chicago: University of Chicago Press, 1977).

10. R.J. Chorley and P. Haggett, 'Models, paradigms and the new geography', in R.J. Chorley and P. Haggett (eds), *Models in Geography* (London: Methuen, 1967) pp. 19–42. W. Isard and his colleagues have addressed themselves specifically to a general theory of locational relativity in a series of publications. See, for example, W. Isard and P. Liossatos, 'Parallels from physics for space–time development models, Part I', *Regional Science and Urban Economics*, vol. 5 (1975) pp. 5–40 and W. Isard and P. Liossatos, 'Parallels from physics for space–time development models, Part II: Interpretations and extensions of the basic models', in *Papers of the Regional Science Association*, vol. 34 (1975) pp. 43–66.

11. F.K. Schaefer, 'Exceptionalism in geography: a methodological examination', *Annals of the Association of American Geographers*, vol. 43 (1953) pp.226–49.

12. See D. Gregory, *Ideology, Science and Human Geography* (London: Hutcherson, 1978) and L. Guelke, 'Geography and logical positivism', in

D.T. Herbert and R.J. Johnston, *Geography and the Urban Environment*, vol. 1 (Chichester: John Wiley, 1978) pp. 35–61.

13. I. Burton, 'The quantitative revolution and theoretical geography', *Canadian Geographer*, vol. 7 (1963) pp. 151–62, reprinted in W.K. Davies, *The Conceptual Revolution* (University of London Press, 1970) pp. 140–56.

14. See, for example, M.E. Harvey and B.P. Holly, *Themes in Geographical Thought* (London: Croom Helm, 1981).

15. D. Harvey, *Explanation in Geography* (London: Edward Arnold, 1969) pp. 17–18.

16. D.R. Stoddart, 'Organism and ecosystem as geographical models', in R.J. Chorley and P. Haggett, *Models in Geography*, pp. 511–48.

17. D.R. Stoddart, 'The paradigm concept and the history of geography', in D.R. Stoddart (ed.), *Geography, Ideology and Social Concern*, pp. 70–80.

18. H.G. Johnson, 'The Keynesian revolution and monetarist counter-revolution', *American Economic History Review*, vol. 16 (1971) no. 2, pp. 1–14. Johnson's thesis had already been invoked by D. Harvey, in his *Social Justice and the City* (London: Edward Arnold, 1973) pp. 122–4.

19. P. Taylor, 'An interpretation of the quantification debate in British geography', *Transactions of the Institute of British Geographers*, new series, vol. 1 (1976) pp. 129–44.

20. D. Harvey, *Social Justice*, pp. 128–9.

21. R.J. Johnston, 'Paradigms and revolutions or evolutions', *Progress in Human Geography*, vol. 2 (1978) and R.J. Johnston, *Geography and Geographers: Anglo-American Geography Since 1945* (London: Edward Arnold, 1979).

22. D. Harvey, *Social Justice*, pp. 128–9.

23. D. Harvey, *Social Justice*, pp. 128–9.

24. See, for example, R.L. Martin, N. Thrift and R.J. Bennett (eds), *Towards the Dynamic Analysis of Spatial Systems* (London: Pion, 1978); R.J. Bennett and N. Wrigley (eds), *Quantitative Geography: A British View* (London: Routledge & Kegan Paul, 1978); and R.J. Bennett (ed.), *European Progress in Spatial Analysis* (London: Pion, 1981).

25. M.D.I. Chisholm, *Human Geography: Evolution or Revolution* (Harmondsworth: Penguin, 1975).

26. R.J. Johnston, *Geography and Geographers*.

27. R.J. Johnston, *Geography and Geographers*.

28. Such a claim, of course, does nothing to explain the emergence of different paradigms in the first place.

29. Johnston, *Geography and Geographers*, p. 185.

30. Johnston, *Geography and Geographers*, p. 188.

31. A. Giddens, *New Rules of Sociological Method: A Positive Critique of Interpretative Sociologies* (London: Hutchinson, 1976) p. 136.

32. J. Langton, Review of R.J. Johnston's *Geography and Geographers: Anglo-American Geography Since 1945*, in *Journal of Historical Geography*, vol. 8 (1982) pp. 102–4.

33. D.R. Stoddart, 'The paradigm concept', pp. 74, 78.

34. I. Lakatos, 'Falsification and the methodology of scientific research

programmes', in I. Lakatos and A. Musgrave (eds), *Criticism and the Growth of Knowledge* (Cambridge University Press, 1979) pp. 91–196.

35. See B. Barnes, *T.S. Kuhn and Social Science* (London: Macmillan, 1982). *The Changing Logic of Scientific Discovery* was the title of the book Lakatos intended to write as a development of Popper's classic *The Logic of Scientific Discovery* (London, 1959). He was prevented from doing so by his untimely death in 1974.

36. B. Barnes, *T.S. Kuhn and Social Science*, p. 59.

37. D.R. Stoddart, 'The paradigm concept'.

38. B. Barnes, *T.S. Kuhn and Social Science*, p. 61.

39. I. Hacking, 'Lakatos's philosophy of science', in I. Hacking (ed.) *Scientific Revolutions* pp. 128–43.

40. M. Hesse, *Revolutions and Reconstructions in the Philosophy of Science* (Brighton: Harvester, 1980) pp. 29–60.

41. I. Lakatos, 'History of science', pp. 123–4.

42. See, for example, E.P. Thompson, *The Poverty of Theory* (London: Merlin, 1979).

43. M. Hesse, *Revolutions and Reconstructions*, p. 56.

44. M. Hesse, *Revolutions and Reconstructions*, p. 56.

45. This is to reproduce the narrowness of Lakatos's perspective. See, for example, R.T. Harrison and D.N. Livingstone, 'Philosophy and problems in human geography', *Area*, vol. 12 (1980) pp. 25–31.

46. B. Barnes, *T.S. Kuhn and Social Science*, pp. 117–18. See also A. Giddens's theory of structuration, in A. Giddens, *Central Problems of Social Theory: Action, Structure and Contradiction in Social Analysis* (London: Macmillan, 1979).

47. T.S. Kuhn, *The Structure of Scientific Revolutions*, p. 109.

48. T.S. Kuhn, *The Structure of Scientific Revolutions*, p. 109.

49. T.S. Kuhn, *The Structure of Scientific Revolutions*; B. Barnes, *T.S. Kuhn and Social Science*.

50. J.B. Thompson, *Critical Hermeneutics* (Cambridge, 1981).

51. T.S. Kuhn, 'Reflections on my critics', in I. Lakatos and A. Musgrave (eds), *Criticism and the Growth of Knowledge* (Cambridge University Press, 1981) pp. 231–78; the reference to Feyerabend is to his *Against Method* (London: Verso, 1975) and *Science in a Free Society* (London: New Left Books, 1978).

52. J. Bleicher, *The Hermeneutic Imagination* (London: Routledge & Kegan Paul, 1981) p. 36.

53. I. Scheffler, *Science and Subjectivity* (Indianapolis: Bobbes-Merrill, 1967).

54. J. Bleicher, *The Hermeneutic Imagination*. See also A. Giddens, *New Rules*, p. 144.

55. M. Hesse, *Revolutions and Reconstructions*, p. 181.

56. M. Hesse, *Revolutions and Reconstructions*, p. 181.

57. D. Layder, *Structure, Interaction and Social Theory* (London: Routledge & Kegan Paul, 1981).

58. M. Hesse, *Revolutions and Reconstructions*, pp.57–8.

59. Yi-Fu Tuan, 'Geography, phenomenology and the study of human nature', *Canadian Geographer*, vol. 15 (1971) p. 181.

60. D. Harvey, *Social Justice*; C. Wright Mills, *The Sociological Imagination* (New York: Oxford University Press, 1959).

Part II
Recollections

Experiences of an Outside Man

HAROLD C. BROOKFIELD

I am, it seems, the only representative from among Third World specialists in this collection. My experiences of the 'quantitative revolution' are coloured by the fact that in the critical years of the late 1950s, when the pioneers of the 'new geography' were active on the far side of the world, I was spending as much time as I could in New Guinea, doing work that in its very different way was also well removed from the descriptive approaches of the timid 'possibilist' geography that then prevailed. Moreover, my time away from New Guinea was spent in a research school in Canberra where trans-disciplinary exchange was as important as intra-disciplinary discussion. Earlier, three years in southern Africa had already sharpened both my social awareness and my doubts concerning the value of geography as then practised.

My contacts with the 'new wave' were therefore delayed, and my reaction was influenced by the fact that the changes which I sought were of a different kind. I did not find it easy to come to terms with the new movement, and indeed I did not succeed. My experience with the later upsets in the discipline was of a different order, for I was by then in the North Atlantic heartland. I make no apology for inclusion of discussion of these later events in the account which follows, or for placing them in the context of political views concerning a disturbed and changing world. A quarter century of change in geography has not yet yielded a consensus. It has, on the other hand, yielded a greater degree of pluralism, and for this much we must be thankful.

In what follows I first offer a personal narrative, focused mainly on the few years during which my own ideas underwent the most rapid change, and in which my own career passed through two crises in which perception of my discipline played a major part. I then discuss the meaning of events in terms of ideas. In the end there is perhaps more of continuity than of new beginnings, a continuity certainly based in Third World experience.

My title seeks to reflect this. I do not claim either the physical stamina or the endurance under hardship of the 'outside men' of Papua, those government officers of the years 1918–39 who explored the interior while others worked from their desks. I was, however, 'outside' much of the ferment, and my one period of residence in a department renowned for its role in the revolution was unhappy and brief; I retired 'outside', or at least to the edges. But to say this is already to anticipate what must be said below.

Narrative

When I went to New Guinea for a long field spell in 1959–60 I took with me, along with other and lighter reading, Richard Hartshorne's then newly published *Perspective on the Nature of Geography*.[1] I wanted, I suppose, to find out what geography really was all about, having by that time come myself to the non-conclusion that it was no more than a point of view on subject matter common to a range of other disciplines. I read Hartshorne from time to time, and recall one Sunday afternoon as the sun sank behind the mountains across the valley, muttering to myself that the 'chorological' approach said nothing to me; if this was geography, then I was not a geographer.

Though I can trace origins back to early work in Ireland, Africa and Mauritius, it was during that field spell that my concern with process in man–environment relations first took clear shape. A year later, in a seminar at University College London, I trailed my coat by offering a paper concerned entirely with process and not at all with differentiation. One member of the audience, who shall remain nameless, confirmed for me my fear that this was 'not geography'. Undeterred, I soon afterwards began to write what became a long series of papers and other statements arguing for a process-orientated discipline in which the question 'How?' should be at least as important as the question 'Why?'. Much later, I carried the same basic approach into the inter-disciplinary context of UNESCO's Man and the Biosphere Programme (MAB), but along the way my insistence on asking *how* change takes place, applied in a Third World setting, led me deeply into the field of development studies; it could have led me out of geography altogether had the right opportunity arisen at the right time.

This sounds like undeviating obstinacy of such an order as to be more properly described as pigheaded stubbornness; perhaps it was and is. However, what really happened was more like a series of resurgences than an *idée fixe*. I had many periods of doubt, some of them prolonged, and most of them arose because of the seemingly contrary trends of the 'quantitative revolution'. I became aware of the 'new wave' before I went to New Guinea, and encountered its force for the first time when I spent two months living on my wits and the bounty of departments where I had friends, in the USA late in 1961. I cannot tell what my reaction to the new force would have been had I not gone to New Guinea, because as early as 1950 I had published a paper in which, like David Harvey[2] a few years later, I misapplied regression analysis to painfully collected quantitative data. This arose from a very personal second interest in the marine transport industry, which began early in life when I wanted to become a merchant marine officer, and has re-surfaced from time to time ever since. It would have been a career less fraught with uncertainty. By the late 1950s I, as much as anyone, felt that some sort of 'revolution' was needed in the discipline. By 1960, however, I had found my own, and it led me away from the so called 'mainstream'.

Mine, however, seemed a small distributory, and it led me to keep company with many whose basic views I did not share. I was called several things during the 1960s, including 'an anthropologist who draws his pay masquerading as a geographer', but the term I liked least was 'cultural geographer'. I sought to draw a line between them and myself in more than one paper, for they did not join in my concern with process, and many of them were far more hostile than I was toward the 'quantitative revolution'. Moreover, I was increasingly surrounded by the latter. I had students and colleagues who gently, or not so gently, told me that this or that formula represented some concept that I had known for years; I had a wife who began a prolonged love affair with the computer; I, on the other hand, could not even work my way through Tom Lehrer's lesson in the 'New Math'. As my field data collection programme in New Guinea tailed off, my use of the data was increasingly influenced by the new ideas and methods. I studied distance relationships; I transferred my data, 'massaging' it first, to a grid for computer manipulation; I read von Bertalanffy[3] and became enamoured with systems analysis, I had my own first run in with the computer, and received my own first output composed almost entirely of zero values because I had not understood the first principles of coding.

Doubts came to a head in 1968. In that year I wrote a paper about perception of environment after a tour of US and British universities, and handled some of my New Guinea material in a manner which removed me further from the cultural geographers and brought me closer to the new geography. Then we had a visit in Canberra from David Harvey, which I negotiated. David was immensely popular; he taught us a great deal about the philosophy behind the new geography, even if his teaching of method – based on matrix algebra – went over several other heads as well as mine. I was characterised by some of my students as, not inappropriately, Dr Watson to Harvey's Holmes. It seemed indeed elementary, and at the end of the year I decided to go to the USA to be re-educated and re-created. Before I left, however, I managed to complete my long promised book on Melanesia,[4] the product both of a decade of empirical research and of a set of ideas about long term and short term processes of change that, thus formulated, carried me forward into the next stage through a year of bitter disappointment.

The academic year 1969–70 was not the best year in which to arrive in the eastern USA. The nastiness between 'quantifiers' and 'traditionalists', sharpened by the concern already shown by some of the latter for the problems of environmental pollution, was at its height. Academic debate was overlain by the ideological confront- ation over the Vietnam war, accentuated during that year by Nixon's 'limited' invasion of Cambodia. Student protests led to deaths at Kent State and in Mississippi; the former, being white, achieved more notice on northern campuses. After only a few months I fled gratefully north, across the border into Canada. The 'powerhouse' was certainly exciting, but it contained no party, of the right or left, with which I could wholly sympathise. Moreover, the rest of the world – my world– did not really exist in the perception of any of my colleaques, or of most Americans. Perhaps more important in terms of my relations with geography, the victorious revolution was exposed to me as irrelevant to, and even callous towards, the major social and environmental problems of the day. A year later a large group of US geographers, assembled in Boston, took the same view. By that time, however, I was already ensconced in the turbulent but less intolerant environment of Montreal.

Canada, at least from Toronto eastward, was in that day an oasis of pluralism that survived even kidnapping and murder by the Front de Libération du Québec, and the over-reaction to these events by government. Canadian geography was pluralistic, though perhaps also directionless. Physical geographers co-existed with human geographers, quantifiers with traditionalists, microgeographers with macrogeographers. They could not be said to co-operate, and often did not like one another, but the tone of debate was several decibels lower than across the border. In an internationally orientated city and university there was plenty of scope for a Third World specialist, and plenty of encouragement for him to relate Third World experience to that of Canada itself, and of Quebec in particular. There was a modicum of inter-disciplinarity, there was some genuine bilingualism which I liked, and with only light teaching I had plenty of freedom in which to re-develop and re-define my own interests after two bruising years. I was for quite a while very happy.

The direction which I chose was to get myself deeply into the literature on Third World development, particularly with reference to the Caribbean and Latin America, which I visited several times. Meanwhile I wrote up remaining material from the Pacific, wrapping up my final quantitative efforts on the New Guinea material in a single paper, to which they did not contribute very greatly. Even this much earned me the anger of some cultural geographers, who maintained that I was 'selling out' to the opposition. Meanwhile I was becoming deeply involved in the development field for its own sake. I recognised that development, being the study of social and economic change, was providing me with the dynamic theory which I had long sought, but communicated these thoughts to geographers only through criticisms of the 'geography of modernisation'; its pretensions seemed to me to embody some of the worst and most arrogant excesses of the 'revolution'. When I came to write a book on development theory intended mainly for geographers I spent very little time on the writings of my colleagues. I was quite astonished by the success of *Interdependent Development*,[5] and still more astonished to hear it described, by a development economist, as a 'strong plea for inclusion of a spatial perspective in development studies'. It seems clear that the philosophy of the revolution, if not its techniques, had soaked far more deeply into my thoughts than I had realised.

But this is again to anticipate. Before this, in 1972, I declined an invitation to go back to Australia for a chair interview, having determined that my future lay, for the foreseeable future, in Canada. The very next day I received a letter that was ultimately to sweep this away, and change the course of my life once more. The letter was from UNESCO, and it asked me to participate in planning the new international Man and the Biosphere Programme (MAB), by designing a long term plan for the study of islands. This was timely, for by 1972 it was over three years since I had ceased to work actively in the man–environment field, had lost a rearguard action to avoid the splitting of my old department in Canberra, and had begun to turn toward the road of development studies. Behind me, however, lay a whole early career during which I had worked within the man–environment paradigm, and throughout which I had sustained a consistently strong interest in the work of my colleagues in geomorphology and biogeography. It was time to think about reviving my older interests in the context of what I had learned since 1968. Though the first report which I wrote for UNESCO laid stress on the spatial systems within which islands, as human habitats, were now incorporated, I soon found myself again involved with natural and physical scientists. This time the involvement was in an avowedly integrative context, as opposed to the context of growing separation between human and physical geography of the previous decade.

During the following two years while I was first preparing to write *Interdependent Development*, then actually writing it, I was involved increasingly (on a part time basis) with MAB. My first island research proposals to UNESCO proposed work in the Caribbean, for I hoped to be involved in the research from Canada; moreover, I was keen to develop new means of strengthening links between Canada and the US tropics in a period when Canadian research funds were not flowing quite so freely as in earlier years. Unfortunately for my plans, UNESCO determined that the first pilot project should be in the Pacific; they asked me to go to Fiji to negotiate it, which I did, and then set about the task of recruiting a team with myself in an advisory role. Along the way, my newer interest in the dynamics underlying the spatial structures of development, which I had hoped to pursue in Latin America, led me instead to Malaysia in the hands of the World Bank. My colleagues in Montreal looked askance on these activities.

Finally, in 1974, while I was on leave at the Institute of Development Studies in Sussex, a comic opera series of chance events put the Fiji project in peril just as it was about to begin. I had to make a choice: abandon Fiji and return to Montreal, seeing two years' work go down the drain and with it a set of connections which gave me much stimulus, or quit Montreal, save the project, and throw my future into the hands of fate. It was also a choice between returning wholly within geography, or continuing to develop an international and inter-disciplinary field of work which I found exciting. Put in an either/or position, I opted for risk and Fiji. The gamble paid off only in part, for I had afterwards to return to and remain within geography. I was however able to sustain international and inter-disciplinary connections, continue to develop work that I wanted to develop and, by good fortune, ultimately regain the advantages of location in an inter-disciplinary research school which I had so wantonly cast away in 1968.

Discussion

I have focused attention on the period 1968–74 in the above narrative for two reasons. First and obviously because it was critical in my own development in response to the 'revolution'; second because it was during this period that the new geography, never universally accepted, first came under very powerful assault from a wholly unexpected quarter: the successive and overlapping 'socially aware', radical and Marxist movements that arose largely from within its own ranks, and which involved rejection of logical positivism. The second 'revolution' should have been greater than the first, for by sensitising geography to major trends and cyclic movements in political thought it has had an effect opposite to that of the earlier 'revolution' under review in this volume. Whereas the 'quantitative revolution' had the effect of closing 'geography – and particularly Human Geography – against outside influences, the 'radical revolution' sought to throw the discipline wide open, giving it a societal as well as a purely academic role. The contrast can be overdrawn, for the later 'revolution' has not achieved its potential, while the new geography of the 'quantitative revolution' itself acquired an applied role. However, the opening of the discipline to society, which was long overdue, may have a permanent effect, outlasting the present and perhaps now fading vogue for a set of political theories rooted in the 19th century.

To geographers of my generation, brought up in the man–environment paradigm, the second 'revolution' presented fewer problems than the first. It questioned our beliefs, and made some of us re-think them, but it did not of itself demand that we change our paradigm into that of location and spatial pattern while at the same time changing our working methods. Moreover, having already endured the abuse of Young Turks and the contempt of their students in the first revolution, we were not about to be so readily fazed by the second. To those of us who had worked in the Third World during the years of decolonisation and the first hopeful stages of the 'development drive', there was nothing new in the idea of social relevance; most of us were well aware of social and political problems, and had sought to make our work useful in this context. Many of us had taken up particular causes in our own writings, though generally writings not seen by other geographers. The discovery of social relevance by the Boston rebels of 1971 inspired some acerbic comments about 'Johnnies-come-lately'. The adoption of Marxism was another matter, and some of us – like myself – could not find it in our consciences to seek 'full Marx' because our experience demanded a more pluralistic ethos. A Marxist interpretation of history, on the other hand, presented many fewer problems.

To understand the reaction of geographers such as myself to the second 'revolution' is of help in understanding our reaction to the first. In attempting to interpret it I fall back on the first person singular, even though I do not believe that my response was in any way unique. The response of each of us to the new wave of the 1960s was, however, a very individual matter; whereas I hope I also speak for others, I may not necessarily do so.

My own first reaction, before 1961, was conservative and hostile. Even though I felt that the practice of geography made it more a 'point of view' than a discipline with its own clearly defined field of subject matter, I took great pleasure in being able, from time to time, to demonstrate the role of place and of environmental variation in human affairs, and the converse role of changing technology and changing society and economy in determining the nature, physical form, prosperity and decline of places. I use the verb 'to determine' advisedly, as I did in the title of a paper written in the later 1950s. I was convinced that rigorous methodology must have the purpose of seeking cause and effect. I was contemptuous – too contemptuous – of the premature generalisations of regional geography, for in seeking to establish cause I felt it necessary also to establish the operational link between supposed cause and observed effect. Hence my emphasis, in those years, on the question 'How?'. Late in the 1950s I found that it was far easier to seek cause and effect at microscale, where individual decision makers could be seen in action. I therefore advocated this scale of work to my colleagues.

Empirical observation of spatial and diachronic regularities, especially when these could be explained in terms of some theory, was essentially a bonus in this approach. However, search for such regularities could be made by comparative method, which I also advocated throughout the 1960s. There was a contradiction in my logic between my insistence on seeking cause and effect on the one hand, and my preference for inductive method on the other, and it took me a long time to realise this discordance.

Moreover, it was only later in the 1960s when the new geographers themselves came to grips with the deeper issues in the philosophy of science that they were of much help to me in dealing with this problem. My early reading of the work of the quantifiers failed to impress me. It seemed sometimes simply to 'prove' the obvious, at others to provide a rather low level of explanation of complexity. Some of it seemed like 'old description writ large in new statistics'. Above all, it seemed to deny the need to *understand* causality, as opposed to *explaining* it in terms of a theory/hypothesis structure.

Yet this was far from being the whole of my reaction to the 'revolution'. Quantifiers became human beings for me after my visit to the USA in 1961, human beings who, moreover, expressed considerable interest in the work that I was doing. Thereafter I took much greater interest in theirs, and in particular in the methodological and philosophical discussions that began to appear from the mid-1960s onward. It was particularly illuminating to read the assessment from outside anglophone geography provided by Paul Claval in 1964,[6] and his analysis of 'retrospective' and 'prospective' geography; he, in common with many of the new geographers, saw geography in the future as a science of spatial forms and patterns. Harvey's later analysis[7] which – like Claval's – was extremely fair, led ineluctably to the same conclusion: geography's 'indigenous theory' concerns spatial form, though it requires 'derived theories' regarding temporal process to be elevated into a general theoretical system for the future development of the discipline. All this, as Wrigley pointed out in 1965,[8] led to an increasing separation between the two parts –

physical and human – of traditional geography.

Here was the rub. Not only had I been brought up in the traditional man–environment paradigm, but I was actively working
within it and, moreover, was developing it in ways that my teachers
had not taught me and of which they would probably not have
approved. My contacts with geomorphologists, biogeographers,
palynologists, pedologists, agronomists and environmental pre-
historians were growing constantly closer, along with my more long
standing involvement among anthropologists. Within a limited
domain we were on an exciting research frontier; within the same
domain I was also in growing contact with economists, and with
practical administrators and professional civil servants, on the
emerging problems of development. Back on the ranch, in geography, these interests were of small concern; the man–
environment paradigm was derided as lacking in theoretical
significance, and my work was valued principally along a scale
determined by its use of 'advanced techniques'.[9] My own doubts,
uneasy attempts at compromise, and ultimate surrender and
temporary disorientation are described above. They were made less
tolerable by my respect for the very real intellectual advances
achieved by the new geographers, in particular the new rigour in the
formulation of research questions which was their signal and
enduring contribution.

Conclusion

I have come full circle, back to 1968. Two years later, totally
disillusioned with the new geography, I was already deep into the
development studies field. Two years further on I was hauled back
into the man–environment field by UNESCO, in the context of a
programme not set up by geographers but by natural scientists who
had become aware of the scale of the human dimension in their
subject matter. MAB has in recent years sometimes unofficially
been dubbed the 'International Geographical Programme', but this
was certainly not so at the outset. In that it has become so, it is due
to geographers of varied specialisms joining in a trans-disciplinary
effort and being able, through their training, to provide a measure
of integration.

Notwithstanding some of the statements of its intellectual leaders
in the 1960s, the 'quantitative revolution' left the man–environment

paradigm on one side, to be taken up very actively by others. In so far as there has been a *rapprochement* within the discipline, it has come more from physical than from human geographers. In human geography, almost all the subsequent movements have perpetuated the direction initiated by the 'quantitative revolution', even though the 'opening up' of the discipline should have led to greater eclecticism. So long as 'spatial form' remains the central research paradigm of human geography, those environmentalists who are also geographers will continue to find themselves somewhat detached. Fortunately, we no longer lack colleagues and there is an alternative view of the scheme of things, with which I conclude.

I have also come full circle in another and more complete sense. While I would gladly have seized any good opportunity to shed the label 'geographer' for most of a decade, I no longer see the need to do this. I would define my field of work as the study of development processes in the broadest sense, including their spatial expression, in relation to management of resources and adaptation to process within man's environment. This process-orientated enlargement of the old man–environment paradigm takes in 'areal differentiation' and 'spatial form' as the expressions of process interaction on the ground. Research questions in geography may begin with these physical expressions, but the real questions conern the manner in which they have come about. More briefly, I could alternatively say that I am concerned with structure, process and transformation within man–environment systems, taking care to define each term very carefully, a task I do not attempt here.

Others might define their field of interest in similar terms, and by no means all of them would call themselves 'geographers'. They might use a range of newly coined terms to describe the field, but there is no need for such terms, since the word 'geography' has described this integrative inquiry for more than a century. In this broad sense 'geography' might be better used to describe a school rather than a discipline, but its core lies in the interpretation of pattern as first identified on the ground, which is what some students of geography are, as I was, still trained to do.

At this late stage in the day, then, my conclusion is that the man–environment paradigm is the real 'mainstream' of geography, now joined by a range of others from several disciplines. It is a mainstream that has its origins in the beginning of modern geographical inquiry, which took off from earlier compendia of spatially-organised knowledge around a set of questions about that knowledge in the post-Darwinian period. It can be better likened to a braided than to a meandering mainstream, and the 'quantitative revolution' becomes in this analogy a major anabranch, one that has contributed a new rigour and a set of new methods to problem formulation and solution. On the somewhat dubious assumption that the world as human habitat still has a future, there is a great deal that my kind of 'new' geography – constantly infused by new ideas and constantly in touch with its disciplinary neighbours and with the real world – can contribute to its better management.

Notes and References

1. R. Hartshorne, *Perspective on the Nature of Geography* (London: Murray, 1960).

2. D. Harvey, 'Locational change in the Kentish hop industry and the analysis of land-use patterns', reprinted with a comment in A.R.H. Baker, J.D. Hamshere and J. Langton (eds), *Geographical Interpretations of Historical Sources* (Newton Abbot: David & Charles, 1970).

3. L. von Bertalanffy, *General Systems Theory* (1956).

4. H. Brookfield, *Melanesia* (London: Methuen, 1971).

5. H. Brookfield, *Interdependent Development* (London: Methuen, 1975).

6. P. Claval, 'Essai sur l'evolution de la geographie humaine', *Cahiers de Geographie de Besançon* (1964), no. 12.

7. D. Harvey, *Explanation in Geography* (London: Arnold, 1969).

8. E.A. Wrigley, 'Changes in the philosophy of geography', in R.J. Chorley and P. Haggett (eds), *Frontiers in Geographical Teaching* (London: Methuen, 1965).

9. Here it is necessary to distinguish between the intellectual leaders of the 'quantitative revolution' and their more numerous followers.

A Foundling Floundering in World Three

R. J. JOHNSTON

For more than a decade, many Anglo-American geographers have been attracted to the model of scientific progress developed by Thomas Kuhn as a framework for interpreting the recent history of their discipline.[1] The notions of 'paradigms' and 'revolutions' have remained in the literature, despite the criticisms of Kuhn's work by many other historians of science, the problems of transferring ideas from the natural to the social sciences, the rejection of those ideas by other social scientists, and the increasing weight of evidence from within geography which confronts the essential concepts of Kuhn's model. Thus the changes in methodology and philosophy which have been introduced to geography since the American based 'quantitative and theoretical revolutions' of the 1950s have been interpreted as paradigm shifts or revolutions terminating periods of normal science which create disciplinary consensus over means and ends.

According to Kuhn's model, new members are socialised into a science, its methods and its aims, during their years as students. Their texts define the means and the ends; their postgraduate supervisors (or patrons) provide the academic stimulus and leadership; and their completion of what is accepted as a major piece of research provides the passport into the profession. Many of the supervisors are disciples of a particular leader (who may well be the author of an influential text, too). Occasionally new leaders emerge, preaching alternative means and ends and attracting disciples who, in turn, stimulate others and convert the adherents of previous views. If this attempted 'revolution' succeeds, then a paradigm shift occurs and all members of the discipline have been

39

converted to the new orthodoxy: new texts are written and a new consensus takes control.

Like many models this is a seductive representation of reality, and it appears to describe what has happened in human geography since 1950. But it is wrong – in detail and in general outline – as my personal account here of academic geography since 1959 will indicate. The general theme which I develop is that I was not socialised into an academic environment characterised by disciplinary consensus: the world of minds (World Two in Popper's terminology) in which I have worked has in no sense ever conformed to Kuhn's conception of 'normal science'. Rather, I have experienced the ferments of the last years through my non-random walks through Popper's World Three – the world of ideas as inscribed in the written word. It has been 20 years of floundering. Some of its peculiar characteristics may reflect my personal wanderings of that period, but I believe that much of my experience is common with that of many others. Presentation of this brief autobiographical sketch should illuminate general processes of geographical acculturation, and aid those who would write a history of academic geography that rejects the Kuhnian analogy and produces a state of 'paradigms lost'.

From Swindon to Manchester, Masham and Monash

It was an enjoyment of maps which first kindled my interest in geography at school. By the time I had decided to apply for university, there was no doubt that it would be to read geography (economics was the only other social science I had heard of). But neither my sixth form years nor my undergraduate experience at Manchester provided any coherent philosophy of the discipline. During the latter, an interesting range of individuals lectured on some intriguing things and places, but there was no evidence of a 'whole'. Nor did I finish with an arsenal of skills, though I recall drawing weather maps, constructing a Mercator projection, and ordering all the streams on a one-inch Ordnance Survey sheet (I chose one with lots of limestone!). Nothing from my formal training had any lasting positive effect.

First research
The academic component of my undergraduate career which made

much the greatest impact on my later work was my dissertation – an essay on my home town, Swindon. In reading for this I first encountered central place studies (though not central place theory; our training at Manchester was constructed in what must have been total ignorance of the current ferment in American geography). Bracey's book on *Social Provision in Rural Wiltshire*[2] gave me intriguing insights into the techniques of defining hinterlands and hierarchies, and I decided I wanted to do something similar. I applied to do research at Leeds (I had discovered Dickinson's books[3]) but was rejected, and so I stayed at Manchester.

My ideas were far from formulated when I started. I had the notion (it certainly couldn't be called a hypothesis)[4] that patterns of social provision in rural areas were influenced by the nature of the settlement pattern (basically the degree of nucleation), though I cannot remember how this notion developed. I had decided to study the topic in northwest Yorkshire, for the main reason that my family home was then in Leeds; I was warned off, that this was 'Leeds territory', but stuck to the area. In formulating the work programme I was very much on my own. The current system at Manchester was that as a graduate with a II.1 first degree there was no requirement for a supervisor, or so I was told: fortunately, Walter Freeman was very kind, and was extremely helpful when I started writing my MA thesis.

Very early on, I became convinced of the need to express conclusions quantitatively. In part this reflected the influence of a fellow student, Peter Lewis, but it was largely an impression gained from my early reading on central place studies. I had discovered the Proceedings of the 1960 International Geographical Union Urban Geography symposium,[5] Godlund's work on bus services in Sweden,[6] Green's on the same topic in Britain,[7] and Bunge's *Theoretical Geography*:[8] the last entranced me, though I certainly misunderstood much of it. Percy Crowe helped me to understand regression, R.G.D. Allen's book on statistics for economists provided some insight,[9] and then in 1963 Stan Gregory's *Statistical Methods for the Geographer* provided the needed cookbook.[10]

I collected lots of data on central places and bus services in my study area and manipulated these almost *ad infinitum*: much of the number-crunching came to nothing and very little of it entered the thesis, but I remember playing with the uses of chi-square and the analysis of variance for regional definition, only discovering Zobler's papers on the same topics much later. My ideas also related population change to the central place pattern (there was a von Thünen-like element somewhere) and I was intrigued by Gordon Dickinson's paper on the electoral roll as a data source:[11] after completing the thesis, I spent three months collecting data in County Hall, Wakefield. Eventually, all of this work was published. Meanwhile, I was married and entered the job market. For several years I had been sure that Australia was the place to go to – again, I have no idea why – and in early 1964 we set out for Melbourne.

Monash

Although my research experience was based on rural areas I was appointed as an urban geographer at Monash, to work on the largely unexplored Melbourne metropolitan area. Before leaving England I had discovered the writings of the 'Chicago School', especially E.W. Burgess,[12] and Dave Herbert and George Gordon had introduced me to social area analysis. More importantly, I discovered Emrys Jones' superb *A Social Geography of Belfast* and decided that was the work which I wanted to emulate.[13]

From the outset in Melbourne I overwhelmed myself with data – on buses again, on central places, and on census collectors' districts. I was very unsure as to what to do with them, except that I 'knew' that it had to be quantitative. I had no detailed supervision or help – nobody knew much about either topics or techniques and I was probably not the best at taking advice: I remember my anguish at trying to understand both the writings on ecological theory of Duncan Timms and the factorial ecologies of Frank Jones.[14] The problem was clearly the lack of training; my undergraduate and early postgraduate years at Manchester had in no way fitted me for such research, and I had a very vague understanding of the 'positivist paradigm' into which I was socialising myself. After about two years I sorted out a theme on the relationships between social areas and aspects of the townscape (street patterns, building fabric and shopping centres) and then produced a PhD thesis in the next six months. Looking back at the various parts of that thesis, I remain impressed at my independent ideas on intra-urban central place patterns (despite technical deficiencies), on high status residential areas, and on street patterns; technically, too, I seem to have learned much, as indicated by the papers on classification and regionalisation (several papers on the latter were rightly rejected by psychometric journals, however, and it was only a much later comment by Brian Berry which suggested to me why the paper 'Choice in Classification'[15] was so rapidly accepted for the *Annals*).

I was considerably influenced during two of the three years at Monash by Peter Rimmer. We did a lot of simple data collection and pattern description together, on a variety of topics ranging from the origins of Australian Rules footballers to derelict gold-mining areas in Bendigo. We found it easy to get our short papers accepted, and built some of the pieces into a monograph *Retailing in Melbourne*.[16] It was during those years that I developed the urge to write and an exhilaration with the task; perhaps more important, I decided that only when I got a lot of things in print would my ability be recognised so that I could get a job away from Monash. And so I did lots of little empirical pieces, few of them containing much more than a simple analysis of a small data set testing a trivial hypothesis: I thought that this was all that the 'new' geography involved.

Apart from the research, my main gain at Monash was the first insights it gave me into academic life, something which I entered with few preconceptions. These insights were far from exciting. I discovered the extent of petty academic jealousies, gossip, and backstabbing; I found that senior colleagues were totally unaware of the current literature, even in their own 'field'; and I discerned that many academics were frightened of ideas rather than ex-hilarated by them (one senior reaction to Chorley's critique of Davisian ideas[17] was that we should drop geomorphology from our courses altogether until it was sorted out again, and an early staff meeting included a long spirited debate on the relative merits of exercise books and loose leaf folders). It was made clear that at least some members saw the department as a teacher training in-stitution and thought that research was unnecessary; after two years the only back set of geography periodicals in the new library was of the *National Geographic Magazine*.

New Zealand

We never settled in Melbourne, and very soon determined that we would not stay there beyond the contracted three year period: income, heat and flies were major influences on that decision, though I was far from being a good colonist. But I was unable to get a university post 'back home', despite my belief in my list of publications. Fortunately, however, I had impressed Barry Johnston at a conference and was invited to apply for a post in his very reputable department at the University of Canterbury in Christchurch, New Zealand. There I spent 7½ years reaping the benefits of working among a group of young enthusiasts whose researches and publications were encouraged. Although we worked in separate fields we learned much from each other, and there was much valuable discussion and mutual help involving virtually the whole department.

Despite two research degrees, about a dozen research papers in refereed journals, and a reputation as a 'quantifier', I took up my first permanent appointment (tenure was automatic in New Zealand) with no coherent philosophy of the discipline, and no real knowledge of either methodology or techniques. I was an empiricist – though I didn't know it. Data existed to be manipulated, increasingly by computer, and I was a pragmatist in that any data which looked worth analysing were acquired. Indeed, one referee's report on a paper written in 1967 suggested that it was a case of 'I've found some data, here is a general story woven around their manipulation'; my response was that I had a general theory of how the city was organised and tested this whenever I came across valid data – the paper was published, elsewhere!

The years in New Zealand were very important and I learned a great deal from my research and teaching. The latter was perhaps the most formative even though, in line with the departmental ethos established at the top, I had what most academics would regard as a light teaching load. I taught two courses in urban geography (later expanded to three), one on research methods, and one on introductory statistics. For the last named, I was forced to read and understand the textbook willed to me by Bill Clark, Blalock's *Social Statistics*,[18] and this gave me my first basic understanding of probability, for example. I later changed to a shorter text – there is too much in Blalock for a pass degree undergraduate – but without that experience I would have floundered much more than I did.

My first research in New Zealand continued along the lines initiated at Monash, emphasising the social geography of cities but no longer paying much attention to the townscape. I became intrigued by factorial ecology, learned how to program in FORTRAN, and slowly mastered the differences between factor analysis and principal components analysis. *Urban Residential Patterns*[19] took shape during this period, although the writing largely predated my wholesale immersion into factorial ecology. At the same time I was excited by Peter Gould's 'On Mental Maps'[20] and decided to replicate his work in New Zealand, as well as extend it to the intra-urban scale. A large data collection and analysis exercise resulted (as with virtually all of my research, it was undertaken without much assistance; the main source of help was a series of small grants from the University Research Fund which was used to pay someone – usually my wife – to code the needed data ready for punching). I tried to link this work on mental maps to the urban ecologists' theories about residential patterns and intra-urban migration. In this I was joined by a sequence of research students, notable among them Bill Donaldson, Peter Newton and Mike Poulsen. We were intrigued by the papers we were able to get from the USA in mimeographed form and in particular were stimulated by John Adams' ideas on directional bias in intra-urban migration.[21] We had a general theory of urban spatial organisation and behaviour based on the principle of least effort, and sought to verify it – never to falsify.

Many other ideas were stimulated by particular pieces of reading. My usual response was to assemble a relevant New Zealand data set and to experiment with techniques. Many data sets were collated, partly processed, and then discarded, partly through incomplete specification of ideas, partly through poor comprehension of procedures, and partly through overload. Computer time (which was free) was consumed at an enormous rate and there was much wasted programming effort (we had no SPSS!). New Zealand has much excellent data, and it offered wide opportunities for testing other people's ideas; but it never occurred to me that it was important to set those ideas in the local context and to obtain a mastery of the peculiar features of the New Zealand social and economic conditions. As far as the social geography of the city was concerned, Burgess, Hoyt *et al.* were kings: Chicago ruled, and our task was to prove it.

Three new pieces of work developed (apart from a number of one-off jobs). The first followed my early investigations of high status residential areas. Several papers by Leo Schnore on the cities of North and South America were intriguing,[22] and I became determined to study where the élite lived in Latin American cities. An invitation to an IGU Quantitative Commission meeting in Europe (received because of my classification paper)[23] and money from the university enabled me to spend a month in South America in 1969

(I also went to the Ann Arbor Association of American Geographers and Bill Bunge's field trip to Detroit: both were very disturbing to my empiricism). Just before leaving I became entranced by the writings of William Margin and John Turner on squatter settlements,[24] and I spent much of the time I was in Caracas, Bogota, Quito, Lima and Mexico wandering around such places. (Very conspicuously. The British Council representatives warned me from going, especially in my light coloured jacket which made me look American; so I wore my dark suit. I shall never know how I had the nerve to do it; I always walked, never being prepared to catch a bus.) On returning, I wrote only one academic piece about it, for *Progress in Geography*[25] (someone who read that in draft said that it could have been written by Keith Buchanan; I took that as a compliment though I'm not sure one was meant). But much more important than the exercise in 'theorising' was the fact that the visits, plus attendance at the Ann Arbor meetings, stimulated a social and political awareness (which has never developed into a philosophy, for I retain the liberal 'hopeful hopelessness' of Chapters 7 and 8 of *Geography and Inequality*[26]): I began to look outside my data and at the 'real world'.

Secondly, I was intrigued by Kevin Cox's paper in *Progress in Geography 1* on the neighbourhood effect and voting decisions.[27] I didn't believe it, so as usual collected New Zealand data to test for patterns consistent with the 'friends and neighbours' voting model (unconscious Popperism!). But the results were strongly as Cox's models predicted, so I collected some more data: the results were the same. And as I did the analyses so I did some reading, becoming so intrigued by elections and politics that this became my major research interest, culminating in the joint book with Pete Taylor, *Geography of Elections*.[28] Like so many of the other things I studied, positivist empiricism ran riot, and it was only in the late 1970s that I developed an interest in the state and in putting elections in that context.[29] One interesting comment is that the work began because I was sceptical about the neighbourhood effect, about the influence of environment on behaviour; a little introspection and realisation of the influence of what I read on what I did would surely have convinced me of its validity!

Finally, during the early 1970s, I decided that all of my research had been in small pieces and that I should undertake a single large project, during the year's study leave which was nearly due. I chose to investigate spatial aspects of world trade; why, I do not know. I had done a little on regional development in New Zealand (then of considerable political import) which interested me in the general topics of the spatial division of labour and trade; the world trade data were sitting there, and I had some ideas about problems fitting the gravity model, because its resulting regression ceofficients with regard to trade patterns were counter-intuitive. But mainly it was the thought of crunching a large data set which attracted. I did it, and learned a lot incidentally (about handling large files, for example, and about gravity models – the latter from graduate students at Toronto). But the result was a slim book, in every sense of that adjective.

Unease

Whilst this empiricism occupied most of my time, and I played endlessly with data and techniques (often becoming dissatisfied with the latter almost as soon as I had written a paper applying them), uneasiness was growing about the loose framework within which it was set. There were several components to this unease. The first, and probably the most important, developed through my teaching of urban geography. I was unhappy at having to put across a series of descriptions, and their technical bases, for which I had no real explanations. For the course on urban systems, for example, I found central place theory both boring and irrelevant to New Zealand. I wanted to explain urban systems: the ahistorical Christaller presentation offered no help and although Jim Rose's early piece on primacy was of value[30] it took a long time to sort out a 'theory' which I found convincing (it was eventually written down in *City and Society*).[31] There were similar problems with lectures on intra-urban residential patterns based on Burgess and factorial ecologies. I tried hard to weave a convincing explanation – which perceptive reviewers of *Urban Residential Patterns*[32] found wanting – but the continued focus on distance and efficiency (the basis for both *Urbanization in New Zealand* and *Spatial Structures*[33]) misled me and I found no convincing alternative in what I read, or in the so-called behavioural revolution, parts of which I rapidly found of little use.[34] By the time that I did, in the early 1970s, I was firmly committed (in reputation at least) to an approach which the 'radicals' discredited and which I was increasingly uneasy about.

Secondly, I developed a feeling of academic impotence with regard to the issues and problems of 'the world outside'. This had an early root in a report we were commissioned to write on a shopping centre development, for I could not see the planning relevance of the facts we had gathered on hinterlands. We were encouraged to expand this work, but fortunately political squabbles prevented the funds being granted. What I later realised were the problems of *status quo* theory were extended by my involvement (in a small way) in New Zealand's nascent regional planning and our opposition to a planned New Town near Christchurch: they were really driven home when I wrote the conclusion to *The World Trade System*,[35] but only one reviewer apparently realised my difficulties[36] – perhaps no other reviewers got that far! Writing my chapters of *Geography and Inequality* only furthered my feelings of impotence, and my frustration that I could see no solution (revolutionary or otherwise). And the only apparent application of my research was in a way of which I disapproved: my work on voting in Christchurch was part of the encouragement for an attempted gerrymander.

And yet the 'real world' attracted me, even though getting involved meant questioning my entire background and research. Two pieces brought this point home. One was an essay I was asked to write for the Canterbury Chamber of Commerce on the planning system. I chose to analyse the impact of zoning on land prices: my case – which I felt to be both logical and empirically validated – was attacked in the editorial columns of the *Christchurch Press*, on Boxing Day that year (when I rehearsed the same basic argument seven years later in Johannesburg, I was branded as a 'red'!). The other was an essay on planning for balanced neighbourhoods commissioned by the Diocese of Christchurch, in which I attacked currently popular notions of 'social mix' and 'community'. None of this fitted in well with my empiricism.

Finally, I became convinced that geography was a formless discipline. I read widely within the subject and got considerable pleasure and stimulation from editing the *New Zealand Geographer*, but I found that nearly every piece, like all of my own, was an item of empiricism, closely tailored to a minority audience but fitting into no overall theoretical framework. And so I sought guidance in the other social sciences, built arguments around 'urbanisation as modernisation' and behaviouralist reductionism,[37] and debated the need for a closer integration of geography with the social sciences. I made no discoveries in World Three which provided a convincing geographical philosophy, however. I had decided that human and physical geography should be divorced,

because techniques along were insufficient to hold them together –
according to one of my senior colleagues, this makes me a spatial
sociologist. There was nobody to guide me to Popper or to Marx,
and I failed to find them on my own: *Explanation in Geography*
was the alternative,[38] but it was too cold and unreal, too lacking in
empirical content, to be convincing. And so I left New Zealand
temporarily in 1972, to discover a new World Two, first in my four
months at Toronto and then in the ensuing eight at the London
School of Economics.

To Sheffield

It was while I was away from New Zealand that I did much of the
work on the ill fated world trade book.[39] But the contacts made
during that year covered a much wider field and I became aware of
many currents of debate that were not yet transmitted to the
Antipodes in the published record. And so I decided that I wanted
to remain in this much livelier place. By the time I was appointed to
Sheffield I was back in Christchurch and well aware that I needed
to escape from the small pool in which I seemed destined to become
an uncomfortable big fish (I had realised that three years previously, when I declined a chair at Auckland because I didn't want to be
'trapped' à la Peter Principle).

Academically, the move heralded a fruitful period, in many
senses. Some of my teaching continued as before, on urban residential patterns, but apart from a little technical dabbling I have
done no research in this area. The managerialist and structuralist
approaches to urban geography have proved attractive and have
been incorporated within an eclectic teaching framework, but they
offered no obvious empirically based research avenues – there were
no easily available data sets to be chewed through. And so as an
urban geographer I am now mainly an observer and commentator.
This is reflected in my theoretical outline for the subject (*City and
Society*)[40] and in my attempt to apply that outline to the United
States (*The American Urban System*).[41]

Two new teaching interests evolved. The first was in electoral
and political geography and developed out of a course entitled
'Spatial Systems and Society' – before arriving at Sheffield I had
offered to teach a course based on David Harvey's book on social
justice;[42] the title was not favourably received, so a compromise

had to be sought. My interests in elections broadened, thanks mainly to contact and collaboration with Pete Taylor; a range of topics was investigated, several of them involving simulation work and allowing me to create my own data sets! This was empiricism run riot, but slowly a more coherent framework emerged, both for the positivist study of elections themselves (*Geography of Elections*)[43] and for linking elections into political geography (*Political, Electoral and Spatial Systems*).[44] Reading in political geography convinced me that Brian Berry was right to call it a 'moribund backwater' in 1969, though his argument was based on techniques whereas mine rested on theoretical issues. It became obvious that political geographers were ignoring the great problem of the nature and functions of the state, and I was led to explore the spatial patterns of state activity, in relation to electoral considerations. Here again there was great scope for empirical data manipulation, and even more computer time was burned up (the results were put together in *The Geography of Federal Spending in the United States*[45]). Continued consideration of the problem of the state in geographical theory involved me in a debate with Michael Chisholm (in the pages of *Progress in Human Geography*[46]) and in writing *Geography and the State*.[47]

The other teaching interest was a course I was asked to give on current philosophical and methodological issues in human geography. This encouraged me to continue reading widely, and I had to develop a framework within which to teach what became a history of the subject since 1945. Kuhn's paradigm model[48] provided that framework – because it was there – but the more I read and organised material, the more I became convinced that it was wrong. The course changed several times in a few years, until it settled down in what became *Geography and Geographers*.[49] The reading on which it was based confirmed my views that geography is a formless discipline, lacking any rigour in either content or training programmes.

During this period, the expanding structuralist and Marxist literatures had considerable appeal, for they threw much light on the problems with which I had for long unsuccessfully wrestled. In particular, my attempts to structure the study of towns was placed into a more coherent framework. But there were many new problems, associated largely with my empiricist background: I was unable to break out of my data based approach or to kill my fascination with computer program development. And despite its appeal, the new literature led in ways that I was unable to follow. A general cynicism (perhaps an implicit belief in original sin) led me to deny the conclusions of the Marxist creed, and there were many difficulties in adapting positivist empiricism to the structuralist arguments. The latter pay very little attention to individual real-isations, to particular patterns on the ground, preferring to focus on more general processes: my own deep involvement with the analysis of the actual was not only a store of capital which it was hard to jettison but also a belief that empirical testing of structuralist theories is necessary to convince both the generations of empiricists that geographers have produced, and the outside world. The problem remains and I remain a prime example of what Geoffrey Hawthorn describes as 'contrasting sets of assumptions [which] have often coexisted in the same places and even occasionally in the same men'.[50]

My attempts to grapple with these problems – which are essentially to do with scale – led to a paper in the *Transactions of the Institute of British Geographers* in 1980 and a debate with John Eyles and Roger Lee in a 1982 issue.[51] My entry into the North Atlantic World Two has been exhilarating, therefore, even if challenging and leading to much reconsideration of my philosophy – of life in general, not just of social science. In a sense, it continues the process started at Ann Arbor and in the South American squatter settlements. Whilst the nature of individual pieces of research is little different in style from what I was writing a decade ago, the framework within which they are set has changed considerably, and attempts to produce overviews have been person-ally satisfying. Contact with others, notably with Alan Hay, has been crucial in this, but I rapidly realised that although the North Atlantic World Two is denser than its Antipodean counterpart, in many senses it is just as small. I re-discovered what I had found in Australia but was very largely absent from New Zealand: many academics seem to be frightened of ideas rather than stimulated by them; a large number avoid the current literature and are less than competent in the techniques and procedures that they insist all students should be taught and that they even use in their own research; academic debate is avoided in favour of political trivia and many retreat out of the world of ideas and uncertainties into a life of bureaucratic impotence; course organisation indicates by its very anarchy a lack of consensus as to what should comprise a geographical education; there is a great deal of parochial boundary drawing around disciplines and sub-disciplines; and, perhaps most disturbing of all, academic debate is frequently replaced by personal point scoring, as I discovered to my distaste when a technical issue that I raised generated a response which questioned my social values.[52] Very clearly, Kuhn's model is irrelevant to academic geography. There is no consensus about means and ends, which might be understandable in a period of 'revolutionary fervour'; but there is also no constructive debate over competing philosophies, largely because of ignorance. World Three is much more attractive.

In Summary

If this autobiographical sketch is of any value to an understanding of what happened in academic human geography during the 1960s and 1970s, its main contribution must be to indicate how unstructured the so called 'revolutions' have been. It may be that as one who has tried to assimilate the content of those 'revolutions' and to contribute to at least some of the methodologies espoused within them, my own almost entire reliance on World Three was relatively unique, because I spent nearly 11 years in Australasia, and because of the conservative early training that I received at Manchester. I was on my own, dependent on what I found in the literature. Many were similarly placed, I believe, and still are. A few large graduate schools, mainly in the USA, may provide a thorough grounding for their students in at least one philosophy of the discipline, but most academic geographers who have entered the discipline in the last 20 years have, I believe, like me, been negotiating a poorly signposted, randomly constructed route network.

Reliance on the literature is a major aspect of academic life, of course; it is encouraged in at least some universities. But the socialisation via World Three should be guided, and a pathway through the literature charted. During the 1960s there were no guidebooks available. We knew that there was a revolution going on, we saw the output in the journals, and we attempted to build on what we read. But that literature provided insufficient straw for the bricks. We thought we were adopting *the* 'scientific method', but apart from a vague progression of model–hypothesis–test– conclusion–theory and a vague conception of inferential statistics we neither comprehended that 'scientific method' nor applied it rigorously. There was virtually nothing in the bibliographies of the papers which we read to guide us into the philosophy of the 'new geography', the only real debate was a pin-pricking one with regard to quantification, and *Explanation in Geography* came too late. We had been convinced of the need to quantify, and so selectively scoured the cookbooks and package program manuals to find the 'right' methods for our data. Few of us had the depth of training or had undertaken the necessary self-education which would have allowed a proper appraisal of our endeavours. My own reading in sociology during the 1960s was highly selective, for example, concentrating on the empirical pieces and avoiding the theoretical critiques. And so it continues: World Three is treated like a bran tub, with every dip producing a stimulus that requires a response, regardless of the other stimuli lying unwrapped and awaiting the next dip.

And so for a decade or more my experience of the 'quantitative revolution' was one of continued experimentation, of hours of thoughtless number crunching and program development (the latter brought its prestige; for some years I had the only principal components program in New Zealand that generated scores). Much of this experimentation was to little avail; many errors crept through the referencing filters of the journals (and continue to do so). The learning was extremely public. A lot of the lessons are best forgotten, salutary though they are in retrospect. They lie in World Three for future historians to discover and recoil from, and they have left their mark on one's approach to new problems. They certainly contributed very little to an understanding of the world.

My experience of the 'quantitative revolution', therefore, was that it was very largely unproductive because it was unstructured; I lacked any rigorous training yet despite this gained status which was based on quantity rather than quality. This general situation remains. Although the 'quantifiers' came to dominate the professional literature they do not dominate the profession, and never have; as a consequence most training for research is inadequate and lacking in rigour because many academics are not fully committed to the need for such rigour and many students shy away too. The 'revolutions' since have fared no better. A pluralism of approaches may be desirable, but not when it becomes a soggy trifle lacking any substance in even one part. As a result, we all continue to burrow away in World Three, uncovering snippets that we apply in a 'geographical context'. Because those snippets are unconnected to their sources, we too frequently misunderstand and misapply them; floundering prevails.

Early in this essay, I characterised my undergraduate education as involving interesting people lecturing to us on intriguing things and places, with no evidence of a 'whole'. My experience since has been very similar, with lectures replaced by reading. For me the 'quantitative revolution' was a decade or more of floundering; it was often exhilarating, frequently frustrating but, in retrospect, largely unproductive and disillusioning. The period since has been much the same. How much of this floundering reflects personal characteristics which have gone unexplored here, and how much reflects a general malaise in the educational experience I shared with my peers and have since provided for later generations is not clear. But floundering it has been.

Notes and References

1. T.S. Kuhn, *The Structure of Scientific Revolutions* (Chicago: University of Chicago Press, 1962); for its use in geography, see R.J. Johnston, *Geography and Geographers: Anglo American Geography Since 1945* (London: Edward Arnold, 1979).

2. H.E. Bracey, *Social Provision in Rural Wiltshire* (London: Methuen, 1952).

3. G.C. Dickinson, 'The nature of rural population movement – an analysis of seven Yorkshire parishes based on electoral returns 1931–1954', *Yorkshire Bulletin of Economic and Social Research*, vol. 10 (1958) pp. 95–108.

4. See J.L. Newman, 'The use of the term "hypothesis" in geography', *Annals of the Association of American Geographers*, vol. 63 (1973) p. 23.

5. IGU, *Proceedings of the Urban Geography Symposium* (1960).

6. S. Godlund, 'Bus services in Sweden', *Lund Studies in Geography*, series B (1956).

7. F.H.W. Green, 'Urban hinterlands in England and Wales: an analysis of bus services', in J.P. Gibbs (ed.) *Urban Research Methods* (Princeton University Press, 1961).

8. W. Bunge, *Theoretical Geography* (Gleerups, 1966).

9. R.G.D. Allen, *Mathematical Analysis for Economists* (London: Macmillan, 1938).

10. S. Gregory, *Statistical Methods for the Geographer* (London: Longman, 1963).

11. G.C. Dickinson, 'The nature of rural population movement'.

12. See, for example, E.W. Burgess, 'The growth of the city', in R.E. Park and E.W. Burgess (eds), *The City* (University of Chicago Press, 1967).

13. E. Jones, *A Social Geography of Belfast* (London, 1960).

14. For an example of Timms' work, see *The Urban Mosaic* (Cambridge University Press, 1971).

15. R.J. Johnston, 'Choice in classification', *Annals of the Association of American Geographers*, vol. 58 (1968) pp. 575–89.

16. R.J. Johnston, *Retailing in Melbourne* (Canberra: Dept Human Geography).

17. See, for example, R.J. Chorley, 'A re-evaluation of the geomorphic significance of W.M. Davis', in R.J. Chorley and P. Haggett (eds), *Frontiers in Geographical Teaching* (London, 1965).

18. H.M. Blalock, *Social Statistics*, 2nd edn (New York, 1979).

19. R.J. Johnston, *Urban Residential Patterns* (London: Bell, 1971).

20. P.R. Gould, 'On mental maps', reprinted in R.M. Downs and D. Stea (eds), *Image and Environment* (London: Edward Arnold, 1973) pp. 182–218.

21. J.S. Adams, 'Directional bias in intra-urban migration', *Economic Geography*, vol. 45 (1969) pp. 302–23.

22. L.F. Schnore, *The Urban Scene* (New York: The Free Press, 1965).

23. R.J. Johnston, 'Choice in classification'.

24. W. Mangin, 'Latin American squatter settlements: a problem and a solution', *Latin American Research Review*, vol. 2 (1967) pp. 65–98; J.F.C. Turner. 'Uncontrolled urban settlement: problems and policies', in G. Breese (ed.), *The City in Newly Developing Countries* (Englewood Cliffs, N.J.: Prentice-Hall, 1969) pp. 507–34.

25. R.J. Johnston, 'Towards a general model of intra-urban residential patterns', in C. Board, R.J. Chorley, P. Haggett and D.R. Stoddart (eds), *Progress in Geography*, vol. 4 (1972) pp. 83–124.

26. R.J. Johnston, *Geography and Inequality*.

27. K. Cox, 'The voting decision in a spatial context in Board *et al.*', *Progress in Geography*, vol. 1 (1969) pp. 31–118.

28. R.J. Johnston and P. Taylor, *Geography of Elections* (London, 1979).

29. R.J. Johnston, 'Electoral and political geography', *Australian Geographical Studies*, vol. 18 (1980).

30. A.J. Rose, 'Dissent from down under: metropolitan primacy as the normal state', *Pacific Viewpoint*, vol. 7 (1966) pp. 1–27.

31. R.J. Johnston, *City and Society* (Harmondsworth: Penguin, 1980).

32. R.J. Johnston, *Urban Residential Patterns*.

33. R.J. Johnston, *Spatial Structures* (London: Methuen, 1973).

34. R.J. Johnston, 'Mental maps: an assessment', in J. Rees and P.T. Newby (eds), *Behavioural Perspectives in Geography: A Symposium* (Hendon: Middlesex Polytechnic, 1974) pp. 1–12.

35. R.J. Johnston, *The World Trade System* (London: Bell, 1978).

36. I. Wallace, in the *Canadian Geographer*, vol. 22 (1978).

37. R.J. Johnston, *Content Foci in Urban Geography*, Monash Publications in Geography, vol. 4 (1972).

38. See D. Harvey, *Explanation in Geography* (London: Arnold, 1969).

39. R.J. Johnston, *The World Trade System*.

40. R.J. Johnston, *City and Society*.

41. R.J. Johnston, *The American Urban System* (London: Longman, 1982).

42. D. Harvey, *Social Justice and the City* (London: Arnold, 1973).

43. R.J. Johnston and P. Taylor, *Geography of Elections*.

44. R.J. Johnston, *Political, Electoral and Spatial Systems* (Oxford University Press, 1979).

45. R.J. Johnston, *The Geography of Federal Spending in the United States*.

46. R.J. Johnston, in *Progress in Geography*, vol. 5 (1980).

47. R.J. Johnston, *Geography and the State* (London: Macmillan, 1982).

48. T.S. Kuhn, *The Structure of Scientific Revolutions*.

49. R.J. Johnston, *Geography and Geographers*.

50. G. Hawthorn, *Enlightenment and Despair* (Cambridge University Press, 1976) p. 253.

51. R.J. Johnston, 'On the nature of explanation in geography', *Transactions of the Institute of British Geographers*, n.s., vol. 5 (1980) pp. 402–12.

52. E.D. Perle, 'On normative analyses and factorial ecologies – a response to Johnston', *Environment and Planning A*, vol. 10 (1978) pp. 1, 207–1, 209.

Recollections of the 'Quantitative Revolution's' Early Years: The University of Washington 1955-65

RICHARD L. MORRILL

Introduction

I will admit at the start that I am proud to have been part of this period of challenge and re-direction (as others have shown, 'quantitative revolution' is not properly descriptive), and also that my memory for detail does not extend to who said what, and when. Nevertheless, I hope to present a reasonably faithful picture of what it was like as a participant – how I as an individual changed, and how the group of students and faculty interacted and changed.

Background

My original intention, upon entering Dartmouth in 1951, was to become a high school history/civics teacher. In a time-honoured tradition, I discovered geography by accident at the end of my sophomore year, and was converted to the field by the sheer excitement and quality of the introductory course (Professor Trevor Lloyd, later at McGill). Although in those days we were required to obtain a rather broad liberal education (for which I am very thankful) there was something of a physical emphasis within geography (and there was not the remotest hint of a quantitative approach). Having come from Los Angeles, I resisted the Arctic emphasis of most of my fellow students, however, and undertook a study of water-power development in the northwest for my senior thesis. On the basis of help from Marion Marts of the University of Washington and advice from Al Carlson to study with Edward Ullman, I applied to the University of Washington rather than Wisconsin, and arrived in September 1955. I believe it was in that first week or so that some new friend took me on my first hike in the Cascades, an episode that started an insidious addiction to the northwest.

The University of Washington in the late 1950s

The participants
Students arriving that fall included Brian Berry, John Nystuen, John Kolars, Waldo Tobler and myself. We were preceded by Duane Marble in 1954, and followed in 1956 by Michael Dacey, Art Getis, Bob Mayfield, Ron Boyce and Bill Bunge – an eclectic group from all parts of the country and the world, from many intellectual and personal backgrounds.

The faculty included Donald Hudson, the Chairman (and no mere figurehead), Edward Ullman, Marion Marts, John Sherman, Howard Martin and Frances Earle who represented a continuity with the University of Washington of the 1930s; Rhoads Murphey, Doug Eyre, Doug Jackson, and William Garrison, who had been brought in by Martin back in 1951 (the above named students were those most affected by Garrison – there were many of other persuasions, and these enlivened our experience; there were many shorter and longer term faculty visitors, again of all persuasions).

The atmosphere
The critical question for this history is why and how innovation occurred (1953?) and succeeded (1955–56...) at Washington. One element was the structure (or seeming lack thereof) of graduate training. No core programs, even for small sub-groups, have ever been implemented, then or since. Rather, all students' programs have been individually fashioned, with the help of their committee, but primarily by themselves. Despite this freedom, the faculty had high expectations of students. There was not only the freedom, but also the expectation that the student would reach high levels of proficiency in related fields e.g. economics or sociology or Russian studies.

A second element was the tolerance (or more) of a competitive even confrontational, spirit (I could never forget the corridor arguments between Donald Hudson and Bill Bunge). Neither Donald Hudson nor Edward Ullman were apostles of the 'quantitative revolution', but they understood what science was about – that if geography were to become respected, it had to be concerned with theory, and that the search for and testing of theory required better methods than they themselves knew; and they defended our often over-zealous endeavours along these lines.

But the critical influence was clearly William Garrison– a low-key revolutionary from Tennessee (via Northwestern). 'Discipleship' may not be too strong a word for the fervour with which we came to accept and welcome a role as spreader of a new word. There was something electrifying about tilting with the dragons of the establishment. Perceiving ourselves as a subversive and feared minority gave us foolish strength and helped us to maintain a breathless pace of intellectual ferment, complaint and conspiracy. It was easy to personify Richard Hartshorne, whose work we studied in detail, as what we struggled against.[1] We found heroes – notably Schaefer[2] and Christaller[3] – and many villains. Of course, there was strong resistance, which made us all the more determined!

Although Garrison was the leader of what we thought to be a 'revolution', the role was actually carried out in the context of a number of classes and seminars, through thesis and dissertation advice and in his role as our employer on research projects. In every aspect, he was an exceptional teacher and helper.

Motivation

But there must have been more than graduate philosophy and personalities. A strong (pre)conditioning element was an as yet vague discontent with the low status of geography – in our universities, in science, in the eyes of our peers in other fields; with the lack of funding; with our dependence on unglamorous teaching careers; and in the provision of descriptive service courses for others. We were deeply disturbed by the fundamental question of whether geography deserved to be in the university at all, but became determined to show that it did. We were also embarrassed by the rejection of environmental determinism, but uneasy about the retreat from theory as justified by the geography establishment, which we contrasted to the theoretical ferment or statistical applications we encountered in our geology, anthropology, economics or sociology courses.

The formative years: 1955–7

In 1955 Washington was a much smaller institution, as was geography itself with perhaps only 25 graduate students. While some were married Korean war veterans (e.g. John Nystuen), most of us were young and single. This contributed to a camaraderie outside the classroom – long hours at taverns, parties, studying languages together, hikes (to this day the university maintains a high level of such shared activities, including at least monthly parties and twice-annual picnics, activities which contribute to morale and solidarity).

Our 'baptism of fire' in the autumn of 1955 was Geography 426: 'Statistical Methods' – no euphemism for cartography. I had done no real maths since high school, and had spent much time at Dartmouth reading philosophy, politics, language and the like. Geography 426 was a severe shock, an experience that probably deterred some forever, but excited many of us tremendously. It was instant conversion – not just to standard statistical techniques, but to the computer (albeit very primitive). I might add that this course was the first, and last, in which I was better or quicker than Brian Berry.

Winter 1956 introduced us to Ullman – central place theory, gravity models in urban geography – and to a location theory seminar with Garrison (for which there was of course no book).

The strategy, as I recall, was that each of us would review the critical literature on some particular model or location theory and present it to the seminar. In this first seminar, I think, Brian Berry was contrasting Löschian and Christallerian concepts;[4] others were discussing Hotelling, Graham's comparative advantage model, or the transportation problem and the like.

Spring was incredible. It brought us into Geography 442; 'Commercial Geography'. However, this turned out not to be a study of commercial land use or the CBD frame, but a crash introduction to the new movement called 'regional science' via Isard's just published *Location and Space Economy*.[5] Although we criticised it as unreadable, we were subtly converted to something more exciting than statistics: the search for *theory*, and the idea that this could be expressed by mathematical models. On two afternoons we proceeded to econometrics with Arnold Zellner (later of Chicago fame). This proved fairly tough for those of us who were barely conversant with statistics. In my case the course was truly significant, because I reviewed for the class Samuelson's spatial equilibrium models,[6] which became the basis for my MA and PhD theses, and subsequent interest in transportation and health care. On two other afternoons we were entranced by the application of statistics to physical geographic problems in a seminar with visiting Ross Mackay.

The 1956–7 academic year was, for some of us, devoted in part to our theses, but was highlighted also by a seminar in more advanced statistical methods; a seminar class with the visiting Les Curry; and with an intense bout with industrial location theory, via Garrison. By this time, we naively thought that we knew enough to start writing up some definitive models, but Garrison soon disabused us of this.

Cohesion among the group was enhanced, and both the practice of field research and the importance of funded research opportunities furthered, by participation in summer 1957 in the Washington Civil Defense project – in which each of us was responsible for assessing the distribution of, and accessibility to, essential services and supplies (mine was medical – an accident that influenced later research).

Perhaps the period of peak activity (at least in my time there) was the 1957–8 academic year. Brian was already completing his dissertation, Ullman was back from Italy, offering work on transportation, and we had such different visitors as Norton Ginsburg and Preston James.

As quasi-faculty Brian taught economic geography; then I taught human geography. Both graduate students and faculty made presentations of research to the departmental colloquium and critique and discussion were not always gentle. Debate raged among students concerning 'idiographic and nomothetic approaches'; on the mistreatment of Schaefer; on the shortcomings of Hartshorne and James.[7] The students at the university were not all rebels; there were eloquent spokesmen of traditional approaches, and even the most radical of us took and enjoyed traditional regional courses. We were also exploring new statistical procedures, uncovering or translating possible models.

Perhaps the most significant innovation of the year was the establishment of the Discussion Paper series, an outlet for seminar papers, preliminary thesis findings etc. Their circulation to other outposts of the 'new geography', especially Iowa and Northwestern at first, was of great immediate (feedback, encouragement) and long-term benefit (spreading the word!).

The summer of 1958 again brought most of the 'Garrison group' together in the pioneering highway impact studies, in collaboration with Civil Engineering. Most of us were out in the field interviewing farmers and townsfolk about the effect of the Marysville Bypass. These studies were the basis for several theses and dissertations, including mine, and resulted in the, I think, revolutionary book, *Studies of Highway Development and Geographic Change.*[8]

The Los Angeles Association of American Geographers meeting in 1958 was the first for many of us. Our papers were not met with sympathy, but we did participate and were able to spread the word; and besides, John Nystuen and I were interviewed for (and got) our first positions.

The year 1958-9 was memorable for the beginnings of Bunge's 'theoretical geography', which was the basis for endless discussion, for the involvement of some of us in radical anti-war causes, for rejection of our papers and rough treatment of our ideas at professional meetings (Los Angeles 1958), but from my perspective the most influential event was the visit of Torsten Hägerstrand in the spring of 1959. The combination of theory and thorough field work expressed in the demonstration of diffusion processes, before they were available in English, had an electrifying impact, and has greatly influenced my work ever since. It was his first visit that led me to apply for and receive National Science Foundation (NSF) research support for a year in Sweden (1960-1) – a year which resulted in my breaking into the *Annals* (1963) and in my Lund monograph on Migration and Settlement,[9] as well as later work on the black ghetto.

The 1950s: University of Washington's contribution

It is reasonable to assert that from 1954-61, the University of Washington was the dominant and most innovative department in the development of both quantitative and theoretical geography. After 1961, this role spread to several institutions, most notably Iowa, Chicago, and Northwestern, and later Ohio State, largely through a 'second generation of Washington graduates (e.g. Berry, Dacey, Bunge and Marble). Washington shifted from quantitative methods as such to a major contribution in the 1960s and 1970s in economic geography and social geography (regional development, industrial behaviour) and urban and regional analysis.

Quantitative methods were a very major part of the later 50s at the university: it began with Garrison's fairly advanced statistics course Geography 426 in 1954–5, and led to more advanced seminars, as well as econometrics (in Economics). In general, we kept up with developments in statistics themselves, and with early computer methods. In the seminars, stress was placed on geographic applications since we were not primarily mathematicians; although some more basic work was done in spatial analysis (Dacey); residuals mapping; spatial sampling (Berry); and applications to cartography (Tobler). Inferential methods, especially, found early application in 'Impacts of Highway Improvements' (the famous Marysville Bypass study) in 1957.[10]

The clearest consequence of the 1950s work was the Berry–Marble book on *Spatial Analysis*[11] and the 1959 Office of Naval Research sponsored symposium on quantitative geography; as well as the applied work in the Discussion Papers. Subsequent to 1960, however, the development of statistical methods shifted more to Iowa and Northwestern, and the methodological contribution of the University of Washington came from regional modelling: input–output (Beyers) and simulation (Morrill).

Quantitative methods beyond statistics received much of our attention from the very beginning, and experiments and applications of gravity models, linear programming (not just transportation models), input–output and – after Hägerstrand's 1959 visit – simulation and probabilistic models, were carried out.

Although the initial 'revolutionary thrust' may have been methodological, the emphasis fairly quickly shifted toward the development of theory (a change which, I believe, helps explain the relatively greater long term contribution to geography of Washington and Chicago, over, say, Iowa or Northwestern). The excitement of theory actually came first from Edward Ullman who introduced us to theories of trade and interaction, urban systems and structure, comparative advantage, and regional development. Garrison then continued with theories of industrial and commercial location, and with more mathematical formulations of all these theories. Without doubt, Washington's contribution to theory was greater than to statistics or methods. Most dissertations stressed theory – Berry's central place theory; Marble's and Boyce's rent theory and urban structure; Nystuen's urban movements; Tobler's theoretical surfaces, etc. and this emphasis was apparent in the now 'historic' *Studies of Highway Development and Geographic change* (1959).[12]

I early became interested in models of movement – for my MA dealing with wheat (1960 paper with Garrison, 'Projections of interregional flows of wheat'), and shifting to movements of persons for my PhD ('Normative model of trade areas and transportation') – actually patient–physician flows.[13] I often found myself in the role of trying to conciliate between opposing views and forces – among the faculty, as well as among students.

Northwestern: 1959–60
My first job was at Northwestern – a tremendously exciting year. Most important was probably the interaction and mutual support with Ned Taaffe, and again, immediate involvement with Ned and Peter Gould in another large transportation study, this time involving Africa as well as the US. Teaching statistics to what were really my peers – Peter Gould, Barry Garner, Maurice Yeates – proved to be a real learning experience for all. Certainly the Northwestern atmosphere rivaled in enthusiastic ferment that which I had experienced at Washington. The year also brought the first 'quantitative symposium', in Chicago (sponsored by the ONR) and bringing together the Washington, Iowa, Northwestern, Chicago people, and others, and resulting in the later book, *Quantitative Geography*.[14]

Sweden: 1960–1
The NSF sponsored year in Sweden, at the University of Lund, not only permitted me to accomplish the research on the evolution of settlement and the role of migration (a study which brought my first break into the *Annals*[15]), but to learn so much more from Torsten Hägerstrand and other colleagues in Sweden; to meet Walter Christaller and many other famous European geographers at the IGU in Stockholm and the Lund Symposium in Urban Geography; and to travel widely in Europe.

Washington: 1961–6
I returned from Sweden not to Northwestern, but to Washington, because I feared being in the shadow of my advisor, Bill Garrison, who had moved to Evanston. It was not at all easy to replace

Garrison, and it took a few years to establish an independent position. The continuing series of NSF workshops and symposia were a vital source of reinforcement and knowledge. In part because most of the economic geography students were pre-empted by more senior faculty, and because of my contacts in Sweden, I came to advise students with social geographic and population interests. Inevitably this led to a shift in my own research and interests in these new directions. My wife and I were deeply involved in CORE[16] and the AFSC[17] in these years, and it was only natural that I should (begin to study race relations, the ghetto and the geography of poverty.

By 1966-7, which I spent in Chicago as Director of the Chicago Regional Hospital Study, the so called 'quantitative revolution' was essentially over, and a second generation had emerged.

The role of Office of Naval Research and National Science Foundation sponsored quantitative geography and regional science workshops and institutes; 1960-6

During the 1958-60 period, the quantitative group was very small indeed, and relatively scattered. Individuals perceived themselves as 'missionaries'. Although there was intense communication at meetings, an especially important mechanism for both group reinforcement and for 'spreading the word' were the early institutes and workshops. Most were intended as instructional, but since the instructors were novices themselves the sessions were often arenas of discovery and demonstration of new methods and findings. The 1960 Office of Naval Research (ONR) sponsored symposium, noted above, was both a reporting of research, and for the first time, a meeting between the human geography group and the mathematical, physical geography and cartography groups. In both 1961 and 1962, NSF sponsored instructional workshops were held, where, for example, I taught linear programming.

Regional science institutes, in (I think) 1964 and 1965, increased contacts with related disciplines, and were instrumental in spreading the 'revolution' to Britain via a converted participant, Peter Haggett.

Later in 1965 and 1966, NSF again sponsored more research-orientated symposia. It was at these later symposia that we sensed the problems of lack of publication outlets, which spawned the idea of a theoretical orientated journal, later to become *Geographical Analysis*.

Competition and External Pressure

Competition – both in the form of competition with other practitioners of 'other geographies' (descriptive, regional, cultural) and the editorial establishment, and with each other for the discovery and application of new methods or the statement of better theories – provided an impetus for progress. Of course, it also led to often unpleasant relations between camps, and at times to carelessness with (or too hasty or inappropriate application of) methods.

The external pressure was not just an imagined paranoia. There really was a measure of hostility and a large measure of suppression, which was variously manifested through programme committees, session chairmen and editors of journals. Such rebuffs were discouraging, but probably more effective in fostering a more committed and unified sense of cause. In any event we did get employed; we spoke out at meetings, did occasionally get published, and did attract good students, so that by 1966 it was clear that the 'revolution' was complete, not in overthrowing traditional geography but in gaining recognition, especially in the more prestigious institutions and journals and – more important – in beginning to turn geography around from a state of gradual decline to one of gradual recovery and growth.

A different kind of competition occurred through our strong participation in the early days of regional science. Having to meet the standards and face the criticisms of economists and others was sobering but tremendously beneficial. It got us into the habit of reading widely outside geography and (partly by necessity) of publishing outside geography, thereby gaining the valued critique of peers in related fields.

A 25-year Assessment

It is appropriate, after 25 years (1954–79) in geography to assess where I've come, what has happened to the discipline, whether I have any 'second thoughts' about direction, methods and my role in them. How do I feel about the critiques, the re-appraisals and the re-formulations?

Twenty years or so ago were Brian Berry and I wrote an essay on Geography as a Science. We never tried to publish it, because we decided it would be more fruitful to fight by doing rather than by philosophical argument. The essay was in the nature of a manifesto. We looked around and observed that geography was intellectually and numerically weak, and held in low esteem by other disciplines. It was viewed from outside as a describer of places or areas (regional geography), or of distribution of industries or farming (systematic geography), for the purpose of training teachers and preparing atlases. Its methods were descriptive – enumerative, even intuitive – and the absence of theory was stoutly defended by recourse to a concept of geography as the interpreter of the uniqueness of places. As such, it was no wonder that geography was being eased out of prestigious institutions, that it had no representation on or funding from national research bodies – in short that it was viewed as second rate (even though there had been many excellent individual geographers and published works over the preceding 50 years).

Our vision may have seemed radical to those satisfied with an inferior status, but was actually conservative in the sense that we wanted to save geography as a field of study and to join the mainstream of science. We viewed the objective of all disciplines as the pursuit of understanding, and of geography in particular as the attempt to understand the organisation and evolution of landscape. Our courses in economics, anthropology, geology, even sociology were pervaded by a dedication to explanation of human or physical behaviour, and to tests of such an explanation. Presumably there were reasons, however difficult to find, for the landscape looking like it did; and searching out these reasons seemed not only more exciting than 'just describing' landscape,[18] but indeed essential if we were to make any meaningful contribution to knowledge – either as individuals, or as a discipline.

It was no great secret that it had been the purpose of science for centuries to seek such an explanation, and that powerful methods of analysis and mathematical abstractions of processes had been built up to aid in this search. Therefore we intended to pursue 'explanation in geography' – to discover theories, and test them with appropriate methods.[19] I repeat all this because I am now asked: 'Should we have perceived the problem differently?' 'Are there alternative approaches to understanding we might better have used?' I have grave trouble with such questions, because they seem to ignore the sweep of history – that it has been science, however imperfectly executed, that has amassed the vast knowledge of societal and physical processes, that has liberated so many from superstition, and made possible through technology and organisation an escape from slavery, poverty and disease.

My simple answer is 'No'. I will not apologizse for my dedication to science: I see no alternative. I remain as convinced as ever that the principal objective of geography is to seek explanations of behaviour, and that science offers the means to do so (in retrospect, I might have pursued these goals somewhat differently, but I would not have altered the basic approach). I do not at all object to others who may wish to pursue other approaches, which they may perceive to be beyond or better than science. But I wish, in their zeal to do so, that they would not reduce science to but a narrow caricature of what it encompasses. I feel I must briefly address two of these several critiques – the humanist and the radical/Marxist.

It appears that many critics wish not merely to supplement science with other approaches (an idea that any searcher for truth should embrace), but to supplant it. Why? Some (Marxists) feel its practice is irretrievably tainted by the power relations of western society. Others may still fear the potential of science for penetrating mysteries, which they prefer unstudied. Many appear to suffer from a childish impatience that the theoretical–quantitative approaches have not already ushered in a new millenium of disciplinary prestige and societal transformation. In contrast, I assert that for a few people (going in many and varied directions), we have made considerable progress, both theoretically and practically, for so ridiculously short a time (20 years).

We have barely started the process of construction and testing of geographic theory. Instead of seizing upon other divining rods to discover truth by short cuts, we should learn patience, re-dedicating ourselves to the slow, tedious and difficult process of pushing back our ignorance – by the careful observation of behaviour, the hypothesis of the genesis of such behaviour and tests of the consistency of the behaviour i.e. through science. I by no means deny the humanist tradition in geography, nor its value in increasing our understanding of landscape. But this is not in opposition to geography as a science. As Yi-Fu Tuan observes 'Humanist geography contributes to science by drawing out the facts hitherto beyond the scientific purview'.[20] A humanistic approach can broaden and enliven a science of geography by much improving the questions asked; the variety of facts observed and treated; and the quality and completness of theories constructed. It is not then 'anti-science', but 'science liberating'. Scientific inquiry, especially in its behaviouralist form can indeed be reductionist, in part because the easy facts to come by may be misleading as well as incomplete. The humanist critique does not knock down the house of science, but it does reveal the simplicity and crudeness of the present edifice, revealed by objective analysis. The re-discovery of the variety of subjective feeling about the meaning of places does not pain me – I find it enriching. What pains me is the misconception that a scientist–by exclusion – may not be a humanist as well.

What about the Marxist critique? The argument that western science is biased toward the *status quo* is not an argument against science as a means of analysis, but against a parochial manipulation of its pursuit and recognition that individuals are typically creatures of their culture. The fact that many investigations do escape the constraints of a particular society's values proves science's more fundamental nature (I don't see Marxist methods as antithetical to science, but rather the working out of a particular hypothesis with particular methods). Indeed I like very much Peet's definition of radical science as a study of the interrelation of social processes and natural environment and spatial relations.[21] And, as I have argued elsewhere, our various theories are not *'status quo'* or 'capitalist' theories (most indeed assume income equality). Rather it is precisely the inequality of power over other people (and resources) that constrains processes to produce particular results. US quantitative geography has certainly been in the service of the establishment, and our models and analyses have usually served at best to ameliorate the abuses of the social system, but this reflects on the role of individuals, not the inherent nature of science and its methods.

Let me summarise this methodological morass with reference to my own research – to indicate that it is foolish to force us to choose a camp, to categorise us or our work too quickly. My article on the 'Negro ghetto',[22] was at one level, the application of a model (spatial diffusion) incidentally to a racial context. But three years of intense involvement in CORE on and off the picket lines, obviously influenced and enriched the study beyond that which a totally detached analysis would have been – because of both a radical political experience and an idealist commitment to racial cause. On the other hand, my emotional commitment to integration did not prevent me, as a scientist, from accepting the fact that there were good reasons for racial separation, including preferences of the minority itself.

What would I have done differently? Among many failings, my most serious, I think, has been the failure to follow the advice of Gilbert White to concentrate my efforts of a fairly narrow subject area, so as to insure a greater impact, not only on the discipline itself but far beyond (as his career exemplifies). Instead, I could not resist the tempation to pursue both theoretical and practical problems in too many areas – transportational, urban, social, political etc. Many of these studies shared an internal consistency of concern with models of spatial processes, but that was not the route to recognition. My personal commitment to social causes has ironically probably been more helpful to my career (although this was not my motivation or expectation) because of the visibility of early writing in the areas of segregation and poverty.

The same critique is valid for the discipline (but there may have been little choice). A very small number of persons, most of us not as well trained as we should be, tried to make progress in too many areas. Such dilution of efforts resulted in inadequate internal and external communication and critique. Perhaps, too, there was too much fascination with method, and not enough attention to quality of data, the validity of questions asked, and the construction of coherent theory.

A major error with respect to theory was the too ready acceptance of the establishment critique of environmentalism, and therefore the exclusion of an enormous and crucial area of inquiry – on what really might be the influence of environmental characteristics.

Geography is far stronger and more respectable than it was 20 years ago. It has considerable influence on some institutions and with some funding and operation agencies (here I'm speaking only of the US). It has even made a methodological impact of a sort on other disiplines (e.g. anthropolgy and planning). But it appears fragile – there are still few of us; our journals are not much read by outsiders; our representation at private universities and in national bodies is very weak. Individually and collectively, we are ever asked: 'But what does a geographer *do* at a university?' Can anyone really believe that we can afford an utterly eclectic view – that geography is what geographers 'do'; that a retreat to a concept of geography as the contemplation of the uniqueness of places will be anything but disastrous; that there is really any alternative to science except that we must do it better? If we are to retreat, then I suggest going back to older days, and bringing back into the forefront the question of environmental influence. That was geography's first attempt at theorising, and our methodological and ideological weakness (here our values really did dictate our science) discredited our efforts. Our retreat to the idiosyncractic and banal almost buried us. The 'quantitative' transformation was potentially liberating but most have remained unable to rise above the trivial, methodologically sophisticated or not. Now it is time to remember that geography concerns our understanding of *landscape*, that it is the 'joint evolving product of physical and human forces'.[23]

Notes and References

1. R. Hartshorne, *Perspective on the Nature of Geography* (London: Murray, 1960).
2. F.K. Schaefer, 'Exceptionalism in geography', *Annals Ass. Am. Geog.*, vol. 43 (1953) pp. 227–49.
3. W. Christaller, *Central Places in Southern Germany* (Englewood Cliffs, N.J.: Prentice-Hall, 1966).
4. A. Lösch, *The Economics of Location* (Yale University Press, 1954).
5. W. Isard, *Location and Space Economy* (MIT Press, 1956).
6. See, for example, P. Samuelson, *Linear Programming and Economic Analysis* (New York, 1958).
7. R. Hartshorne, *Perspective on the Nature of Geography*; P.E. James, *American Geography* (Syracuse University Press, 1954).
8. W.L. Garrison *et al.*, *Studies of Highway Development and Geographic Change* (University of Wastington Press, 1959).
9. R.L. Morrill and C.F. Jones, 'On the spatial organisation of the landscape', *Lund Studies in Geography*, series B, no. 46.
10. W.L. Garrison and W.E. Marks, *Geographic Impact of Highway Improvement* (University of Washington Press, 1958).
11. B. Berry and D.F. Marble, *Spatial Analysis* (Englewood Cliffs, N.J.: Prentice-Hall, 1968).
12. W.L. Garrison *et al.*, *Studies of Highway Development*.
13. R.L. Morrill, 'Normative model of trade areas and transportation', unpublished Ph.D.
14. R.L. Morrill *et al.*, *Quantitative Geography* (Chicago: Northwestern University Press, 1967).
15. R.L. Morrill, 'The development of spatial distributions of towns in Sweden', *Annals Ass. Am. Geog.*, vol. 53 (1963) pp. 1–14.
16. Congress of Racial Equality.
17. American Friends Service Committee.

18. I don't use this phrase to demean 'description', since I agree with M.D.I. Chisholm that 'good description is the basis of scientific progress', *Human Geography Evolution or Revolution* (Harmondsworth: Penguin, 1975) p. 171, but to demean our dependence on it.

19. To this day, many do not grasp that scientific methods, statistical procedures and mathematical models – even many theories – are *general*: no one can claim unique theories, let alone methods. The complaint is that we had to 'borrow' the theory and method; that this is 'demeaning' is groundless, and reveals an ignorance of how knowledge has been amassed over the centuries.

20. Yi-Fu Tuan, 'Humanistic Geography', *Annals of the Association of American Geographers*, vol. 66 (1976).

21. R. Peet, *Radical Geography* (London: Methuen, 1977).

22. R.L. Morrill, 'The negro ghetto', *Geographical Review*, vol. LV (1965) pp. 339–61.

23. M.D.I. Chisholm, *Human Geography*, p. 172.

Toward a Sermon of Modernity

GUNNAR OLSSON

Pre-text

This recollection is a tribute to the god Janus. Janus is a pivoting symbol of gate keeping, whose major characteristic is not that he can see in opposite directions at the same time, but that he manages to merge seemingly contradictory categories into a meaningful whole; in the same evaluating glance of the present he can catch a glimpse both of those pasts which once were, and of those futures which have yet to come.

Janus's concern is with *creativity*. This makes him a deity of our own time, for the crucial presumption of modernity is that creative praxis grows out of criticism; while created objects appear fixed, they are in deed temporary; while creative activity seems always in flux, it is in fact permanent. Thing yields to process, stability to change, certainty to ambiguity, noun to verb, being to becoming. And yet, even Janus himself is hung on the momentarily stable reality of the present; the time is therefore now, for in actuality there can be no other time. In the tale I am about to tell, the present is nevertheless doubly tied to the memories of the late 1960s and to the prospects of 1984.

In the Sisyphean spirit of modernity, I shall strive to place myself inside Janus's head, well remembering from Nietzsche that it was not God who created man in his image, but Man who created god in his. From that privileged position, I shall try to understand how Janus makes sense out of the logical contradictions he sees around him. What I would really like to understand is how he manages to deal with this double bind in such a fashion that he is celebrated as a god, and not put away as a schizophrenic. My examples will seem to come from that special case of 'thought-and-action' which is 'geography-and-planning'. In reality, however, I shall illustrate some principles of forgetting, for even though parts of what I write reflect what I know without knowing it, the most crucial fragments are those I have forgotten without knowing that I forgot them.

If my distortions happen to be further distorted in the reader's mind, then so much the better. I will then have helped creativity along, for creativity never stems from the perfect rerendering of simple truth but always from the errors inevitable in any translation; at those moments, interpretation yields to inter-penetration and subjective ambiguity is allowed to rule over objective certainty. Translation without introduction of 'me' is therefore impossible. It follows that the meaning of my words reigns over yours regardless of whether the sign 'me' denotes the writer or the reader. The central purpose of this discussion is consequently to reveal some hidden aspects of the collective unconscious which are in the story of the geography of the late 1960s. As it will appear, 'ideology critique' is another word for the same activity. My tribute to Janus is not in glorifying him, but in being so immersed in his spirit that I cannot do without it.

Confession of Sins

Science is an integral part of modern mythology. Like other myths it aims for truth, defines truth, and supports truth. Obeying its ritual I must therefore specify a set of preliminary definitions.

To define is necessary, for without definitions our thoughts-and-actions are anchored in the ever shifting nothingness of solipsism. And yet, to define is to take the first step towards the fallacy of misplaced concreteness and the alienation it embodies. Thus, to define is to distinguish what is inside a boundary from what is outside it; to split open a natural whole; to sift friend from foe like wheat from chaff; to employ an intellectual technique for grasping and communicating what is otherwise non-graspable and noncom-municable; to use Ockham's razor on Samson's head. But in prison, Samson's hair grew long again, and in the revenge of the end he killed more Philistines than in his entire life.

According to the *Oxford English Dictionary*, to define is 'to bring to an end', 'to state exactly what (a thing) is', and 'to declare the signification (of a word)'. All definitions involve elements of 'thingification', and are therefore well ingrained in the current metaphysics of presence. But the necessary Cartesian separations are never more than the first step in the recognition of the interdependence of subject and object, self and other. For bridges to connect, there must first be a separation:

Whatisculturehidinginthesilentspacesbetweenitswords?

But to define is not merely an intellectual necessity. It is also an issue of making others accept your cleaving categories. Whenever you do, you exert power. As a consequence, I shall strive to write, and therefore act, in such a way that I erase my original definitions, even though I acknowledge Heidegger's and Derrida's point that whatever is erased always leaves a trace. And so it is that this recollection is loosely patterned after the liturgy of the Protestant church itself. I am already in the midst of a collective confession of sins (admitting the impossibility of staying within given categories); I then proceed to a confession of faith (defining what the specific congregation takes to be its categorial boundaries). Then I move on to the reading and explication of the gospel text (applying the definitional principles to a special case). Finally, I end with renewed prayer that our trespasses be forgiven:

Oh, to sin is to trespass. To trespass is to cross a boundary. To cross a boundary is to break a definition. To break a definition is to create. To create is to be different. To be different is to sin. To sin is to be aware of self-reference.

So, Janus! Help me become a sinner! Let me understand how you break definitions! Teach me how to erase what others see as irresolvable paradoxes! Teach me the equation of that third lens inside your head whereby you transform contradictory images into coherent wholes!
    Speak, memory, speak!

As memory speaks, it should nevertheless be remembered that my memory is like yours. What is crucial is not what it remembers, but what it forgets. Memory has little to do with what once was, more with what is right now and most with what is left for the futures which never will be. In that perspective, memory appears as a hypothesis yet to be rejected. Its claim to truthhood is not that it happens to be true but that the concept of truth is in the service of legitimation. In ancient Greece, *aletheia* meant 'true', whereas its opposite, *lēthē*, meant not 'untrue' but 'forgetfulness'; etymology itself suggests that remembering is a sanctioned technique for purifying one's individual and collective conscience. By telling half truths now I make it easier to tell whole lies later. And yet, a new time has just begun, for what else can time ever do? Heads chasing tails, tails chasing heads.

Confession of Faith

In the disciplinary environment of post-war Sweden, there were tight ties between geography and planning. If not then, then at least now, I believe planning to be a modern strategy for wielding power, not over space but over time, not over yourself but over others. I believe planning to be a political and bureaucratic phallic symbol whereby the present penetrates the future. I believe that to plan is to preserve what now is by ensuring that current intentions are turned into the stones of physical and institutional structures. The values of the strong today are thereby ontologically metamorphosed into the facts for the weak of tomorrow. The result is a modern version of the castration complex in which some fear the loss of something they once had, while others experience that lack of something they never possessed. Thus, from the suppressor's elevated perspective, planning appears as a way of extending a heritage of hopes and fears from one generation to another. From a different perspective, it looks like an efficent technique for raping the future. From either perspective, it seems like other cases of penis envy: inseparable from authority.

The authoritarian elements in planning exploit hierarchical organisation levels, and this is the reason why geographers could use Christaller as a key to the vaults of consulting firms and planning departments. The main issue to understand is how the welfare functions of different decision units are traded off against each other: planning interferes deeply in the dialectic between society and individual. This fact posits planning in the holey cross between the social sciences and politics, for neither activity poses a more central question than that about the relation between the individual and the collective, one and many, subject and object, I and you, us and them. Myth – old as well as new – shares the same concern. And yet, it is through dialectical analysis that one learns about others through oneself, and about oneself through others.

My conceptions of 'geography-and-planning' lead to issues of power. So do my notions of ideology. But what exactly is that untouchable for which people continue to kill and get killed? What is the structure of those belief systems which require some architects to build Auschwitz and others to construct dehumanised apartment complexes and commuter trains? What are those forces which reflect and influence the ontological transformations through which things are turned into relations, and relations into things?

These questions are in the spirit of Janus, for they are questions of ideology critique. They are therefore themselves part of that ideology of modernity which Marcel Duchamp and Octavio Paz have lived and expressed. And yet they are all embedded in the classical definition which takes ideology to be a form of social philosophy which aspires to merge description and prescription, theory and norm. An ideology is a system of coherent beliefs, whereby we try both to understand the world as it is and to change it into what it ought to be. It follows that different ideologies express different sets of internal relations. They have the power of bringing theory and practice together, and of enabling their followers to distinguish permissible from nonpermissible, go(o)d from (d)evil, Heaven from Hell. It is in the nature of all ideologies to be thoroughly dialectical; what they do is to forge together what logic takes to be contradictory, to combine what conventional knowledge says is impossible to combine.

Choir

My conceptions of ideology and planning are closely related. Both activities are nourished by the legitimating interplay of mystification and domination. It follows that planning is an ingredient of that ethical bond whereby the 'is' of the past and the 'ought' of the future are glued together. Everyone has his ideology, for without it he would not know how first to dis-member the world into graspable pieces and then to re-member it into a whole again. It is important to realise that those who deviate too much from accepted norms of categorisation always end up in some form of social asylum: crackpots crack pots.

There are few works more thoroughly ideological than those of Karl Marx; not only did he understand the world, but he changed it as well. His insight was that the two verbs 'is' and 'ought' are dialectically 'consumed' in the ideology of the ruling class. In the first sentence of *The German Ideology* he and Engels wrote that 'men have constantly made up for themselves false conceptions about themselves, about what they are and about what they ought to be'.[1] Thus, they claimed that, in the collective unconscious, actions become harmonised with possibilities just as possibilities arise in the interest of the *status quo*. But, as Wittgenstein later came to note, this harmonising legitimation is neither intentional nor conscious, for intentions are thoroughly embedded in their situation, in human customs and social institutions; intentions are in internal relations and thereby in the belief systems which support and reflect them. Saying that an actor has evil motives is therefore deeply misleading. The situation is rather like classical tragedy, where everything is right in the beginning and everything horribly wrong in the end. But nothing is on purpose, because in reality beginnings never reach their end even though every end grows out of a beginning. The development of 'geography-and-planning' offers a good case in point.

To understand human action is never to blame. It is instead to recognise that we as actors are so entrenched in our own roles that we take the shadow play to be reality and reality to be the play. It is indeed an integral part of all internal relations (and thereby of all ideologies and all mythologies) that we obey their commands without hearing them, and without knowing where they come from. To break the spell completely is impossible, for under the mask I shed there is always another. And the next veil I always fail to notice because it is one with my own sight; I see the mote in my neighbour's eye, but not the beam in my own. Perhaps the fashion of today's ideology critique is nothing but a legitimating activity for modernity itself.

The internal relations of mystification and domination were never as skillfully disentangled as in Marx's critique of fetishism. Since he conceived of money as the fetishist commodity par excellence, he saw the money form of things as a reflection and determinant of what he called 'the categories of bourgeois economy'.[2] With his dialectical mind he could grasp how the seemingly contradictory forms of use and exchange value exposed nothing but different sides of the same commodity. The major shortcoming of the men who hitherto had made up false conceptions for (and of) themselves was that only one of their Janus eyes functioned: their 'thing eye' saw, while their 'relation eye' was blind. And so it comes about that the captives of capitalist ideology are better equipped to explain the nature and use values of a commodity than to understand relations and exchange values. But in the more discerning mind of Janus, the relations connecting the labour of one individual with that of the rest appear, not as direct social relations between individuals at work but as what they really are – material relations between persons, and social relations between things. It is a characteristic of those in power that they have internalised this ontological law of the double so well that they automatically turn it to their advantage – unconsciously, un-wittingly and often unwillingly.

But even though I have recognised some of Janus's features in Marx, the history of Marxism is different. Instead of actions conceived as ontological transformations, it speaks of social and economic reality fitted into the categories of dialectical materialism. In the world of qualitative leaps, however, two times two can sometimes become five, just as in some geometries parallel lines can sometimes cross. And so it is that Hegel and Riemann, Marx and Einstein all have something important in common. What they share is a concern with severed relations and a pursuit of categories gone astray; while Hegel and Riemann formulated new principles of thought, Marx and Einstein used these alternative reasoning modes to catch and order new sets of material data. Their collective spirit loomed high in the group of young geographers in the 1960s – unconsciously, unwittingly and often unwillingly.

Gospel

Although beginnings never reach their end, they nevertheless indicate the degree of belief I have in the future. Thus, 'in the, beginning was' is the beginning of myth; 'once upon a time' is the beginning of fairy tales; 'in the end' is the beginning of the being of nothingness.

For the truth of today, we now turn to the gospel text in Figure 1. It is Chapter 1132 from the *Book of Certainty and Ambiguity*.

Preaching

Janus's message is in the white spaces of the gospel text itself. They connect stages on life's way, and in this sense they silently speak

Text		Causal relations
Wold	$I_{ij} = f(d_{ij})$	
Isard	$I_{ij} = k \dfrac{P_i P_j}{d_{ij}^{b}}$	Social gravity
Curry	$I_{ij} = k \exp[-bf(d_{ij})]$	Negative exponential
Dacey	$P(x) = \left(\dfrac{x+k-1}{k-1} \right) p^k (1-p)^x$	Negative binomial
Lukasiewicz		Many-valued logics
Gang of Five		Geographic inference
Marx / Hegel		Dialectical relations

$$\text{FORM} \; -\,-\,-\,? \,-\,-\,-\; \text{PROCESS}$$

$$\text{T I F}$$

Self-conscious re-evaluation

Russell/Frege — *Principia Mathematica* — $E!(\backslash x)(Qx) = (\exists b)(x)[(Qx) \equiv (x = b)]$
$U(\backslash x)(Qx) = (\exists b)\{(x)[(Qx) \equiv (x = b)] \,\&\, (Ub)\}$

Gödel — Incompleteness theorem — $(\exists y)(x)\sim\text{Dem}(x,y)$

von Wright — Predicament — $O(p|q)\&O(\sim p|q)$

Sartre — Ontological transformations — Existence/Subsistence

Wittgenstein/Joyce/Derrida — Language prison — Self-reference

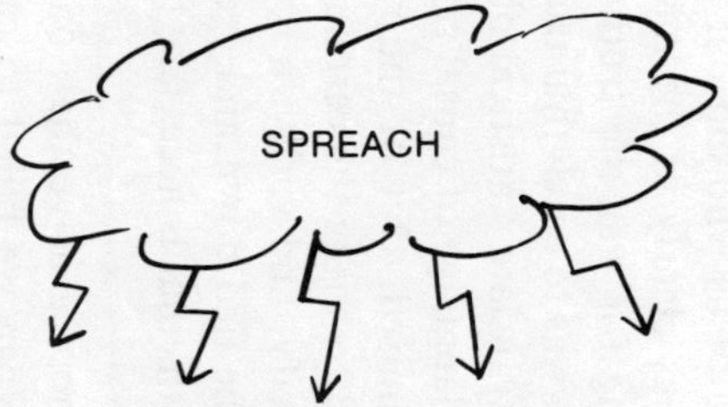

Spencer Brown/Nietzsche/Lacan — Symbolic relations

SPREACH

FIGURE 1 *The Gospel Text*

for, of and to themselves. They should perhaps be left alone.

Convention nevertheless demands that I submit to the common theme of this volume and explicate the story of the gospel's first verses. These are not about the success of the spatial revolution in geography but rather about its failure, not about the major over-throw but rather about the subsequent putsch. To stress this lack of obedience is a point of intellectual honesty paid in reverence to those who went before. For, if there ever were a 'quantitative–theoretical–spatial' revolution in human geography, I and my generation had little to do with it. When its course was chartered and its manifestoes secretly passed around, I was still in high school, much closer to the acts of motorcycle maintenance than to the thoughts of academic hothouses.

And yet, for those of us who did our dissertations in the early 1960s a new time was clearly in the making. What I and some others were searching for was the truth of human spatial inter-action. Our ambition was to catch that truth in the most precise net we knew, that is to translate statistical observations into the clear and non-ambiguous language of causal relations in which the error term had been minimised. Out of the rich manifold of specific experience we wished to wring the certainty of general knowledge. The goal was to specify, and verify, a set of parameter values by which reality could be tied down and eventually tamed. We were after the kind of 'truth' that is necessary for the construction of an optimal world.

But reality was more evasive than our naive minds had been taught to believe. When we failed to catch truth by our simple deterministic models, we gradually drifted into probability estimates, stochastic models and even into a brief encounter with many-valued logics and fuzzy sets. The idea was that the observed variations in human behaviour had a metaphoric counterpart in statistical variance; the structure of action was assumed to be more akin to probability theory and non-Euclidean geometry than to algebra and conventional Euclidean space. The major approach remained the same, however, for it was still a Cartesian question of translating 'observational' data into a 'theoretical' language whose structure was as close as possible to the structure of the investigated phenomena – if these obeyed stochastic principles, then we could not hope to say anything precise about them unless we employed a stochastic model. And yet, the game of certainty and ambiguity had already changed: we were no longer chasing truth, truth was chasing us.

Or so it can be told: a search for clarity and security in a world of increasing confusion and indeterminacy. Mostly, though, it was simply a matter of passing time, of innocent war babies playing in a field of intellectual blind shells.

The activity nevertheless continued. And then suddenly, around 1968, something drastically different burst upon us. *First* was the suspicion that those parameter values in which we had hoped to encapsulate our general knowledge of human behaviour had more to do with the spatial distribution of origins and destinations than with interaction *per se*. Put differently, we were measuring form rather than process, map rather than behaviour, geometry rather than human action. *Then* came the insight that the form/process relation involved some extremely challenging issues of geographic and causal inference. Experiments with the negative binomial proved that even perfect rendering of spatial form was not sufficient for determining the process which had generated it. What the analysis yielded was not more knowledge of the phenomena the model was speaking *about*: what it revealed was instead the hidden structure the model was speaking *within*.

The implications were doubly shattering. Not only did they strike at the heart of the discipline, whose main claim was that spatial analysis lead to knowledge of human behaviour. They also initiated fundamental questions about the relations between geography and planning on the one hand, and geography and ideology on the other. It was a basic tenet of the planning of those times that changes in spatial organisation lead to social change and ultimately to a better world, more fair and more efficient. Given the problems of spatial inference, however, this assumption about the symmetry of explanation and prediction had to be abandoned: to argue for social engineering was no longer ethically defensible. What initially had presented itself under the disguise of humane methodology now appeared as crude, inhuman and power-ridden ideology. What our elders had told us to be emancipatory we found out to be the opposite.

In my own mind, my heritage always antagonistic to the practices of Swedish social democracy, I could now begin to understand why the results of planning so often turned out to be the opposite of its stated intentions. The resulting paradoxes, double binds, predicaments and tragedies became my major concern. More than a decade later they remain unsolved. They are likely to stay in that tantalising state because they are central to the human condition of modernity. Torsten Hägerstrand seems to have sensed something similar, for in his time–space studies he has shown how social and personal life is bound by temporal and spatial constraints. *La condition humaine* is one of predicaments lived behind prison walls. We knew it all along, even though we can express it first now: the walls are invisible because they are internally related not only to our ideology but to our culture, to our shared norms, to the silent spaces of our language itself. But the air we breathe is invisible too. We do not realize the need for it until we begin to suffocate. SPREACH! Break and preach, search and reach. And Babble's walls come mumbling down.

Communion

And so it came to pass that what briefly had appeared as the phalanx of geography penetrated the discipline so deeply that it got seriously wounded: the spear head itself split apart. In the shadow of North Armorica's 1968 nothing else was to be expected. The story has been told many times, by many withnesses, from many perspectives. Its details need not be repeated even though its social and intellectual pattern is likely to be.

It may nevertheless be instructive to note what subsequently happened. The discipline as a whole got caught in the backwaters and had to sink in the whirlpool before it could re-emerge somewhere else. The individuals with whom I shared the interest in wine and geographic inference seem still to be headed in the same gener(ation)al direction, albeit along circuitous routes; thing has yielded to process, stability to change, being to becoming, thought to action, youth to middle age.

One was the Australian Reginald Golledge, who gave himself away to behavioural psychology and for a while served as the editor of the *Geographical Analysis*, the phallus symbol of quantitative geography. Another was the New Zealander Leslie King, who from being the first editor of the journal moved on to the heights of university administration. A third was the American John Hudson, who turned his devotion to pigs, railroads and historical geography eventually to become editor of the *Annals of the Association of American Geographers*. A fourth was David Harvey, who got himself thoroughly and thoughtfully immersed in world Marxism. A fifth was myself, the Swede, who began wondering about philosophical problems – first about birds and eggs and then about eggs and birds. To outsiders it may seem strange that all of us continue not only to be called 'geographers' but also to meet whenever there is a chance; not for the sake of geography, but for the lack of discipline. Perhaps we are now safely back in the homes we never really left.

Blessing

Conventions die more slowly than revolutions. As revolutions fade away, recollections fill the empty spaces. Rebels, however, have a passion for Russian roulette. Some win, some lose. It is significant that Diana was Janus's favorite: when peace came and she could return to the temple, he closed its gates. In self-reference, silence speaks through the culture which fills its empty spaces. Praxis is totalisation, totalisation is praxis.

For nothing spake to me but the Fair face of Heaven and Earth, when yet I could not speak. I did my Bliss, when I did silence, breach.

SPREACH, Janus, SPREACH!

Notes and References

1. K. Marx and F. Engels, *The German Ideology*, ed. C.J. Arthur (London: Lawrence & Wishart, 1970).
2. Ibid.

From Here and Now to There and Then: Some Notes on Diffusions, Defusions and Disillusions[1]

ALLAN PRED

Quite obviously, any person writing of his or her recollections of the 1950s and 1960s from the vantage point of the 1980s cannot produce the same document that would have resulted if he or she had kept a contemporary diary or record. Almost inevitably, when looking back from here and now to there and then our selection of foci and our interpretation of events are coloured by our 'life content' during the interval (or by the external actions and internal experiences we have accumulated in weaving a path through time–space on both a daily and lifelong scale), and by the inseparable context within which that 'life content' has unfolded.

That I begin this essay by lapsing into some of the vocabulary of time-geography is no accident, no spur of the moment inspiration. At the constantly receding here and now from which the editors of this volume have asked me to reconstruct 'the decisions and difficulties' which confronted me personally during the 1950s and 1960s, I am preoccupied with time-geography. More precisely, I am much engrossed with employing time-geography as a means of gaining a greater understanding of: the impact of institutional and technological innovations upon individual 'life content' and, more generally, the dialectical relationships existing between individual behaviour and the workings of society. Consequently, what follows is (at least in part) an attempt to bring my current time-geographic view of both the world at large and my own life to bear upon a small selection of particular past decisions and difficulties. However, since time-geography is often mistakenly construed as nothing more than a form of constraint analysis, it is appropriate to begin by digressing so as to illustrate some of the ways in which that still evolving perspective allows one better to appreciate what, in general and personal terms, was involved in the 'quantitative [and conceptual] revolution'.

The 'Revolution' as a Series of Innovations With Personal Consequences

The 'revolution' which human geography underwent during the 1950s and 1960s is often depicted in broad and crude terms as having involved a pronounced shift in emphasis from the ideographic to the nomothetic. In less conventional terms, it also can be viewed somewhat more exactly like any other 'revolution' – intellectual, political, or economic – as having comprised a series of innovations that gained widespread acceptance. Each innovation – whether it was a specific quantitative technique, a specific location theory, or a specific conceptual framework borrowed from another discipline – did not merely in an academic sense alter the face of human geography. Each innovation also had a variety of obvious and subtle consequences for the intellectual development and general 'life content' of numerous individuals.

The students, teachers and researchers who became associated with any one of the 'revolution's' component innovations by definition could do so only by allocating some of their limited time resources to it through participation in one or more 'projects' (from the time-geographic viewpoint, a project consists of *the entire series of tasks* necessary to the completion of any goal-orientated behaviour; and the carrying through, learning, or use of any type of innovation always requires the performance of a project by an individual, group, or larger coalition).[2] The tasks associated with such projects (like those associated with any other), normally had an internal logic of their own which required that they be sequenced in a more or less specific order. Moreover, each of the logically sequenced component tasks was not undertaken in individual isolation, but was synonymous with the formation of activity bundles, or with the convergence in time and space of the paths being traced out either by two or more humans, or by one or more people and one or more physically tangible inputs or resources (e.g. books, classroom space, computer terminals). To take a mundane example, when I participated in certain graduate seminars at the Pennsylvania State University and the University of Chicago in the late 1950s and very early 1960s – thereby learning and applying innovative methods and concepts – it was necessary for me to sequence my enrolment, attendance of weekly meetings, reading of particular materials, and writing of papers in an order that had little if any room for flexibility; and it was necessary for me in each instance to bring my path into convergence – *usually at specific times and places* – with those of specific students, professors, journals, desks etc.

It is critical to realise that participation in completely new projects always requires the elimination, modification, or re-scheduling of existing time uses, or the rejection of other potential time uses (forms of project participation). The projects springing from innovations are always time (and space) consuming; any movement which is necessary to bring an individual path into conjunction with other project participants is also time-consuming; and the individual's time resources are limited to 24 hours per day. Hence, those reading particular publications or carrying out research in connection with any one of the 'revolution's' innovations were wittingly, or unwittingly, rejecting or postponing the possibility of reading other publications or performing other research. When project commitments at the University of Chicago in the autumn of 1959 demanded that I devote considerable time to a painstaking reading of Christaller's writings, I forsook, at least for the moment, the possibility of reading the works of Vidal de la Blache or any of a number of other intellectually seminal geographers and non-geographers. (When numerous individuals make a commitment to the innovation based projects of a 'revolution' or some slower form of institutional or societal change, they in essence are consciously or unconsciously contributing in aggregate to the partial or total abandonment of previous innovations, or to the 'defusion' of innovations. Thus, just as the limited time resources of any areally defined society bound the capacity of that society to maintain many of their traditions and customs or cultural heritage in the face of change, so do the limited time resources or finite reading and communication capacity of the total membership of any discipline bound its capacity to maintain much of its intellectual heritage, or to keep alive simultaneously old and new knowledge, viewpoints, methods, and concepts.)[3]

When individuals participated in the various tasks which were part of the innovation based projects tied to the 'revolution' of the 1950s and 1960s, they not only displaced or completely sacrificed academic alternatives but, owing to the temporal and spatial locations at which the tasks in question were carried out, their own physical indivisibility, and the operation of other time-geographic constraints and 'realities'.[4] They daily eliminated or modified opportunities for interacting with other people and objects in activities inside or outside the 'household' – on any given day the path synchronisation and 'synchorisation' demanded by, for example, a seminar or the use of computer facilities, constrained when, where, and for how long friends, lovers, spouses, or parents and children could intermingle with one another. This set of circumstances often must have held consequences for the outcome of subsequent 'revolution'-based project tasks, since the information and experience acquired from 'non-academic' interactions is likely to have impinged occasionally upon writings, discussions, or other 'professional' actions, either by influencing values and attitudes, or by influencing moods and intentions.

In a not unrelated vein, in time-geographic terms there is a constantly ongoing dialectic between the external (or corporeal action) and internal (or mental experience and intention) dimensions of an individual's life. Consequently neither I, nor anybody else who participated in specific projects that were part of the 'revolution' of the 1950s and 1960s came to do so independently of our past life path and the societal context in which that path was lived out. No person can spin out his physically observable daily and life paths – corporeally participating in projects, activity bundles, and interactions with other persons and objects – without amassing internal experiences that are fundamental to the shaping of his values, perceptions, attitudes, capabilities, preferences, and conscious or sub-conscious motivations, and hence his goals and intentions. Yet in choosing among roles, activity bundles, and interactions that are possible within the environment's time-geographic constraints, and in thereby eventually adding corporeal actions to his daily and life paths, no individual can do otherwise but, consciously or unconsciously, fall back on his previous mental experiences and consequently derived goals and intentions. In addition – insofar as participation in academic (or other institutional) projects is dependent upon holding certain independently existing roles access to which is generally governed by rules, competence requirements and economic, class, or other constraints

– participation normally depends partly on whether or not the actions and experiences of one's previous life path has made one eligible for such an independently existing role.[5] In other words, whether or not a person became part of the 'revolution' during the 1950s and 1960s depended on where he or she succeeded in occupying an independently exisiting graduate student or faculty role. For, clearly, the daily exposure of graduate students and faculty to personal contacts, first- and second-hand ideas, books, articles, and informational impulses in general varied greatly from department to department (for example, students who found their way to the University of Washington's Department of Geography during the late 1950s were educated and professionally socialised in a manner which differed greatly from the way in which their counterparts at most other US geography departments were trained).

Berkeley in the Early 1960s: Difficulties and Delights

For those in the USA and Canada who were the most active espousers of the 'quantitative revolution', the geography department at the University of California, Berkeley, served as the ultimate anti-revolutionary symbol. In the eyes of the 'revolution's' most avid proselytisers (and even in the eyes of many of the 'revolution's' more broad minded advocates), the Berkeley department was seen as the most entrenched bastion of resistance, the home of antediluvian views and practices, and above all, the intellectual fiefdom of Carl Sauer and his particular brand of cultural geography (outsiders were so prone to associate Berkeley with Sauer that even a decade or more after his retirement many still imagined him to still be running the department completely in his own image). Given this set of circumstances, some recollections of my years as a junior faculty member at Berkeley during the early 1960s may be of more than passing interest to historians and interpreters of the 'revolution'.

My arrival in Berkeley in June 1962, to take on the independently existing role of Assistant Professor, would not have been possible if I had not previously occupied several independently existing roles which facilitated or necessitated certain daily path interactions. Had I not been a graduate student at the University of Chicago I would not have had frequent daily encounters with Marvin Mikesell, and he would not have written a letter (unbeknown to me) to

Jim Parsons, then the departmental chairman at Berkeley, concerning my qualifications for a vacancy that had occurred (Mikesell
knew of the unadvertised opening because of the contacts he himself had developed when occupying a graduate student role at
Berkeley a few years earlier). Had I not attended Antioch College
in the role of undergraduate between 1953 and 1957, I would not
have developed personal relationships which enabled me to visit
Berkeley while writing the fourth chapter of my dissertation during
February 1962, and I would not have had an extended informal
interview with Parsons (while still unaware of the fact that Mikesell
had written to him). Had I not taken on the short lived role of participant in the annual meetings of the Association of American
Geographers at Miami Beach a few months later, my path would
not have intersected (unintentionally) once again with that of Jim
Parsons, he would not have congratulated me upon my being hired
at the University of Washington – only to find out that I knew
absolutely nothing of such an appointment – and he would not
have consulted quickly with those of his colleagues attending the
meetings concerning the wisdom of offering me the Berkeley post.[6]

Discussions with faculty members and fellow graduate students
at Chicago had given me a sometimes discouraging and sometimes
bright impression of what to anticipate at Berkeley. In retrospect,
things turned out to be both a lot worse and a lot better than I had
expected.

One unanticipated difficulty sprang from my age. When I
arrived in Berkeley, some months before my 26th birthday, I was
somewhat younger than half or more of the graduate students in
residence and considerably younger than my colleagues. Whether
or not it was because the Berkeley environment encouraged
students to regard intellectual merit as a function of age, I
perceived my lack of years as a factor contributing to the prevailing
lack of interest in my research shown by the department's MA and
PhD candidates. Much more difficult to accept was the fact that
influential colleagues, while personable and amiable, were steering
graduate students away from me; telling them that there was no
place for either theory or models in geography; telling them that I
was not a 'true' geographer because of my inadequate concern for
physical geography and 'field work'. (My basic view of field work
at that time was essentially the same as that I hold now, although
somewhat less thought out. To wit: the distinction made between
'field work' and other more everyday observations and experiences

is but one manifestation of a general unwillingness to accept the fact that our 'professional' and 'non-professional' lives are not in dichotomous opposition to one another, but dialectically inter-related.) As it was, the silent expression by graduate students of their lack of interest in my type of research turned out to be something of a blessing in disguise. Being largely (but not entirely) deprived of the exhilaration and intellectual stimulation that was to come from working simultaneously with several gifted graduate students during the 1970s, I found myself with large blocks of time that could be devoted to reading, research, and the writing of articles and books.

Given the alluring portrait of Sauer that had been painted for me in Chicago by Marvin Mikesell and Philip Wagner, and given the role of intellectual villainy that had been assigned to him by many of those committed to the 'quantitative revolution', it was only natural that curiousity spurred me to seek out this almost legendary figure. Sauer, who came into the department daily throughout his retirement, kept his office door figuratively if not literally open at all times, and it was therefore easy to engage him in frequent conversations. Listening to Sauer could be extremely fascinating. With ever-present pipe in mouth, he would often ramble on at length, unveiling the breadth of his knowledge and in effect providing a sweeping account of the changes that had occurred in the fields of anthropology, economics, history, and geography during the 1920s and 1930s. On the other hand, listening to Sauer could be extremely disturbing because of his narrowmindedness. While he was a great proponent of 'historical geography' and 'the historical approach', Sauer appeared to have little appreciation or understanding for my attempts to model *processes* of urban growth and socioeconomic change over time and space. My broaching of these topics would almost inevitably lead by an indirect route either to a calm but unmistakeable criticism of the objectives of just about every stripe of contemporary social science, or to a defence of the virtues of studying history for it's own sake. Not unexpected-ly, in both his general observations and his reactions to my views Sauer frequently expressed an unwavering distrust of what he liked to refer to as 'the use of numbers'.

In the end, it was not Sauer's refusal to tolerate a more pluralistic view of the nature of geographical inquiry which led to my breaking off our occasional conversations by the middle of my second year at Berkeley. It was rather his narrowmindedness with respect to the American social scene which forced the rupture. In particular, his interpretation of the black civil rights movement could be paraphrased, in essence, as follows: 'Negroes are simple, happy folk whose natural place is close to the soil. If only they hadn't been driven from the southern countryside into the cities we would have none of these problems now'. Suffocated by numerous variations on this theme, I had little choice but to terminate my visits. The cessation of my conversations with Sauer caused a certain uneasiness, primarily because I feared – justifiably or not – that comments he might make to some senior members of the department could jeopardise my chances for promotion.

One minor difficulty which ironically confronted me during the early years at Berkeley took the form of repeated expressions of sympathy made by friends and acquaintances in other geography departments. At annual meetings and elsewhere I was often asked how I could stand up under my plight: How could I possibly function in such a department? How could I work in isolation from anybody else who was interested in 'modern' geography and the 'quantitative revolution'? Despite my limited interaction with graduate students, and despite the worsening of my relationship with Sauer, I hardly felt myself to be in a position worthy of sympathy. Not only was Berkeley a great university, with exceptional facilities and an enviable physical setting, but intellectual stimulation was available in such tremendous quantities from a variety of sources that the absence of fellow 'revolutionaries' within the department was more than compensated for.

If I wished to discuss location theory and regional growth, there were young people of the calibre of Michael Tietz and William Alonso, who were hired by the Department of City and Regional Planning at about the same time that I arrived. During my first few summers in Berkeley I also had access to a host of 'revolutionaries', including Brian Berry and others, as a consequence of the regional science institute organised by Walter Isard. (The first or second summer also brought me into fleeting contact with Peter Haggett, who was teaching geomorphology in the department's summer programme. Haggett's role as summer instructor enabled him to have frequent daily interactions of a formal and informal nature with participants in Isard's institute – interactions which undoubtedly influenced the direction which his longer range work shortly began to take.)[7] If I wished to discuss processes of urban growth and socioeconomic change there was the joint Berkeley– Stanford faculty seminar on the history of economic development, which was held once monthly. (The other participants were economists and historians who were contributing to a 'quantitative revolution' of their own – the so called 'new economic history'. I perceived many (but not all) of them as resembling the worst of their geographic counterparts insofar as they were preoccupied with methodologies and quantitative techniques as ends in themselves, were at best interested in comparative statics rather than complex, probabilistic processes, and were rarely concerned with intellectual or philosophical issues of substance.)

Much more importantly, *sans* the presence of other young modern geographers, the Berkeley department was still a place of enormous intellectual vitality. Although he was uninterested in quantitative methods, often highly singular in his views, and not inclined to share my appreciation of models and theories pertaining to information circulation, innovation diffusion, and decision-making, Jay Vance had a deep concern for the modelling of processes – something which unfortunately was absent among the great majority of form orientated champions of the 'revolution' – and a seemingly boundless knowledge concerning recent and past urban growth in North America and Europe. While the models of past US urban growth that I began formulating in the early 1960s were quite removed from Vance's way of looking at things, their birth was much facilitated and inspired by his interest and our almost daily conversations over mid-morning coffee. Inspiration of a more general sort came from Clarence Glacken, who occupied the office next to mine. During the early 1960s Glacken was nearing completion of *Traces on the Rhodian Shore*, a book which has become a classic in its own time and which, it can be argued, will have a more lasting impact inside and outside of geography than any work penned by an individual identifiable with the 'quantitative revolution' of the 1950s and 1960s.[8] Glacken was a person with whom I could discuss philosophical issues. He was also a person who because of his wide ranging command of the history of ideas could provide entertainment and enlightenment through a few casual comments made on something he or I had read recently. The painstaking and extremely careful way in which he conducted his work also provided a standard of scholarship which I could only weakly begin to emulate in my own books. And then there was Paul Wheatley, another individual possessing considerable intellectual breadth and depth. Although my interactions with him were relatively infrequent, I almost always found the combination of his informed scepticism, sharp wit, and biting tongue a challenge to my ideas of the moment.

In sum then, for someone who was young and devoted to the development of conceptual frameworks, being in Berkeley was not without its considerable difficulties but it was, on the whole, probably as nourishing and stimulating an experience as I could have hoped to encounter at any US university with a major geography department. Probably most crucially – because Berkeley was clearly not one of the cauldrons of the 'revolution' – I could more easily make conceptual contributions, however meagre, to that 'revolution'. Being periodically somewhat isolated, it was easier for me to continue pursuing questions of process and to avoid committing myself to some of the more fashionable quantitative and theoretical research of the period – research that all too often either reified space or distance, making them ends in themselves, or naively attempted to derive conclusions about human and societal behaviour from spatial form.

Swedish Counterpoints

To this observer at least, it appeared as if quantitative 'revolutionaries' regarded Berkeley and Sweden as polar extremes. If Berkeley was considered widely as the principal 'anti-revolutionary' bastion, then Sweden's geography departments in general were often considered as vital contributors to, and defenders of, the 'revolution'. With respect to both my exposure to 'revolutionary' innovations and my general intellectual development, it was my good fortune to spend a portion of the 1960s (and 1970s) in Sweden rather than Berkeley. However, my experiences in Sweden were not as one-sided as the stereotyped image of geography in that country initially had led me to anticipate.

Owing to the great influence that Swedish contacts have had upon my work, it is rather clear that my initial decision to do dissertation research in Göteborg during the academic year 1960–1 was as critical a professional decision as I have ever made. Yet, like many a decision of eventual magnitude, its far reaching importance was not apparent at the time. Consequently, it was made somewhat hastily and without the forethought normally associated with critical decisions.

I had been in Chicago only a few months after completing my master's degree at the Pennsylvania State University when Gilbert White involved me in what was to be a pivotal conversation. He informed me that it was the opinion of the faculty that I ought be considering the formulation of a dissertation project which could be set in motion by the beginning of the following academic year. I was also informed that there was some urgency in the matter, as several grant application deadlines were looming on the horizon. Subsequently, a combination of role-based circumstances resulted in my choosing to draw up a proposal focusing on the impact of initial modern industrialisation on the external relationships of cities.

While a novice at Chicago I held the independently existing role of research assistant to Brian Berry, a position which required that I read hundreds of articles and books on central place theory so as to assemble an annotated bibliography on that topic. This concentrated confrontation with the central place literature quickly led me to conclude that it was too preoccupied with spatial form and too little concerned with the dynamic processes affecting urban size and function. It further occurred to me that there were far more significant issues surrounding the interdependence of cities and their growth or decline over time, and that my accumulated knowledge of industrial location theory, agricultural location theory, and migration theory could be brought to bear on those issues (had I not previously occupied the role of graduate student at the Pennsylvania State University and come under the tutelage of Allan Rodgers, I might not have been in a position to consider such an application of classical theories). At the same time, owing to the presence of individuals I had first met while in the role of undergraduate at Antioch College, many of my acquaintances at the University of Chicago were either historians, or social scientists devoted to historically based model formulations. Repeated informal discussions with these people helped me to centre upon a period of 'industrial revolution' in seeking an outlet for my newly acquired intention to apply location theory to urban change issues. Finally, I first became aware of the rich variety of 19th-century Swedish data appropriate to the kind of study I was beginning to contemplate through a chance encounter made possible by a role dictated visit to the library. After that, it was only a matter of a day or two before I decided to use Göteborg as the locus of my research.

Although most of my 1960–1 sojourn in Göteborg was devoted
to dissertation related tasks – data gathering, extensive reading,
and the development of some competency in Swedish – certain
other actions and experiences proved more fruitful in the long run.
As my language skills improved, I took the opportunity to give
Torsten Hägerstrand's monograph on innovation diffusion a
careful reading.[9] I had previously given some attention to
Hägerstrand's writing and ideas while in Chicago, but it was not
until this lengthier and more slowly digested reading that I was able
fully to appreciate the interpretive possibilities that can arise both
from designing process models with probabilistic feedbacks and
from incorporating information–circulation elements into such
models (this exposure, as it turned out, also paved the way for my
first personal meeting with Hägerstrand).[10] Göteborg was also the
scene of my initial linking up with Sven Nordlund, an economic
historian whose manifold interests provided much in the way of
stimulation both during the winter and spring of 1961, and during
the subsequent years of our friendship.

While Göteborg acted as the site for these important influences,
it failed to provide any opportunity for face to face contact with the
'revolution' and its ongoing innovations. Through student contacts
I met Sven Dahl, Olaf Jonasson, and other members of the small
geography department at what was then known as the Gothenburg
School of Economics. Although treated warmly, and given the
chance to deliver a series of lectures on location theory and its
applications, I found little genuine concern for the types of
conceptual issues with which I wished to come to grips, and
virtually no 'frontier' research being undertaken (Dahl, however,
was employing central place theory in a rather straightforward
manner). Unfortunately, in the course of my few visits to the then
separate geography department of the local university, I did not
come into contact with either Sven Godlund, or Olof Wärneryd
(still a graduate student at the time), both of whom were doing
work which would have made me feel considerably less professionally isolated.

It was during my 1966–7 visit to Sweden (when a research grant
and a leave of absence from Berkeley allowed me to be based in
Stockholm), that my path first became intertwined directly with the
paths of Swedish geographers who were the generators and
proponents of specific 'revolutionary' innovations.

Early in the summer of 1966 I met Torsten Hägerstrand in order to discuss some final questions that had arisen in connection with my translation of his innovation diffusion monograph. From the outset I was greatly impressed with the qualities of the man. He was modest and soft-spoken despite his already considerable accomplishments and fame both inside and outside the discipline. He possessed neither the bluster, nor the intellectual one-sidedness, nor the arrogance that I had witnessed in some other leading 'revolutionary' (and vocal 'anti-revolutionary') figures. His primary concern, quite clearly, was the acquisition of a greater understanding of processes rather than with either Monte Carlo simulation *per se*, or the application of any other methodology or technique as an end in itself. Above all, he commanded respect by virtue of the ease and frequency with which he tossed off original ideas and verbalised freewheeling creative mental associations. Fresh insights concerning urbanisation, changing land use and human activity patterns and other basic processes mushroomed freely as he allowed his familiarity with Swedish cultural history, his awareness of contemporary societal conditions and his wide ranging knowledge of the biological and social sciences to interact. From the time of those initial exchanges at Hägerstrand's summer cottage in Ramsjöstrand, I frequently found a creative chemistry of interaction coming into being. For while being exposed to Hägerstrand's often innovative thoughts under informal conditions − strolling in the countryside or sipping coffee or wine − I have frequently been inspired to take long imaginative leaps of my own.

All personal interactions of the moment are at one and the same time rooted in the past and a potential root for subsequent interactions.[11] The set of circumstances which led to my first meetings with Hägerstrand created conditions which, in turn, enabled me to come into contact with three other Swedish geographers − Gunnar Olsson, Gunnar Törnqvist, and Olof Wärneryd − all of whom were doing innovative 'revolutionary' work and all of whom either fortified or influenced my own development.

During the autumn of 1966 Hägerstand made arrangements for me to travel from Stockholm to Amsterdam in order to participate in a symposium on 'Urban Core and Inner City'. My acceptance of Hägerstrand's arrangements gave me a completely unanticipated opportunity for becoming acquainted with Gunnar Olsson. Our almost immediately established rapport gave us occasion to spend three lengthy evenings of animated discussion at Indonesian, Hungarian, and French restaurants comparing interests, perspectives, and philosophical views. Gunnar's philosophical concerns of the moment were centred on the consequences of analysing spatial form (as most 'revolutionaries' were intentionally or unintentionally doing) rather than analysing the processes which generate the cultural landscape and spatial behaviour. His twin positions – that it is possible to reason from process to form but not from form to process, and that human geography should concentrate on the analysis of behavioural processes and social relations instead of the analysis of spatial patterns and geometries – was totally in keeping with my own position.[12] The clarity, persuasiveness and breadth which Gunnar brought to the statement of his position were instrumental in my decision to continue to be among that small minority of mid 1960s geographers who thought of themselves as 'modern', but chose explicitly to pursue matters of process rather than to join the 'revolutionary' mainstream which was largely preoccupied with the static, quantitative analysis of form (while such a decision was easy from an intellectual and philosophical standpoint, there were occasional moments of discomfort, as there were peers elsewhere in the profession who mistakenly perceived my commitment to process – and the frequent use of historical materials – as nothing more than a perpetuation of the 'Berkeley tradition'). Subsequent to Amsterdam a friendship developed with Gunnar that was as much based on our shared bicultural mode of existence as on our common interests. The geographically widespread meetings engendered by that friendship repeatedly served to stimulate and challenge me throughout the remainder of the 1960s (and all of the 1970s) by forcing me to confront the fundamental philosophical issues which were inseparable from both the work being conducted at the 'revolutionary frontier' of the discipline and the larger context within which that work was occurring.

During the course of one of our initial conversations at Ramsjöstrand, Hägerstrand suggested that I seek out Gunnar Törnqvist. I had read and reviewed his innovative monograph on industrial location which pioneered the application of multiple location analysis.[13] The autumn of 1966 found Törnqvist completing some work on the diffusion of television in Sweden and commencing his first efforts to deal with the location of economic activities through focusing on information flows. Inasmuch as I was just starting to work on *Behavior and Location*,[14] and also attempting to link information flows and the location of economic activities – albeit from a somewhat different perspective – there were more than ample grounds for us to meet frequently in a variety of informal surroundings. Our Stockholm encounters (like those of later years in Lund) resulted in a relaxed but lively exchange of new ideas and influences. If nothing else, our 1966–7 path convergences left me convinced of the then somewhat 'revolutionary' idea that the organisation (private or public) was generally a more realistic and meaningful unit of economic locational analysis than was either the single establishment or the sector (or sub-sector).

Another suggestion made to me by Hägerstrand at one of our first Ramsjöstrand meetings was that I try to establish contact with Olof Wärneryd. Although Wärneryd was then on the faculty of the geography department in Göteborg, various responsibilities required that he make occasional visits to Stockholm. We came to meet several times in Stockholm during 1966–7, and once for a period of a few days in Göteborg when I was giving some invited lectures there. At the time Wärneryd was conducting research which was to culminate in the appearance of a pioneering work whose theme was interdependence and growth transmission within systems of cities.[15] This theme coincided with long-term research commitments of my own and our conversations helped me – through disagreement – to bring some of my own previous thinking into sharper focus (particularly with regard to hierarchical versus non-hierarchical channels of diffusion and growth transmission) and, through initial exposure to begin appreciating the ways in which the spatial structure of organisations affects processes of city system change.

If 1966–7 was a year in which personal encounters with the developers of 'revolutionary' disciplinary innovations proved personally rewarding, it was also a year in which I became increasingly aware of the fact that Swedish geography was anything but uniformly. and unquestioningly devoted to the 'revolution'.

One scene of disillusionment was Stockholm. While there I kept an office in the Department of Economic Geography at the Stockholm School of Economics (this arrangement was made possible by Gunnar Alexandersson, who had made my acquaintance a year or two earlier when he was passing briefly through Berkeley). Over frequent lunches and coffee breaks with Alexandersson and his few fellow department members it became painfully evident to me that these people were not only intellectually blind to the kinds of things

Hägerstrand, Törnqvist and others were trying to do, but also that they possessed an irrational and often bitterly expressed antipathy toward the most innovative of their Swedish colleagues. I found all of this highly ironic, for over 25 years earlier William William-Olsson, who was still a highly visible and tone-setting figure in the department, had undertaken two pathbreaking urban studies the conceptual components of which were in large measure compatible with some of the conceptual frameworks still associated with the 'revolution' in the mid-1960s.[16] It was also ironic that while the geographers at the Stockholm School of Economics at best express-ed a diplomatic coolness toward my work, faculty members in other departments, including Bertil Ohlin, showed a sincere interest – I was asked to give several seminars in other departments, but only an undergraduate lecture or two in the Department of Econ-omic Geography.

Lund, Hägerstrand's own bailiwick, proved to be a second scene of (at least partial) disillusionment. As anticipated, lecture and seminar visits to Lund brought me into contact with a number of young and gifted scholars who were connected with the Depart-ment of Social and Economic Geography in a variety of research and graduate student positions. These people were for the most part working under Hägerstrand and clearly receptive to new ideas. In contrast, it was readily apparent that a very large share of the department's undergraduate teaching was being performed by indi-viduals who were highly unsympathtic to Hägerstrand's point of view and who reluctantly (if at all) accepted curriculum innovations which reflected recent disciplinary changes.

A Parting Observation

The meanings and interpretations I have imposed upon the past, the there and then in Berkeley and Sweden, are a result of the knowledge, attitudes and values I hold now, the ever fading here and now in Berkeley. Yet, the knowledge, attitudes and values I hold here and now are rooted in my past path, my past partici-pation in projects and the institutional and societal context which generated those projects. Furthermore, the events I have re-counted, interpreted, and imposed meaning upon – the decisions, difficulties, and encounters with 'revolutionary' innovations – were themselves rooted in antecedent project roles and the experience based intentions which grew out of the daily path actions directly or indirectly prescribed by those roles. All of this holds not only for me, but for any reader of this essay and for any participant in the 'revolution' of the 1950s and 1960s. Just how you interpret this article, just how (if at all) you came into contact with the innovations of the quantitative and conceptual 'revolution' is inseperable from the constantly ongoing dialectical relationships – only some of which have been alluded to here – between the workings of society, or the roles and projects defined by institutions', and the external actions and internal experiences associated with the spinning out of your unbroken life path and its component daily paths.

Notes and References

1. This paper was written while the author was receiving research support from the US National Science Foundation.

2. For further elaboration upon the 'project' concept and innovation use, see Torsten Hägerstrand, 'On socio-technical ecology and the study of innovations', *Ethnologica Europaea*, vol. 7 (1974) pp. 17–34; Allan Pred, 'The impact of technological and institutional innovations on life content: some time-geographic observations', *Geographical Analysis*, vol. 10 (1978) pp. 345–72; and Allan Pred, 'Of paths and projects: individual behaviour and its societal context', in R. Golledge and K. Cox (eds), *Behavioural Geography Revisited* (London: Methuen, 1980).

3. For further development of this line of reasoning, see Torsten Hägerstrand, 'On the survival of the cultural heritage', *Ethnologica Scandinavica* (1977) pp. 7–12.

4. Definitions of basic time-geographic 'realities' and constraints are available in several articles, including Torsten Hägerstrand, 'Space, time and human condition', in A. Karlqvist, L. Lundqvist and F. Snickars (eds), *Dynamic Allocation of Urban* Space (Lexington, Mass.: Lexington Books, 1975) pp. 3–14; Allan Pred, 'The impact of technological and institutional innovations'; and Allan Pred, 'The choreography of existence: comments on Hägerstrand's time-geography and its usefulness', *Economic Geography*, vol. 53 (1977) pp. 207–21.

5. Institutional roles exist independently (until terminated or superseded) in the sense that when they are not filled by one person they sooner or later must be filled by another.

6. For further observations on the dialectical relationships between one's life path and one's daily interactions or path convergences, see Allan Pred, 'Of paths and projects'. For further specific examples of the operation of this dialectic in my own career, see 'The academic past through a time-geographic looking glass', *Annals of the Association of American Geographers*, vol. 69 (1979) pp. 175–80.

7. Haggett's experiences in Berkeley represent another excellent example of the dialectical relationships between 'life path' and 'daily interactions'.

8. R. Glacken, *Traces on the Rhodian Shore* (University of California Press, 1967).

9. Torsten Hägerstrand, *Innovationsförloppet ur korologisk synpunkt* (Lund: Meddelanden från Lunds Universitets Geografiska Institution, Avhandlingar no. 25, 1953); later translated by myself under the title, *Innovation Diffusion as a Spatial Process* (Chicago: University of Chicago Press, 1967).

10. The circumstances leading to my first encounter with Hägerstrand represent yet another illustration of the dialectical relationship between the independently existing roles thrown open by one's own life path context and one's daily path. For an account of this, see Allan Pred, 'The academic past', p. 179.

11. See Allan Pred, 'Of paths and projects'.

12. See S. Gale and G. Olsson (eds), *Philosophy in Geography* (Dordrecht: D. Reidel Publishing Co., 1979) pp. xi–xvi.

13. G. Törnqvist, *Studier i industilokalisering* (Stockholm: Meddelanden från Geografiska Institutionen vid Stockholms Universitet, 1963).

14. Allan Pred, 'Behavior and location', *Lund Series in Geography*, B (1967–9).

15. O. Wärneryd, *Interdependence in Urban Systems* (Goteborg: Regionkonsult Aktiebolag, 1968).

16. W. William-Olsson, *Huvuddragen av Stockholms geografiska utveckling*, 1850–1930 (Stockholm: Meddelanden från Geografiska Institutionen vid Stockholms Universitet, 1937); and *Stockholms framtida utveckling* (Stockholm: P.A. Norstedt och Söners Förlag, 1941).

A Pleasant Pain

BRIAN T. ROBSON

> I dreamt I was in love again
> With the one before the last,
> And smiled to greet the pleasant pain
> Of that innocent young past.
>
> RUPERT BROOKE

There is a strong temptation to see clear goals which charted a conscious course from the 'then' to the 'now' in one's own development. Since, no doubt, I shall succumb to the temptation, let me preface what I say by stressing that, while certainly there were firmly developed interests which quickened my pulse and provided a litmus to determine my reactions to events and ideas, it is clear how small a part in my own development seems to have been played by clearly guided aims and how much has been contributed by the collage of rather random influences and serendipitous events to which I both responded and contributed. The same, I am sure, can be said of the subject as a whole. Direction and purpose tend largely to be imposed retrospectively on this jumble of circumstances. Perhaps, then, the only neutral shape can be imposed by time. It is for this reason that I want to look at developments essentially chronologically, and to begin by painting a brief picture of my own experiences against the background of Geography and its *apparat* in the 1950s and 1960s.

School and university geography in the 1950s were unashamedly environmental, concerned with the relation of man and environment. The promptings that drew students into the subject were twofold: the acceptable face was the interest in the tangible landscape, in an essentially visual stimulus; the unacceptable face was that it was a 'soft' subject, a ready retreat from classics and history. Undoubtedly at school the subject attracted a large body of weaker pupils and it offered more than a little opportunity to be king amongst minnows. University courses in the late 1950s carried on the same thrust: with something of a vacuum at its core – a vacuum created a partly because few of its practitioners would offer more than a token nod of obeisance to the argument linking man and environment – the subject rapidly broke up into very separate specialised concerns and a wide variety of unconnected topics. For philosophy, each lecture course would invariably begin with the statutory bow to the largely dead debate about determinism and possibilism, but even for this there was little accessible published literature to which to turn. We were exhorted to read some of the 19th- and early 20th-century French and German authors and the classics of the early geographical literature,[1] but this was largely a forced and artificial 'extra' to a curriculum rather than a real framework and we were cheerfully encouraged to get on with the serious things – learning about the contribution of the merino sheep to New World developments, longshore drift on the East Anglian coast, the meaning of the concept of Central Europe and the growth of California in the post-war years. Much of this, of course, was individually stimulating and, to look to the future, there was too the first twinkling of spatial theory beginning to make itself felt in Cambridge. Peter Haggett introduced the work of Bogue[2] and some of the other American material which was eventually to find such electrifying form in *Locational Analysis*.[3] We also had some bemusing statistical practical exercises to add to the more standard work on map projections and cartography. For myself – and I suspect for most of my contemporaries – these were but a few more of the ingredients of the goulash which was served. What was missing, overall, was any overt attempt to spell out a purpose, to construct an overarching framework, into which the parts might be slotted; and for me personally what was missing was any attempt to consider *people*. Indeed, as an epitaph to this style of geography, I recall a review of a collection of essays edited by one of my Cambridge teachers, in which the American reviewer ended caustically with the trenchant question 'Are these rocks inhabited?'.[4]

Perhaps it is the role of a sound undergraduate course that it prompts one to react against it. Certainly my own developing interest in urban topics came almost wholly from outside the course itself. Specifically I would pinpoint three sources. First, and in good determinist vein, was the obvious stimulus of the northeast, and especially of Tyneside where I went to school. Travelling each day by train took me through those stark terraces of Tyneside 'flats' marching everywhere in straight lines with a remorseless disregard of topography and housing the faceless workers of an already declining industrial area. It prompted questions which might be tackled not by geography as I then knew it but by history, sociology and economics, all of which bar the first were in short supply in the Cambridge course. Indeed, it was to historical geography, always strong in Cambridge, that I first turned when one could specialise in the third year. There was no 'urban' course on offer except for a short 'one off' series of lectures by J.E. Vance, who happened to be visiting Cambridge on sabbatical. Given this general urban emphasis, the second influence which guided the particular thrust of my interest was provided by three sets of writers: Mumford and Geddes; Young and Willmott; and Park and Burgess. The first of these were strongly architectural and visual. The urban histories of Mumford[5] and Geddes[6] neatly complemented the illustrated lectures given in Cambridge by Pevsner (who was then Slade Professor) in a public lecture series on European art and architecture. Geddes and Mumford were writers of similar mould: indeed, Mumford acknowledges his debt to the writings of Geddes, although the two were only to meet once, and that somewhat disastrously. Their writings on cities are inspired by an astonishing eclecticism and an evident anthropomorphism. What I derived from them was a series of what now seem misplaced views: a romanticism in viewing the city; an idea of teleological forces somehow impinging from outside the system; and a predominantly architectural bias to the selection of points of reference – that it is enough to see the external appearance, within the march of time, to know the inner soul and reality of what the city is all about. Viewed from today, the more positive legacies are their sensuous facility with words and, most importantly, a sense of dynamism, of the sweep and flux of change through time. Their evolutionary views, stripped of the teleology, feed into the sense of accretionary history that is so important an element in understanding the present and which is so unhelpfully denied by the static models of most formal analytical approaches. If these writings were the consciously romantic side, the work of the Institute of Community Studies, and particularly of Young and Willmott,[7] provided a harder view of street life. The survey tradition on which their work drew tied in neatly with Geddes's own emphasis on the importance of survey and their strongly empirical sociology equally complemented the predominant flavour of the geography of the time. The difference between the two was that in geography the survey tradition turned all too rapidly into the sterile dilution of place-work-folk which led to regional description with its implicit physical overtones; in the Bethnal Green studies, people always stayed firmly to the fore. It was Young and Willmott who influenced the undergraduate dissertation that I wrote on the effects of rehousing 'slum' households to peripheral council estates, and it was significant that the Cambridge examiners were not much impressed. The comment came back that: 'The big criticism is that many geographers would not accept this excursion into sociology as social geography'. The outrage that I felt at the time was directed not at the pusillanimity of hiding behind the aggregate view, but at the drawing of disciplinary boundaries which university courses themselves hesitated to do. The combination of social and urban interests and the focus on the more detailed level of individual households, then, was not mirrored in teaching, was apparently not seen as 'geography', and certainly sat uneasily within the then accepted format of the subject. The third set of writings, which was to prove the most enduring influence, was the outpouring of work from the Chicago human ecologists, to which I was introduced through Park and Burgess's *The City*,[8] and through a little known book edited by Wirth, *Eleven twenty-six*,[9] which I picked up fortuitously on a secondhand bookstall, and which consisted of a curious collage of material from Redfield, Cohen, Merriam, Thurstone and Wirth himself, all of which recorded the meetings to commemorate the first decade of social science work in the Social Science Building at Chicago. My interest in the ecologists' work was sustained by Duncan Timms and, of course, there was no lack of further material to satisfy an appetite once whetted in this field. Again, as with the two previous sets of writing, the ecologists offered something of the same mixture of survey and evolutionism. Indeed, in retrospect, all three can be characterised as the end products of philosophies which combined evolutionary neo-Darwinism with a strong element of empiricism and of positivism. These provided the matrix of ideas, but their underpinnings I certainly absorbed unreflectively.

My own postgraduate research on the ecology of Sunderland[10] may seem to have been an inevitable extension of these influences, but the line was not as unbroken as may appear since, when I started research, it was fresh from having worked in what was then

Basutoland, and my first intention was to work on aspects of land tenure in that most impoverished and hauntingly striking country. That idea I soon rejected in favour of working on race relations in Bedford, at that stage a town with one of the highest proportions of West Indians, as well as a longer standing Italian community, of any town in Britain. For a year I worked on this and contacted the small body of social scientists in what was later to become the race relations industry – A.H. Richmond, Michael Banton, Sheila Patterson and Ruth Glass. The line which I began to explore was the degree to which an 'ecological' approach could help to resolve or throw light on the conflicting views of a 'psychological cum personality' approach to prejudice as against a contextual socio-logical approach to aversion which emphasised class structure and conflict over limited resources. Seen crudely, this dichotomy was represented, in British writing, by Robb and Richmond on one hand and Banton on the other.[11] The research design – to give it a rather more portentous appellation than I would have done at the time – was to look at samples drawn from different ecological areas of Bedford, controlling for social class, residential mobility experience and degrees of contact with blacks, and concentrating on both personality traits and the areas in which people lived. This took me rapidly into a variety of scaling techniques, such as those of Adorno, Bogardus and Guttman, all from the American sociological and psychological literature.[12] After considerable testing of questionnaires I decided to abandon the idea, well into my three years of research, since increasingly the 'natural area' approach seemed to throw little light on the contextual variables in which I was interested. The ecological framework appeared to prove a blunt instrument for teasing out the elements of a situation where personality could play too important a role. My final – and long delayed – research topic moved back to the familiar territory of the northeast and to an ecological approach to the development of attitudes to education; a concern, focused on a different topic, which still aimed to illustrate the role of the residential context in affecting social life and values, but which centred on attitudes which were more readily measured and in which the conflicts between personal history, the influence of received ideas and the environmental context were somewhat less difficult to resolve.

This long personal digression on my research interests illustrates two things. First is the somewhat haphazard course that one could plot as a research student: it seems unlikely that a postgraduate today would be allowed the same degree of luxury to meander quite so freely and with so few constraints on what was tackled. The strengths and weaknesses are obvious. The strengths are that, *en route*, a good deal of stimulus and interest can be absorbed, that it helps to lay the foundations for a broad multidisciplinary view and that the mistakes and findings which are made are much more painfully and poignantly learned when made so personally and at such considerable cost and delight. The limitations are equally evident; an incredible amount of time can be wasted in re-learning the mistakes that others have gone through, literature searches can be so much more haphazard, the personal anguish of being left to one's own devices can be considerable, and there is a strong temptation to burrow linearly into by-ways far removed from any original goal. In the three years of my research I had one meeting with my original supervisor, changed supervisors at the end of my second year and saw my second supervisor perhaps six times – a far cry from the closer supervision of today and from the incipient moves by SSRC to emphasise formal training in research. While I think my own experience was somewhat unusual, it did carry to an extreme the then prevailing view of intensely personal research which, at the time, so strongly differentiated the British and American research environments. The formal training in methods and the greater development of team research made it unsurprising that it was US geography that was better placed to apply the quantitative techniques that helped lead to a more robustly theoretical geography. In Britain, the lack of scientific background of all bar a few geographers and the looseness of research 'training' meant that the British style was far better placed to tackle library-based work. The literary background produced far more effective early syntheses of work done elsewhere, somewhat to the chagrin of US workers like Brian Berry, whom I recall once mildly complaining that they did the work and the British got the royalties!

The second implication that can be drawn from my own research background is how little trained one was for research activity and how the lack of a formal training structure for postgraduate work made more difficult the transition from student to postgraduate. The subject was predominantly descriptive rather than analytical. The converse of this was that the subject did offer some excellent teaching – of the pulpit style like E.G. Bowen's marvellous synthetic drawing together of the strands of the Celtic saints, or H.C. Darby's famous courses on the English landscape, or R.J.

Chorley's hilarious hagiology of the history of geomorphology, or Vaughan Lewis' stimulating if chaotic forays into glaciology. It could be the lucid orderly style of Peter Haggett, who stamped shape and sense on to anything he spoke about, or of Harold Carter with his widely influential urban courses at Aberystwyth.

Research at the time, of course, was a much smaller business: fewer research students existed, their position was even more ambiguous and marginal than today, computing facilities were very limited, geographical literature was very much more sparse, research assistants and research teams hardly existed. It was a lowlier, a more hazardous undertaking, although with a firmer promise of a teaching job at the end of it. While this was true of the humanities in general, geography's position was exacerbated by its lack of a robust research tradition. If the ideas of the subject were taken from elsewhere – in my own case from sociology and human ecology – and given fresh and sometimes novel interpretation in a spatial or environmental context, such ideas were unlikely to flourish and propagate without the parallel development of a research context through which they could be spread. It is this that I want to look at in the period of the 1960s.

Frameworks of Debate

The context within which debate develops revolves inevitably around formal meetings, individual contacts and publications. I want to look at these in relation to the two areas with which I was then concerned – urban ecology and quantification, both of which became for me increasingly interacted as the 1960s progressed. The particular ecological approach which I developed in my Sunderland work was largely tackled independently of geography and of direct links with the USA. The chief institutional support was provided by the cumbersomely titled Inter-University Census Tract Committee which was initially established to press for the release of small area statistics from the census, but which developed from this as a body which explored the application of multivariate methods to enumeration district data.[13] The membership was informal and overwhelmingly non-geographical. It largely comprised sociologists such as Elizabeth Gittus, Kathleen Pickett, John Westergaard, Peter Collison, Peter Norman, Clifford Jenson, Ruth Glass and Maurice Broady, and statisticians and demographers such as Christopher

Winsten, Bernard Benjamin, Wallis Taylor and Flavia Savigear. The two geographers were David Herbert and myself. In the years around the middle 1960s the concern of the group was almost exclusively technical – not merely formally technical (such as Wallis Taylor's problem of retrieving from the Manchester computer the vast mass of census data that he had fed into it) but technical in the sense that we were trying to develop some form of comprehensive framework through which various of the individual multivariate studies might validly be compared; to isolate those variables which were diagnostic (in the sense of accounting for a large fraction of the variance of a set of variables); to identify the respective uses of principal components and factor analysis; to define functional urban units for purposes of comparison; and to compare the distributions of individual variables between towns. In addition, contacts with census officials were pursued especially with an eye to bias in the 1961 census and a forward eye to the 1966 sample census – to influencing the questions included, access to the data, forms of sampling and the final presentation. These technical concerns were very much a reflection of the still restricted availability of enumeration district data and the continuing limited use of census material, since the Census Office in the 1960s was still just beginning to emerge from its isolationist chrysalis. It was also a reflection of the relatively primitive computing hardware and software to which most of us had access. Those of us who were using multivariate techniques relied on our own programmes rather than packages and most could call on computers with limited capacity. We all had our tedious tales of traumas: I began by using a Cambridge machine in chemical engineering and, when I moved to Aberystwyth, sat for long nights while reams of data stuttered out for matrices which had to be partitioned because of their size. While the pragmatic fascination of the technical set puzzles which often diverted attention from the object of all the effort, I think it fair to say that the several pieces of work which were produced by some of the participants in this group played a part in persuading the census officials of the value of small area data, helped to make such data more generally available and prepared the basis for the widespread development of descriptive census based research by local authorities which, while having rapidly become mechanical, has added enormously to the information base for towns and to a wider appreciation of socioeconomic problems in their spatial context. While attempts to co-ordinate comparative work came to little, the impetus of the group's work did plot the groundwork for one of the most prolific areas of study during the succeeding decade, starting with urban ecology and developing, linearly, through work on residential mobility to the more recent 'managerialist' and 'structuralist' studies of the urban housing market.

The same initial emphasis on technical and contextual matters equally characterised the more purely quantitative work, where the Quantitative Methods Study Group of the Institute of British Geographers played an active and proselytising role. Stanley Gregory has already given one account of some of its early work and aims.[14] When I was Chairman of the group at the end of the 1960s, the influence of its early mentors was still much in evidence, through Gregory himself and through Barry Garner who was one of the early 'Been To the USA' school. The group both campaigned for the introduction of more formal quantitative teaching in geography departments and, to that end, organised surveys of existing courses in a conscious attempt to spread the gospel of quantification.[15] The seminars and meetings which we arranged were almost wholly concerned with techniques *per se* – network analysis, scaling techniques, trend surface analysis, multivariate methods, computer simulation, space–time budgets. The aim was to broaden the range and depth of techniques taught as well as to provide a forum for the exchange of views. The contacts between the converted meant that the core group – Garner, J.B. Goddard, I.S. Evans, A.G. Wilson, P.W. Lewis, Smart Cowie, A.D. Cliff – acted as a very cohesive node, seeing themselves as the advance guard heralding the future. Since the battle is redundant if the opposition retreats, we were at once both gratified and frustrated by the hostility of large audiences at annual conferences of the Institute, as at the meeting in Belfast at the very end of the decade. That was in 1969, and it is a sobering reflection of the pace of change which has seen the too rapid rise and the subsequent retrenchment of the 'geography as techniques' school. The people involved in the group in the 1960s were mostly self-taught statisticians who were caught up in the excitement of new skills, the thrill of the battle and the tangible results that techniques gave. Those who followed in the 1970s began to develop distinctively spatial techniques and brought to their work a far higher level of sophistication which was itself partly the product of the more formal training introduced during the 1960s.

The third avenue of debate is provided by publications, and here again the changes of the 1960s were very marked. The curve of PhD theses gives some indication of the growth of formalised research in Britain. With an inevitable time lag, there was something of the same exponential growth of formal publication. By the end of the decade Methuen, Edward Arnold, Cambridge University Press and Oxford University Press were beginning to look to geography as a growth field. Before that it is surprising how few geographical monographs and books, other than standard texts, were published. During the 1970s the trickle was to turn into a flood. Likewise with periodicals, where on the human side journals such as *Urban Studies*, *Regional Studies* and the US *Journal of Urban and Regional Science* began to appear newly in the 1960s. And to this growing wave of formal outlets must be added the subterranean literature of occasional and cyclostyled papers. In the 1960s one of the marks of membership of the inner circle was inclusion in the mailing lists of US pre-publication papers – the now dust-covered sheets which still fill yards of bookshelf space in the rooms of 1960s geographers, and which were one of the most tangible expressions of the different style of US research. The idea of inviting criticism and reaction, of speeding up the discussion of ideas amongst a 'community of scholars' by shortcutting the gestation period of formal publication, was largely foreign to the indigenous style of British geography. It both introduced a new urgency and cohesion to British research and had the (perhaps intended) effect of drawing a sharp distinction between an 'in' and an 'out' group, since eventual publication of pre-circulated papers could be long delayed, as in Garrison's *Quantitative Geography* which was published seven years after the meeting on which it was based and whose papers had meanwhile circulated widely amongst the cognoscenti.[16]

Such differences reflected the light years that separated the research cultures of Britain and the USA and it was this that made the statutory visit to North America so liberating, refreshing and critical an experience for the geographers of the 1960s. I myself went only in 1967, under the ideal and generous sponsorship of a Harkness Fellowship, to work in the lively context of Brian Berry's Centre for Urban Studies at Chicago. This was at a late stage in the life cycle of the US quantitative ferment, but what I found no doubt parallels the experience of the other British geographers who had preceded me: an eagerness to talk and share ideas; a framework of endless rounds of seminars and informal discussion; large enough numbers of research students to generate lively internal debate within departments; packs of roving 'conferencees' like peripatetic nomads setting up their tents in such unlikely spots as MICMOG's[17] schoolroom at a crossroads in the wilds, equidistant from Wayne State, Detroit and Michigan; a small group meeting arranged by Michael Dacey which he wanted to hold at the airport so as to corral us away from the German beerhalls of Cincinatti but which the indulgent popular voice insisted on holding in the over-blown gentility of a downtown hotel. All of this frenetic activity generated discussion that was urgent, often strident, and in which there was a give and take still then unthinkable in the reticent and formal presentations of British departments other than LSE. It was this which prompted me to introduce a 'Comment' section in *Area* when I edited the journal on returning from the USA, and it is gratifying to see how, over the years, this section has grown – if not always from strength to strength, then at least from length to length.

By this time, of course, US geography was itself starting to change. The 1968 conference of the Association of American Geographers met in Washington and had a breakaway group, organised by Cox and Golledge, and with the sharp tongue and incisive mind of Gunnar Olsson, which held a session on 'behavioural' geography.[18] As harbinger of things to come it was very evident even at the time that a new battle was to be joined. The time lag between this change in the USA and its echo in Britain was considerably shorter than was the case with the earlier 'quantitative analytical' phase. That this was so in the 1970s says much for the changed balance of academic strengths between the two countries. Indeed, the subsequent erosion of academic contacts between the two and the fact that the current US 'frontier' has been phenomenological while the British has been structuralist have both been extensions of this trend. It reflects the coming of age of British geographical research.

I would suggest that it is this which must be seen as the principal achievement of the decade of the 1960s. At first unconsciously, but I think with increasing conscious intent, the impact of the decade was to create a context more favourable to research. At the start of the decade British geography had lacked an institutional framework capable of creating a broad and robust research tradition – certainly it could not produce research rapidly nor disseminate it very effectively, and it would have been incapable of being responsive to practical policy needs. The development of practical policy orientated research in the 1970s would not have been feasible earlier because of the lack of such a framework. The 1960s were a period when the development of a more formal analytical approach began to attract more and better students into the subject who were to have their impact in the following decade, and when the subject's research house was put in order by the creation of an appropriate context, which meant that geography was well placed to contribute to questions of national policy as well as to the more incestuous internal academic debate. This, I think, was one of the largely unrecognised virtues of the 'quantitative' movement; it accompanied, but also helped to further and foster, the externally generated growth of a research community within the subject and so to provide the institutional framework for the growth, change and strengthening of geography as a social science in the 1970s. In my own case, my initial interest in people and in the approach of the broader social sciences got submerged in the technical fervour of the decade, but it is now able to re-emerge in a more informed and resilient fashion. Similarly, for the subject as a whole, if much of what was done in the 1960s bubbled over with an irrelevant enthusiasm for techniques as ends in themselves, and tended to lose sight of the substantive objects of interest in the process, this is not a heinous fault in the life cycle of the subject if the process can be seen as having created the robust research infrastructure which is a pre-condition for geography's further growth – and change.

Notes and References

1. Which included Ellen Semple and Elsworth Huntingdon. Richard Hartshorne, *The Nature of Geography* (Pennsylvania: Ass. Am. Geog., 1939) was the usual avenue of approach to much of the wider literature, and the chief British reference was A.F. Martin, 'The necessity for determinism', *Transactions of the Institute of British Geographers*, vol. 17 (1951) pp. 1–12.
2. D.J. Bogue, *The Structure of the Metropolitan Community: A Study of Dominance and Subdominance* (Ann Arbor, 1949).
3. P. Haggett, *Locational Analysis in Human Geography* (London: Arnold, 1965).
4. J.B. Mitchell (ed.), *Great Britain: Geographical Essays* (Cambridge University Press, 1962).
5. L. Mumford, *The Culture of Cities* (London: Secker & Warburg, 1938).
6. P. Geddes, *Cities in Evolution: An Introduction to the Town*

Planning Movement and to the Study of Civics (London: Williams & Norgate, 1915).

7. M. Young and P. Willmott, *Family and Kinship in East London* (London, 1957); P. Willmott and M. Young, *Family and Class in a London Suburb* (London, 1960).

8. R.E. Park and E.W. Burgess, *The City* (University of Chicago Press, 1925); and the seminal collection of papers in G. Theodorson (ed.), *Studies in Human Ecology* (New York: Harpe & Robson, 1961).

9. L. Wirth (ed.), *Eleven twenty-six: A Decade of Social Science Research* (London: Arnold, 1940).

10. Which was embodied in B.T. Robson, *Urban Analysis: A Study of City Structure With Special Reference to Sunderland* (Cambridge University Press, 1969).

11. J.H. Robb, *Working-class Anti-semitism: A Psychological Study in a London Borough* (London, 1954); A.H. Richmond, *The Colour Problem: A Study of Racial Relations* (Harmondsworth: Penguin, 1955); M. Banton, *White and Coloured: The Behaviour of British People Towards Coloured Immigrants* (London: Tavistock, 1959).

12. T.W. Adorno *et al., The Authoritarian Personality* (New York: Narten, 1950); E.S. Bogardus, *Immigration and Race Attitudes* (Boston, 1928); S.A. Stoutter, L. Guttman *et al., Studies in Social Psychology in World War II, vol. IV: Measurement and Prediction* (Princeton University Press, 1950).

13. The committee eventually transformed itself into the Census Research Group, which now operates from the Institute of Planning Studies, University of Nottingham. A forerunner in its proselytising work is the Oxford Census Tract Committee, *Census 1951: Oxford Area, Selected Population and Housing Characteristics by Census Tracts* (Oxford University Press, 1957).

14. S. Gregory, 'On geographical myths and statistical fables', *Transactions of the Institute of British Geographers*, new series (1976) pp. 385–400.

15. B.T. Robson, 'The teaching of quantitative techniques', *Area*, no. 1 (1970) pp. 58–9.

16. W.L. Garrison and D.F. Marble (eds), 'Quantitative geography. Part 1: economics and cultural topics', *Northwestern University Studies in Geography* (1967) no. 13.

17. Michigan Inter-University Community of Mathematical Geographers.

18. Papers which resulted in K. Cox and R.G. Golledge (eds), 'Behavioral problems in geography: a symposium', *Northwestern University Studies in Geography* (1969) no. 17.

Recollections of a Random Variable

DAVID M. SMITH

When the editors originally invited me to contribute to this volume, my first reaction was to decline. I could not imagine that my revolutionary activities would be of interest of anyone but my nearest and dearest. In any event, my personal involvement in the 'quantitative revolution' was that of a humble street fighter rather than as one of that select band who found glory manning the barricades or storming the bastions of traditional geography with their latest numerical weapons. In fact I do not regard myself as a 'quantifier', except in the obvious sense of having found some use for statistical and numerical methods in my research. And what use I did make (correctly or otherwise) has no claim to originality. Indeed, if there is anything to distinguish my one book-length excursion into numerical methods from others in this field, it is its lack of sophistication and its tendency to gloss over those finer points of probability theory and the derivation of equations so beloved of real quantifiers.

If my personal experiences in the professional geography of the 1950s and 1960s (even 1970s) are of any significance, it must be in a context broader than that of a *quantitative* movement. While the term 'quantitative revolution' is now widely adopted as shorthand for the changes that took place in geography during this particular phase of its development, such a description is narrow and misleading. Not only did the 'new' geography involve more quantification than had hitherto been the case, but it also brought with it a predelication towards a form of theoretical deliberation unfamiliar to geography with its tradition of being (literally) down to earth. It was in the 'models' movement spearheaded by Chorley and Haggett,[1] rather than in quantification *per se*, that geography's yearnings for conventional scientific status found the fullest expression, through the combination of mathematics and abstract formalism associated with the physical sciences.

Looking back, my own professional activities seem to have been a continual struggle to come to terms with (or keep up with) the rapidly shifting focus of human geography. The struggle arises in large measure from the difficulty of breaking free from one's own intellectual heritage, whether it be the traditional 'arts' training in geography offered before the 'quantitative revolution' or a commitment to some subsequent paradigm which itself came under assault. If my own struggles represent anything more than one half life experience, it may well be the theme of the geographer or social scientist as creature of his or her times. Thus I offer my recollections in what I hope will be more than an indulgence of self-revelation and *post facto* justification. If anything is to be learned from the instant replay of such recent events (apart from the fact that geographers are strangely introspective), it is that scientific 'advance' is not conducted in a social vacuum but as an integral part of human history, within which the element of chance arising from individual personality and creativity plays an important part. So let us proceed with the recollection of one of the random variables.

The Traditional Background

Like so many of my contemporaries who reached the sixth form at school in the early 1950s, my first ability in geography was revealed by a capacity to draw sketch maps with extraordinary neatness. What is more, I enjoyed it. For the first time, homework became a pleasure, as my creativity found such an effective outlet in the portrayal of oxbow lakes, U-shaped valleys, cwms (corries or cirques) and the like, via the contemporary medium of indian ink and Derwent coloured pencils. Added to this was the opportunity of cycling through the Warwickshire countryside on autumn afternoons to survey a muddy field with the dubious accuracy of novices with chain and pole. The usual memorising of where the maize is mined and the coal cultivated could be taken in its stride, such was the compensation of the first glimpses of order and regularity imposed on the physical landscape. Through the erosion cycle, some sense of predictability or process began to dawn. Seeing beauty in such neatness, erosion surface and raised beaches took on an aesthetic as well as scientific fascination. Holmes, Lobeck, Penck, Stamp, Steers and Truman are the names I recall from school reading – along with W. G. Moore whose *The World's Wealth* was assiduously committed to memory on the Christmas Eve of 1954 in preparation for an Open Scholarship examination at Nottingham in the New Year.

The award of a scholarship ended the unequal struggle to revive my small Latin (no Greek) in an attempt to get to Cambridge. Once at Nottingham in the autumn of 1955, I began to realise that I had been rather well educated thus far. Solihull School had been flexible enough to enable me to make the most of my late developing talents. My interest in geography, embedded in an extremely introverted personality, was carefully nurtured by Guy King-Reynolds, to whom (with John Way in English) I own my intellectual awakening. In English (my only other A Level subject) the emphasis on literary criticism and use of language added breadth to my narrow preoccupation with landforms in geography.

Geography at Nottingham turned out to be a disappointment – at least for the first two years. A dull succession of regional courses left only Latin America untouched, in what seemed little more than a continuation of school work. The prescribed dose of map projections, cartography and surveying made things worse (though something lasting was learned from field work via over-indulgence in Forest of Dean cider). Even the geomorphology failed to thrill: the fact that I had already read such things as Linton on southeast England and Valentin on coastlines raised an eyebrow, but that was all. It was the second year before I found it necessary to enter the library.

My subsidiary subject of economics was simultaneously the despair and salvation of the first two undergraduate years. In place of the tedious repetition of what I had learned at school I found an analytical discipline that greatly discomforted my 'arts' mentality. I had opted for economics in a state of total ignorance as to its content, and in the face of advice from my tutor that economic history would be more sensible. As it happened, this exposure to economics was a most influential turn of events as far as later professional development was concerned. What I had unknowingly committed myself to was effectively the first two years of the honours degree in economics. Though largely at sea from first lecture to last, the struggle to understand at least gave the mind some exercise. Cost, revenue and indifference curves lacked the aesthetic attraction of the contours of a cwm (corrie or cirque), but opened up a new world of intellectual order. The strength and shackles of conventional economic theory became an important part of my mental equipment, as I moved from the world of nature to the world of men (or *homo economicus*).

Toward a 'New Geography'

In the third year, geography at Nottingham finally came to life. Two courses made a deep impression. In different ways, they pointed receptive students towards methodological issues that were shortly to become central to the new quantitative and theoretical geography. To the disillusioned intellectual like myself, this provided a lifeline back into geography as a medium for the elevated discourse that, in my naivety, I had expected to find at university.

'Nature and methods', the first of these courses, was the seminar run by Professor K.C. Edwards. As I prepared for my own contri-bution, I was struck by the similarity of some of the sentiments expressed by Ritter and von Humbolt, on the one hand, and the poetry of Wordsworth on the other (a lengthy exposure to *The Prelude, Intimation of Immortality* and so on was one of the more pleasurable parts of the A Level English Literature syllabus). It became apparent that geographers did not function in intellectual isolation. I concluded a paper on 19th-century geographical thought (miraculously preserved if not frequently consulted) with the following:

> It is no coincidence that men in such different spheres as Humbolt and Wordsworth expressed closely similar views on nature, for example, and it does seem that to really understand how our concept of geography today grew up it is necessary not only to study the development of geographical thought in the past, but also to consider the contemporary intellectual and philosophical views which so much influenced the writings of the geographers of the nineteenth century.

However commonplace today, such an observation was heady stuff in student circles in 1958, when protracted debates on whether the Paris Basin was really a region could represent the peak of academic debate. To this discovery of the broader societal context within which the geographer works was added the inevitable reading of Richard Hartshorne's *Perspective on the Nature of Geography*,[2] consumed cover to cover in a two week frenzy of masochism, driven on by the imperative of rejecting the conventional wisdom (whatever it might be) and sustained by barely palatable sherry from a bring your own bottle outlet in Beeston. What all this added up to was a hightened sensitivity to the changing nature of geography, and perhaps the beginning of an inclination to participate in the transformation of this sterile subject into one more in tune with the times.

It was the second course that gave me specific direction. Eric Rawstron's third-year 'option' on economic geography was, in effect, an introduction to location theory. Isard's and Greenhut's 1956 books[3] had just been added to the recent translation of Lösch's *Economics of Location*[4] and the existing classics of Weber, Christaller and Hoover. Rawstron not only knew of these works but appeared actually to have read them – an act of extreme professional deviance at a time when an interest in economics was rare among 'economic' geographers. Each student was assigned a text on which to deliver a seminar: I got Lösch. The effect of Lösch's book was deep and lasting – it gave me the first real indication of common ground between geography and economics. But what was perhaps more important, Lösch conveyed (at least to me) a more profound sense of the nature of scientific inquiry than Hartshorne or anything else I had read in geography. I savoured both the analysis and the purple passages. I found inspiration in Lösch's sense of duty 'not to explain our sorry reality but to improve it'.

A more personal inspiration came from Eric Rawstron himself. A stimulating if not always the most structured classroom teacher, he immersed the students in his enthusiasm for his own research. We worked through drafts of the paper shortly to appear (somewhat emasculated) in the *Transactions of the Institute of British Geographers*.[5] It was here that Rawstron outlined his 'spatial margin to profitability' – still one of the few really original geographical contributions to spatial economic analysis. As I played with this concept in my own mind, recollection of those painfully learned diagrams of cost and revenue curves from first year economics led me to what, at the time, seemed a dramatic revelation of some fundamental truth. If you substitute distance for quantity on the horizontal exit, you have a simple graphic model in which cost and revenue appear as *spatial* variables, their intersections defining the spatial margin in just the same way as the 'break even' points define constraints on scale in the conventional analysis. Location theory and production theory are thus shown to be complementary. I spent the next journey home in the cold comfort of Midland Red's bus X99 drafting a paper with accompanying diagrams to elaborate this. But it was seven years before I filled it out, polished it up and sent it to *Economic Geography*.[6] Finals were coming up, and I was then to be hijacked by my heritage.

A Diversion

As an undergraduate, I had not given much thought to the eventual necessity of earning a living. I had no wish to teach, and lacked the initiative and inclination for the business world (a fact that was clear to the University's careers adviser, whose note of 'a poor prospect for industry' I was able to read when he was called out of his office). A good II.1 and the opportunity to do research saved me from more positive moves in the direction of gainful employment, as well as from national service. More important, of course, was the fact that it provided the opportunity to get to grips with the new and exciting field of location theory. What I actually experienced was a diversion – by no means unprofitable but taking me in quite a different direction from that logically suggested by my scribbles on the X99.

It was in the USA and not Britain that the foundations of the 'new' geography were being laid. A couple of years earlier, Brian Berry had left London for the University of Washington and the guidance of Bill Garrison. While I remained at Nottingham, my more enterprising contemporary Barry Garner went to Northwestern, and was soon writing back about working on quantitative research with Berry. Seeking an empirical focus for my own research, I drifted away from location theory to the industrial geography of the east Midlands. My traditional heritage reasserted itself, and I embraced it with enthusiasm. Geography is about areal differentiation, and to understand existing patterns required reconstructing their historical evolution. I was drawn steadily into the past, and into the field.

During my first year as an undergraduate, K.C. Edwards had delivered a lecture the theme of which was the geographer's eye for country'. Among his illustrations was a slide of a Nottinghamshire framework knitter's cottage – a dwelling with elongated windows indicating its adaptation for domestic industry. The prospect of actually going out into the field to observe such things did not occur to me at the time, and I would doubtless have ridiculed the idea as a third year sophisticate dabbling in location theory. But as my historical enquiries led me to the domestic hosiery industry as the key to understanding the economic development of the east Midlands, landscape evidence of the extinct framework knitters began to take on some significance. The next step was to seek physical remains of the early stages of the factory system in silk and cotton spinning. As Margaret and I spent weekends penetrating the Derbyshire Dales in search of the first Arkwright and Strutt mills, workers' cottages, apprentice houses and so on, I lost myself in the landscape of the Industrial Revolution. My first book[7] was to be on industrial archeology now, not location theory.

A university lectureship became the obvious goal – indeed the only job worth considering. But successive applications failed to bring anything other than an abortive trip to Edinburgh for interview. Finally, within ten days of marriage, I accepted a planning assistant ship in what was grandly referred to as the Research and Industry Section of the Staffordshire County Planning Department.

Two year as a planner provided a first exposure to some of the contemporary economic and social issues which were to become a major professional preoccupation by the end of the 1960s. But in a personal sense, planning was a miserable experience. On the first day I was stripped of my recently earned designation of 'Doctor' to become plain 'Mr' Smith again (so that I would not be mistaken for a medical man, it was explained!). In a profession still dominated by architects and engineers it was impossible to see my request to attend the IBG conference in office time as anything other than frivolous: of what relevance could it possibly be to planning? I spent most of the time bashing a calculator and compiling tables for research on population overspill, industrial land use allocation and the like. Eventually, I did rise to a level of responsibility that required me to read the County Planning Officer's copy of *The Times* each morning and identify items likely to be of professional interest to him. The truth was that they had no idea how to use a

PhD in geography, the attainment of which was a singularly inappropriate preparation for the day to day tedium of office routine. And I was not really willing to compromise and face up to the prospect of a lifetime in planning.

What kept me sane at this time was the tenuous link with academic life provided by the continuing pursuit of industrial archeology. Living in Stoke-on-Trent, Margaret and I spent our weekends discovering the beauty of the Potteries, with the elegant architecture of its half-abandoned factories and their old 'bottle' kilns, and seeking relics of the Darbys of Coalbrookdale, Telford's early aqueducts and so on in Shropshire. I gave the occasional lecture entitled 'The Textile Mills of the Midlands – a topic on which I considered myself, with some justification, to be the world's leading authority. I systematically photographed many early industrial sites, copies going to the National Buildings Record. Nothing that I have done in academic life, before or since, matched the pleasure of our discovery of an abandoned 18th-century mill deep in some Pennine valley or a crumbling Georgian potbank façade in a Burslem back street.

Frustration with planning soon led me back to the daily perusal of public appointments advertisements for jobs in geography. After a further dozen or so applications and another unsuccessful interview (Birmingham) I was offered a post at Manchester. Still preoccupied with the landscape of the Industrial Revolution, and with more time now to write, it was a year before I began to tune in again to contemporary professional geography. And what I heard was disturbing to someone whose brief flirtation with location theory had long since been lost in a reversion to traditional modes of inquiry.

It was the appearance of statistics that bothered me most. Walter Isard's *Methods of Regional Analysis*[8] was fairly easy to relate to the classical tradition of location theory, though the mathematics of input–output analysis, linear programming and so on were beyond me. But Stanley Gregory's *Statistical Methods and the Geographer*[9] left me perplexed. Almost 30 years old and with a PhD under my belt, I had no knowledge of statistics whatsoever. In fact, when I overheard colleagues talking about chi-square, I honestly mistook it for pi. The simple linear equation was too much for my mathematically incompetent mind. But it soon became clear that Gregory's book could not be dismissed as a transient aberration. The debate between quantifiers and traditionalists in the USA had already reached Britain. From my *alma mater* came

rumours that John Cole was into some kind of mathematical geography – an important pointer for those of his former students who
admired his creative imagination. With the two Manchester Peters
(Lloyd and Dicken) and the occasional nudge from David Fox (who
had brought back some of the new techniques from the USA and
actually taught the stuff) I began to struggle to come to terms with
the emerging 'quantitative revolution'.

Apart from extreme ignorance, the major obstacle that we faced
in the middle of the 1960s was computer access. At universities such
as Nottingham, this was overcome fairly easily. At Manchester,
access to the great Atlas machine was limited not only by our
technical incompetence but also by incredulity on the part of the
guardians of the computer that geographers might have a legitimate
use for it. I remember a painful few days at a course on Atlas
autocode, and trying to figure out how the hell to get a matrix of
data into the computer via a ridiculous device called a flexowriter. I
gave up in disgust, and spent most of the Christmas break in 1965
cranking out ratios for a study of recent industrial trends in northwest England on a desk calculator (the connection of my planning
experience and Peter Lloyd's interest in Development Area policy
had finally pulled me out of the industrial revolution into contemporary 'regional problems'). Where I did feel at home was with
location theory, which I was able to teach in a third year option
unashamedly modelled on Eric Rawstron's Nottingham course.

The dominant feeling in 1965–6 was of working in isolation.
There was a sense that we were struggling in the dark. The USA was
where the action seemed to be, and the IHBTA (I have been to the
USA) became a necessary qualification for the aspirant 'new' geographer. So, I had to get to the USA for a year. Approaches to
various institutions brought a positive response from Southern
Illinois University (SIU) at Carbondale, which looked close enough
to the emerging midwestern centres of quantitative/theoretical geography to serve my purpose. Leave of absence from the University
of Manchester was promised, then at the last minute refused.
Angry and frustrated, I resigned the lectureship that I had gained
with such difficulty. In September 1966 we left for the USA on
immigrant visas.

The US Experience

As those with similar experiences have learned to their cost, it is easier to leave British geography than to return. It is faithful service rather than enterprise that the British system rewards. So the one-year visiting post at SIU extended to four, as did Margaret's instructorship in sociology. Though hardly a centre of academic excellence, SIU had a fairly strong geography department which afforded a congenial and at times stimulating intellectual environment until it broke up in one of those orgies of inter-personal strife characteristic of US academia.

What had been so difficult to do at Manchester was relatively simple at SIU. There was easy computer access, including an IBM 1620 that was user operated. There was programming and key punching assistance, and graduate students to do most of the chores. With this back up, learning numerical methods by trial and error broke the mental blockage that had been such a constraint in Britain. Shortly after accepting a permanent appointment, I volunteered to teach quantitative methods, and much of what I subsequently learned was from the necessity to keep one step ahead of a lively group of seniors and graduate students. Packaged programmes and the 1620 made computer applications easily integrated into classroom teaching. Tso-Hwa Lee in the cartographic laboratory put the packages together, overcoming my lack of FORTRAN, and we eventually shared a course in computer mapping based on SYMAP. To take on the coveted identity of quantifier was a natural outcome of the ease with which it could be done in an American geography department.

I was soon able to feed this experience into my empirical research on northwest England,[10] completion of which was necessitated by a book contract. Shift share analyses, location quotients, indexes of change and so on could be run in a few seconds. The dizzy heights of multifactor regionalisation were scaled by virtue of a packaged programme, without having to understand the mathematics. If principal components analysis (Q-mode – or was it R?) with Varimax rotation followed by Ward's algorithm was good enough for Brian Berry, why should lesser mortals try anything else? As with most of my contemporaries, I was soon publishing my learning experiences and helping the bandwagon to gather speed.

Of more serious and lasting interest was my return to location theory. The stimulus was (in part at least) another book contract. The framework in the *Economic Geography* paper could be sharpened up on the lecture circuit. I remember in particular a visit to Clyde Kohn's department at the University of Iowa, where Frank Horton and Larry Brown were beginning to make their mark. An hour with Harold McCarty was alone worth the trip (including the burned out engine in the Pontiac station wagon, abandoned with Margaret and Michael in East St Louis while I took to the air). Industrial location, McCarty told me, boiled down to 'loss of weight and a few random variables'. I saw more to it than that and eventually took 553 pages to say so.[11] That I was able to put this book together in a couple of years was, again, as much an outcome of the level of support at SIU as of the intellectual environment of the midwest at that time. Adequate research assistance with statistical analysis and computer mapping was there for the asking. Ten years later, in a British university, this was still not the case and never likely to be.

My sole claim to any substantial contribution to the literature on numerical methods[12] originated from the SIU years. Now the story can be told, there being no longer any innocents to protect. The initial manuscript for *Industrial Location: An Economic Geographical Analysis* ran to even more unreasonable length than the final book itself. To cut it down, I eliminated a chapter of about 100 pages dealing with techniques of pattern description, much of which originated as worked examples and class projects for my quantitative methods course. After leaving SIU for the University of Florida in 1970, and seeing *Industrial Location* through the press, I tarted up the typescript of the deleted chapter and sent it to some American publisher as an outline of a proposed text in numerical methods. It was firmly rejected. Not wishing to assign so many learning experiences to the waste bin, I tried David & Charles. They accepted it, and then sold the paperback rights to Penguin. So, once again, a contract deadline served as stimulus to further struggles. As I got to work, the limitation of my hasty transformation into quantifier became apparent, especially in the more strictly statistical realm. Rectifying some of these deficiencies (if indeed I did) spilled over into the next sojourn of an increasingly itinerant scholar – in South Africa. Completion of the book required my first (and last) resort to weeks of burning the midnight oil, in the form of stale coffee and cheap cigars. After trying to type the first scruffy chapters, the departmental secretary at the University of the Witwatersrand deemed a visiting lecturer's manuscript to be beyond her responsibilities, so I had to tap out the rest myself. When the David & Charles edition came out, they had reversed a couple of maps of Japan (thus no doubt losing the Japanese market for ever), and I discovered that I had screwed up an analysis of variance. Then the Penguin edition was delayed for months when they printed their cover too small. With the major gaffs rectified or unnoticed, the book was quite favourably received. That a text could be built on such slender foundations as my own numeracy is a reflection on the true depth of the 'quantitative movement' in geography, where really competent practitioners are few. In the land of the blind, one glass eye was the most I ever had.

My personal involvement with quantitative analysis as a major preoccupation in fact lasted barely five years. For by the end of the 1960s a new wind of change was beginning to blow through US geography: the message was 'social relevance', and its direction towards public policy issues.

Social Relevance and Radical Geography

Consideration of the social relevance movement may seem beyond the scope of this volume. But it is extremely significant, for it was this that brought the eclipse of the 'quantitative revolution'. That the 'new' geography of the 1960s so quickly became 'old hat', at least to substantial numbers of the emerging younger generation, is of more than passing interest in any reflections on the changing nature of geography in recent years. How we got off the quantitative bandwagon seems just as important as how we got on.

The shift of emphasis from quantification to what I chose to christen 'radical geography'[13] was very much a reflection of the times. Quantitative analyses and model building, with its preoccupation with the geometry of spatial form and its abstraction from social relations, was the geography of the years of public faith in economic growth, cybernetics, technological solutions and managerial rationality. It was the era aptly described by Michael Eliot-Hurst as that of the 'geographer as mechanic'. Length of computer output almost became a professional virility symbol (I once saw Duane Marble taking his input to the computer in a truck).

In the latter part of the 1960s the growing opposition to the Vietnam war fused with disquiet concerning race discrimination, poverty and hunger and so on into a more general questioning of 'the system'. From criticism of particular institutions in contemporary America grew a more fundamental critique of capitalism and imperialism. As students and some younger faculty looked at professional geography, they saw the heroes of the 'quantitative revolution' content to rotate their principal components while the city ghettos burned – not to mention the people of Vietnam.

The existence of 'problems' demanded solution, and geography was conspicuously uninvolved. Indeed, even to address such issues as poverty and racism in the classroom was judged as dangerous political indoctrination by some of the establishment. On a broader level, the end of the post-war era of sustained economic growth, the emergence of interest in 'the quality of life', the rise of the pollution issue, and the beginning of the 'energy crisis' all contributed to a re-direction of societal concern – and hence geographical inquiry – towards distributional, welfare and ecological issues.

My personal re-direction began quite early. But again the heritage of the past held me back, with the continuing attraction of pattern identification, quantitative methods and conventional economic analysis as powerful constraints on fresh thinking. My first real taste of political controversy in geography came from Don Eggert, a colleague at SIU. He was expressing outspoken concern at poverty in Appalachia when I entered the department, and was soon involved in the anti-war movement which took him out of academic life for involvement on the west coast. To his personal concern, which much impressed me, was being added a more direct factual awareness of the reality of American life. Margaret was teaching a course on social problems, Carbondale's squalid ghetto was only blocks away the other side of Main Street and the railway tracks, shopping trips to the nearest large city took us through the slums of East St Louis, and our newspapers were reporting events in Cairo (Illinois) 60 miles away, where whites would amuse themselves by shooting from their cars into black residential areas. First hand experience of the mindless brutality of the National Guard and the police was provided by the occupation of Carbondale at the time of the riots sparked off by the killings at Kent State.

By 1970s I saw my new research field as the geography of social problems. I began to map the incidence of a wide range of social conditions hitherto largely ignored in geography: crime, housing, health care, educational attainment and so on. The need to get away from SIU coincided with the offer of a joint appointment in Geography and Urban Studies at the University of Florida. My disciplinary affiliation as geographer weakened as I worked with other social scientists. Acting as consultant to the Model Cities programme in Tampa brought me back to planning, and exposed some of the futility of public policy. At home in Gainsville, Margaret was into voluntary work in the ghetto, including unionisation of the grossly exploited black domestics. I became 'political' in the classroom, lashing out at everything from racism to the plight of migrant workers, and proclaiming that the USA had made me a socialist. I was drawn towards Dick Peet's *Antipode* group, and participated in his special session on poverty and social wellbeing at the Boston Association of American Geographers meeting of 1971, where radical geography 'went public'.

The logical progression into Marxist activism would have been swift, I suspect, had it not been for another move. Nixon's 'Amerika', and especially its south, was no place to bring up kids, and it was time to return to Britain. Gambling injudiciously on a Chair for which I had applied, I resigned from the University of Florida. The outcome was that a four month visit already fixed up in South Africa (to study apartheid at first hand) became a year, followed by six months in Australia, before Queen Mary College finally detected professorial qualities that had mysteriously eluded Leicester and Newcastle.

The significance of all this was that, once outside America, the quantitative and economic–theoretical heritage was able to regain its grip on the aspiring radical. The hurriedly completed research on the geography of social wellbeing in the United States, useful though I still consider it to be, failed to break out of the tradition of pattern recognition, albeit aided by modern methods of numerical description including the inevitable factor analysis. The contemporary social indicators movement provided a framework outside geography to which this empirical work could be related. I was reacting to a shift of emphasis in the social sciences at large, associated with the search for non-pecuniary measures of human well-being and progress, in a liberal rather than radical context.

When I sought (*post facto*) some more sophisticated theoretical structures for a geography focused on the well-being of mankind, it was natural to go back to my early training in neo-classical economics. Working in South Africa involved isolation from the growing radical critique of the neo-classical model, and especially of the welfare theory with which I now became enamoured. To some extent an escape from reality – from a sense of personal

impotence in the face of South Africa's extreme racism and blatant-
ly exploitive economy – I found solace in the asocial and ahistoric
abstraction of utility functions and welfare contours. It was only
after returning to Britain that the emerging Marxist movement and
the gentle guidance of Roger Lee began my cautious liberation
from the quantitative and pre-quantitative heritage – a process still
far from complete.

Conclusion

To go further would exceed my brief. What the foregoing amounts
to, I am not sure, save for two things. First, as scholars we are to a
large extent creatures of our times. We react, to a greater or lesser
degree, to contemporary professional fashion – itself moulded by
the wider societal context. A new 'revolution' takes shape, the
bandwagon begins to roll, and we push or jump on rather than
being left behind. Some seek fame (even fortune), some professional eminence, power or status, some simply like the sound of their
own voices or the sight of their own prose. We seek personal
identity in an individualistic societal milieu. We use the talents at
our disposal within our chosen (or chance) institutional setting of
professional geography. A few stand aside from the crowd,
ignoring the bandwagon (or falling off), pursuing scrupulous
scholarship as they understand it, avoiding involvement in institutional structures, keeping off the committees, or simply turning in
their lectures and going home to the gardening. Yet they may be no
less captive than the rest of us – trapped in their narrow and
unquestioned paradigms, idle, or just plain dull.

This brings me to the second point – that whatever the pressure
to conform, follow fashion or fade out, we are all individuals with
some unique contribution to human affairs. This may be the
random variable rather than the systematic determinant of the
course of a discipline's continual reconstitution, but it matters
nevertheless. In my own case, I would not have done anything to
warrant the soliciting of my 'revolutionary' recollections had it not
been for one purely personal characteristic: I love the creative
process of writing. I may not do it with any special skill or elegance,
but it turns me on, gives me a 'high', as they say. So to me the
pursuit of geographical inquiry has been a means to an end,
providing something to write about. I had early inklings of the

exhilaration of writing at school (my first published work was a sonnet). I rediscovered it doing a dissertation at university, and as I moved on to books I found the English prose (clichés and all) flowed from my ballpoint so effortlessly as occasionally to transcend meaning. The creative urge, along with the wherewithal to express it, explains why someone of unexceptional insight and ability has contributed so conspicuously to the accumulation of the printed word that passes for knowledge in the field of geography as a spatial science. I like to feel that my writing is not pure self-indulgence – that it serves some limited social purpose, for concern is part of my motivation. But I don't much care whether it is regarded as 'good geography'. I prefer to see myself as a student of society (however inadequate) who enjoys writing, rather than being pigeonholed as a geographer in an academic world ossified by an ancient disciplinary structure, whose work is packaged as geography by a publishing business commercially committed to outdated categories.

To be quite honest, I no longer care very much about geography, with its smug self-satisfaction and nauseating, narrow-minded chauvinism. Who else but geographers would dignify their puerile pursuit of statistics, models and paradigms as a 'revolution', as though it really mattered to anyone but themselves? Who else would want to publish the post mortem before the corpse was cold? And who else would want to read such trivia? How can we take it all so seriously, when it contributes so little to the improvement of the human condition? Most geography is inconsequential claptrap, and never more so than during the 'quantitative revolution'.

So, the random variable strikes again. And rambles on – within the constraints imposed by the reproductive imperative of the capitalist mode of production as it attempts to resolve its inherent contradictions. Or should I really be into phenomenology? I do know that it isn't out of kilter algorithms or spatio–temporal autoregressive moving mean models. That kind of guff went out with factor analysis. Maybe it is hermeneutics, whatever that means. I'd better ask Derek Gregory.

Notes and References

1. R.J. Chorley and P. Haggett, *Models in Geography* (London: Methuen, 1967).

2. R. Hartshorne, *The Nature of Geography* (Pennsylvania: Am. Ass. Geog., 1939).
3. W. Isard, *Location and Space Economy* (MIT Press, 1956); and M.L. Greenhut, *Plant Location in Theory and Practice* (University of North Carolina Press, 1956).
4. A. Lösch, *Economics of Location* (Yale University Press, 1954).
5. E.M. Rawstron, 'Three principles of industrial location', *Transactions and Papers of the Institute of British Geographers,* vol. 25 (1958) pp. 132–42.
6. D.M. Smith, 'A theoretical framework for geographical studies of industrial location', *Economic Geography*, vol. 14 (1966) pp. 95–113.
7. D.M. Smith, *The Industrial Archaeology of the East Midlands* (Newton Abbot: David & Charles, 1965).
8. W. Isard, *Methods of Regional Analysis* (MIT Press, 1960).
9. S. Gregory, *Statistical Methods and the Geographer* (London: Longman, 1963).
10. D.M. Smith, *Industrial Britain: The North West* (Newton Abbot: David & Charles, 1969).
11. D.M. Smith, *Industrial Location: An Economic Geographical Analysis* (New York: John Wiley, 1971).
12. D.M. Smith, *Pattern in Human Geography: An Introduction to Numerical Methods* (Newton Abbot: David & Charles, 1977; Harmondsworth: Penguin, 1977).
13. D.M. Smith, 'Radical geography: the next revolution?', *Area*, vol. 3 (1971) pp. 153–7.

Trajectories and Co-ordinates

WILLIAM WARNTZ

> Scientists are often enumerated, divided into categories, constructed into tables, illustrated by graphs, and pronounced upon in bulk. But it is sometimes forgotten that they are human beings.
>
> LORD FLOREY, *The Development of Modern Science* (First David Rivett Memorial Lecture, Melbourne, 1963)

> As Lord Florey has remarked, it is sometimes forgotten that scientists are human beings. Nevertheless, analysis is necessary in order to understand scientists better, so that the different kinds can be placed in positions in which they can do their best.
>
> J. G. CROWTHER, *Scientific Types*

In a letter to me the editors of this volume wondered whether they could interest me in contributing to a volume due to appear in a new series, Critical Human Geography. They said that they wished to make sure that discussions would be firmly located in their proper intellectual and historical contexts, and since the events of the 1950s and 1960s were obviously of such strategic importance for the development of the subject, they wanted to include a collection of essays written 'by those most closely involved, in one way or another, which would tell the story "from the inside", as it were'. They were seeking 'not yet another general review of the "quantitative revolution" [I perceive it instead as the 'conceptual revolution'], but rather comments about any "decisions and difficulties" which I personally had to face'. They wished me to relate these to the events and experiences of the time.

Such a request is in the first instance flattering enough, with its implications that one's work has been sufficiently important to warrant additional personal statements about it. However, the strong possibility does also exist that it has been judged to be so idiosyncratic, so abnormal, if not bizarre, that only if the deep dark recesses of its author's mind be probed and also his particular unique combination of circumstances of birth, nurture, education and experience be revealed can the reasons for the work's characteristics and the author's extraordinary behaviour be comprehended. And, following modern psychological and psychiatric practices the investigators, alias editors, have encouraged the 'patient' to speak first and fully.

Why then have I agreed to prepare such an essay and to present it here when on two earlier occasions I had declined similarly flattering invitations and enticements to do so? To the first of those requests I simply responded that I did not wish at that time to make such kind of statement. For the second seeker I agreed to write a statement and honestly and conscientiously tried to prepare one. I succeeded in achieving not one, but two essays, each quite different from the other. Neither of them was satisfactory to me and yet they seemed incapable of being 'improved'. The dilemma rested in the situation that the first suggested that throughout my career every decision had I made was the right one, calculated in advance, and with all the consequences unfolding as neatly as I had known they would – and all of my research and writing had built up in a cumulative progressive way inexorably to certain unshakeable 'truths' and myriad insights which, in time, others would come to understand and benefit from.

Well, real life hasn't been quite like that, although perhaps a bit more so than the situation portrayed in the second essay, which emphasised negative things and concluded with a denouncement of the young and all of their works. I abandoned the project, and had to forego the opportunity to be a participant in the 'celebration' for which it had been requested. I did, however, continue to think for a long time about the difficulties I had experienced in preparing such an essay and slowly came to realise that my dilemma lay in the condition of my having provided no adequate background to help the reader of the essay to comprehend and judge events. And yet, I had the information in my own files to rectify this.

A career, like any progression is comprehensible only within a frame of reference – a co-ordinate system – against which its directions and velocities are measureable. Moreover, the frame of reference, if properly chosen and described, may prove to be of more interest and importance than any particular paths traced within it.

In his penetrating assessments of science,[1] J. G. Crowther has recognised the significant roles for scientists (among which a certain balance should be maintained to ensure progress) as including individual investigators, teachers, inventors and organisers although of course individual scientists may fill several roles at once, and other kinds of roles as well. The organisation for the reporting of one's activities in geography might, too, conform to such a pattern. And while I have, I think, had experience in all of these categories I would I believe be recognised more especially as an individual investigator than as any other type. I must here insist, however, that although I regard geography as my medium and perhaps there may be some who regard it as my *métier* – I in no way conform very closely in education, experience, and objectives to the typical US representative of academic geography. My education and experiences have all been quite different and I have been in a detached position *vis à vis* professional US geographers – do others join me in finding the use of the word 'professional' concerning geographers (if not 'profession' concerning the discipline) abhorrent? In truth although many of my published works have been 'geographical' in nature (at least by my own assessment), the majority of them have appeared in other than the traditional geographical journals, but certainly not less respectable nor demanding ones. In fact, the one geographical journal in which I have published with some frequency is the redoubtable *Geographical Review*, for reasons which will be shown below. And although my university associations as student and faculty member extend over more than 40 years (excepting the six years of military service during and immediately following the Second World War), it is only for the past eight years that I have been a member of an independent and self contained department of geography in control of its own research, teaching, appointments, and student selection. Of course the department is in a premier Canadian university, and hence the detachment mentioned above has been preserved.

All of the 'decisions and difficulties' which I have 'personally had to face' and the 'events and experiences of the time' with respect to the 'conceptual revolution' in geography seem in retrospect to be not unrelated to the fact that I was not routinely following the paths and performing the rituals of US Academic Geography. To have been spared this, and to have followed other paths and to have observed other rituals have been at times the causes of much bliss and the sources of supreme satisfaction. But my having been thus isolated from academic geography's mores has at times resulted in inconvenience and in at least one instance apparently inspired several older conservative and (by their own lights) leaders and protectors of the discipline to engage in a frantic, remarkably elaborate, but in fact genuinely ludicrous exchange of correspondence in an attempt to rig the remarks of the people assigned to comment on a conference paper which I, to my initial astonishment, had been invited to deliver.

The correspondence revealed that the objective of their larger scheme was to 'purify' geography by destroying and ridiculing those who advocated the application of certain mathematical and statistical procedures. The plotters, of course, missed the whole point – being frightened by quantitative measures but not appreciating the whole 'conceptual revolution' that was under way. I had been singled out especially, it seemed, because not only had I been seen to do some computation, but I was also regarded as an outside agitator none of whose academic degrees were even in geography and who could hence not be trusted to be respectful in a proper way of geography's past accomplishments, traditions, and institutions.

Whether the secretary who sent copies of *all* letters pertaining to the conference to *all* participants scheduled to take part in the conference did so from sheer incompetence or from a higher and purer sense of justice and right striving than any mere geography professor could ever have, I do not know for sure. I am strongly inclined to believe the latter on the evidence that letters came to me on which I was not included in the 'cc' list (for the younger geographer I must explain that 'cc' then signified 'carbon copy', a now archaic and rarely used replication process). Another interpretation of this evidence might have been that it signified total, complete and inutterably irredeemable incompetence and irresponsibility. Nevertheless 'God bless her', I say. My simple device to frustrate their knavish tricks was to present an entirely new paper at the conference. This had the desired effect of confounding the politics of the programme organiser and chairman. He was at first puzzled, then abashed, but in the end predictably vindictive. He made it known, rather loudly I thought, that the invitation to all participants in the session to the organiser's own reception following it did not extend to me.

There were also, of course, the early 'it isn't geography' responses from the editors of the geographical journals, with the grand and wonderful exception of Wilma Fairchild of the *Geographical Review*. Here, I must admit, I had 'connections', but they did not by any means prevent the occasional deserved rejection. Journals in regional science, history, hydrology, navigation, statistics and a wide variety of other disciplines, along with certain book publishers, offered abundant openings through invitations and incentives so that I have never felt deprived of opportunities to make known the result of my work. Interestingly enough, I find my papers from the non-geographical publications far more extensively cited in geographical books and periodicals than the small proportion of my own works in such vehicles would suggest. I still feel deeply indebted to those early editors in ways I am sure that they could never appreciate.

These things are all just more fragments related to those that Peter Gould so ably described in his brilliantly definitive article analysing the past two decades of academic geography in the USA.[2] I shall return to Professor Gould's masterful achievement (and certain summary statements in it) subsequently, but meanwhile let me return to my own first fumbling gropings two decades before the period of his concern with what I chose to regard as 'geographical problems'.

In the society and culture of Philadelphia, as an undergraduate at the University of Pennsylvania in the latter years of the national economic depression prior to the American entry into the Second World War, I experienced along with all my classmates many sorts of subtle and in some cases not so subtle signals, symbols, and procedures that assured us that we were very special people receiving a privileged education, but most assuredly and unquestioningly entitled to it. The broadening of the base of facilities for higher education had not yet occurred, of course and for the nation as a whole only 6% of the relevant age group entered college then (compared with 45% in the later 1970s).

It seems to me now that at that earlier time and place there was a comfortable and easy feeling about scholarship and intellectual endeavour. Outstanding achievements were admired and respected in others, and one took pride in oneself for the occasional intellectual success, but equally it was considered by all as poor form to be seen as struggling, striving or in any way working hard to attain it. A gentility pervaded all matters, social and cultural as well as intellectual. That is not to say that the faculty and students were entirely oblivious to the sad plight generally of many of the

inhabitants of Philadelphia, and of the nation. Although the re-
fined reactionaries (a substantial number among the faculty and
students) honestly imagined that the poor were responsible, and
hence to blame, for their own condition, the rising group of eastern
public spirited liberals equally strongly felt that it was their
responsibility to use their education in leadership positions (to
which they would most surely rise) for the public good. In fact, the
distinction between the two groups was reflected remarkably
clearly in the attitudes toward the administration of President
Franklin Roosevelt and his advisors and their novel social
experiments.

The ideal education was taken to be one which drew from all
branches of learning with only a very minor concentration (if any)
in a specific subject at undergraduate level. Literature, history and
music courses, and the odd geography course, were equally favoured by economists, physicists, and classicists. 'Expertise' was regarded as desirable and necessary, but the highly trained specialists,
lacking a liberal education, could not be considered as suitable
candidates for leadership positions. However, expertise acquired in
graduate studies or at professional schools following an acceptable
undergraduate liberal education was highly regarded and was encouraged by the public spirited.

It was supposed that the good of the country (following the
Roosevelt example) could be furthered only by a liberally educated
non-self-serving intellectual élite which presumably would find its
way into highest levels of leadership in society's affairs and its
government. It was supposed that such an élite could manage
things better than the citizens themselves, or more precisely that it
could properly define the arenas for the free play of individual
interests and for control.

After another world war, several regional wars, environmental
abuse, rights movements of great importance, prosperity, stagna-
tion, inflation, and now energy shortages, it seems that the
government's own huge interests in the same arena extend its role
beyond that of pure arbiter, and that it is equally subject to the
deep irrationalities of the nation as a whole. The disinterested élite
is ground to dust, along with everything else that seems intellectually, imaginatively and logically derived.

The tragedy seems complete when it is realised that the characteristic objective of much of modern higher education now is training
for service, which simultaneously provides for expertise and (for

the striving individuals) a means for upward social and economic mobility. That this is fraught with temptation and opportunity for disaster becomes increasingly evident. One of the great difficulties with narrow specialised training is that humanity and compassion do not naturally and spontaneously develop with acquired expertise in some technical matter – I shall say more of this later.

My undergraduate studies in economics at Pennsylvania introduced me to that body of literature which subsequently became identified with economic location theory. I found that literature fascinating, and saw in it some relationships to the material covered in the single economic geography undergraduate course I took. Needless to say the geography course was not organised at that time, with theory made explicit. Nevertheless, in an informal, unstructured, and tentative but spontaneous way I perceived the possibility of interesting development on macroeconomic – geographic terms. I did not pursue these ideas then. Other concerns crowded them from my mind and then the USA was at war and my colleagues and I became occupied with decisions about the branch of the armed forces in which to serve.

I chose the Air Force, hoping to qualify for a flying officer's duties. In this I was successful and as a consequence experienced many new and very different things. I had always enjoyed looking at maps but soon they took on 'life or death' aspects on several occasions. I studied them and their properties intensively, far beyond their immediate application. A vast new field opened up to me extending in virtually unlimited ways beyond those immediate experiences and reaching back to antiquity.

Combat postings took me to England and a B24 air base in East Anglia. Nearby Cambridge with its university and its pubs offered extravagant opportunities for the satisfaction of all kinds of cravings. Things said, read, and done in periods of stress remain vivid in one's mind: I especially recall the leave times spent at the Garden House Hotel in Cambridge and in particular the post-hospital part of a wound recuperation period spent there with its opportunity for leisurely reading in stark contrast to combat operations past and yet to come. Ely Cathedral was a god-send to an airman straining desperately to recognise some landmark in the haze and gloom for bearings to safe landings. Such memories do not diminish.

In the meantime Professor John Q. Stewart of the Department of Astrophysical Sciences of Princeton University was conceiving (and then in 1947 organising) his Social Physics Project, with an original intention of considering thoroughly the transferral of methods and principles of physical science to the social field. It was about this time that I discovered Professor Stewart and his work, although some six years were to pass before I met him personally. Following combat flying with the heavy bombardment group in England during the Second World War, I served as a navigator in the US Air Force on Air Sea Rescue Operations in the Newfoundland Base Command, where in the post library of a remote air base I came upon a copy of *Coasts, Waves and Weather* by Stewart.[3] This book had been prepared primarily to explain to marine and air navigators the physical environment in which navigation must be carried on. Fortunately for me, Stewart could not resist the temptation to include an exotic chapter describing potential of population and its sociological importance, as well as giving the lie to the argument that the social field is the exclusive business of sociologists by demonstrating that physics's double contribution consisted not only of mechanical technology but also – and perhaps more importantly – patterns of thought.

From the first I saw in this presentation application to certain problems in social science, especially the 'multibody' problem in geography, that I had found even in my undergraduate days. I resolved to investigate the matter more thoroughly upon my return to academic life at the University of Pennsylvania. I did return in 1948, and at the end of the one year's work needed to complete undergraduate education, I elected to attend Graduate College at Pennsylvania and pursued a course for the doctorate in economics with a minor specialisation in geography, this seeming the best means to continue my earlier work in social science along with the Air Force associated interests in meteorology, navigation and cartography – Keynes and cold fronts, as it were. I was being, behaving like, and becoming, a geographer.

Stewart's work was recalled, and a trial application to a particular problem in the geography of prices seemed so interesting and useful that when thesis time came around, I had a well defined topic. My personal discussions with Stewart which soon followed, his graciousness and patience combined with brilliant insight into my study both in its inner detail and its broader implications, established the roots from which a wonderfully pleasant and rewarding friendship developed, intellectually and socially.

My dissertation, 'Toward a Geography of Price',[4] was judged to be successful at Pennsylvania and led to promotion from the rank of instructor to Assistant Professor with continuing responsibilities in economics and also in geography in the very same course I had taken before the war. I was eager to introduce new ideas, and tried to. However, within a year I yielded to the splendid inducements and persuasive arguments of Dr Charles Hitchcock, Director of the American Geographical Society (AGS) in New York City, and in 1956 joined his senior staff there to carry out research of my own choosing. I was much impressed with the confidence he exhibited and the willingness he showed in granting such an opportunity to a relative stranger to the geographical profession. I soon discovered, however, that the society's understanding of its own unique role and its appreciation of its sources of sustenances made it more an eastern liberal institution than a professional geographical one.

Wilma Fairchild, who then was editor of the society's *Geographical Review* has commented[5] upon Dr Hitchcock's attitude concerning the philosophy of research:

> The work of the research staff is channeled neither toward particular projects favored by the Director or the Council nor toward cooperative ventures involving the Society as a whole. Instead, the Society's policy has been to select as members of the senior staff individuals of proved merit with faith in, and enthusiasm for, their own research. The Society and scholarship in general stand to gain most from uncommitted research carried on by such individuals in an atmosphere of freedom.[6]

And Mrs Fairchild noted further that when she had become editor of the *Geographical Review*, it had struck her that 'one thing [she] really needed to know was who read the *Review*. Accordingly, I sent down to the business office for a run of the addressograph plates and spent the better part of a week analyzing them. I got some shocks. Miss Wrigley [the former editor] had told me that the greater number of the Society's Fellows were not geographers, but in examining the plates I learned for myself a lesson I never forgot. Only a relatively small proportion could I recognize by name or address as being professional geographers. On the other hand, there were quite a few names I had no trouble recognizing in other areas of endeavor....

Among them were: from the realm of industry and finance, three du Ponts, two Rockefellers, and Thomas J. Watson; from the halls of Congress, Hiram Bingham, Robert A. Taft, and Frances Bolton; from the field of publishing, Alfred Harcourt and Arthur Hays Sulzberger; from the realm of political commentary, Walter Lippman; from broadcasting, Ben Grauer, from the world of letters, Bernard De Voto and two novelists, F. Van Wyck Mason and George Harmon Coxe. 'There were bankers and lawyers and businessmen, engineers, architects, and musicians, physical and social scientists of all descriptions'.

The society was served and governed by an active and dedicated council of perhaps even greater lustre although drawn for reasons of practical necessity principally from the Boston – New York – Philadelphia – Washington DC axis.

In addition to all this, one had then the absolutely priceless benefit of having not only Dr Hitchcock and Mrs Fairchild, but also O. M. Miller, David Lowenthal, W. O. Field, Calvin Heusser, Alice Taylor and others as frequent luncheon companions. The AGS, its nature, and its roles seem to have been much misunderstood by professional geographers and certain recent speculators about the society's present undeniably moribund state seem particularly ill-informed. Charles Hitchcock will forever be one of my heroes. When the opportunity came to join the inter-disciplinary programme in the Department of Astrophysical Sciences of Princeton University it was he who made it possible for me to participate there while continuing as a full time staff member of the AGS. In addition he encouraged me to accept Walter Isard's invitation to lecture in the graduate programme one day a week in term time in the newly founded Department of Regional Science at the University of Pennsylvania in Philadelphia. Residence in Princeton midway between New York and Philadelphia made the commuting 'easy'.

Mrs Fairchild called attention to these kinds of arrangements for staff members when she wrote that 'it should be added that members of the research staff were encouraged to maintain ties with colleagues in their own fields of endeavor. Thus they attended conferences and meetings, lectured at universities, acted as consultants, published in specialized journals, and generally were in touch with large numbers of people who shared their interests and expertise. The *Review* benefited from this crossfertilisation both directly and indirectly. Also, of course, we were privileged to carry in our pages some of the best of the research as it was completed'.

So, for the decade, 1956–66, I was pleased, privileged and favoured beyond all reasonable expectations by being not merely allowed, but actually strongly encouraged to serve at the same time, as Research Associate of the AGS New York, Research Associate in Astrophysical Sciences in Princeton University, and Visiting Professor of Regional Science of the University of Pennsylvania. This was an arrangement that proved more than merely feasible – the activities were complementary and the individuals involved to whom I was answerable very much respected and admired each other's objectives and principles.

The original study of numbers of people, distance and time as primitive 'dimensions' of society was continued and enlarged, and ways were sought to break out of the purely mechanical framework which (however successful for a certain class of problems) left much to be explained by other means. These initial formulations, however, in fact became part of the body of knowledge to be considered in relation to interaction modelling.

It surely is no accident at all that the 'enlightenment' of geography in the 1950s was characterised by a deep concern for (and active research into) economic and social interaction and flow modelling, and that the very recent remarkable upsurge in the discipline again derives not only from the improvement in the means of calibrating such early models but especially from the substantial gains toward securing their theoretical foundations. The nature and significance of 'constraints', and the incorporation of them by way of entropy considerations owing to Wilson *et al.*[7] are now much better understood than earlier and the techniques for considering matrices of asymmetrical geographical flows (Tobler, Goodchild[8]) are developing rapidly and most impressively.

In the meantime at the AGS my research had broadened to consider 'income fronts', the geometrical and topological properties of surfaces, geodesic paths, statistical methodology for areal distributions, hierarchical systems and the history of geography with special emphasis upon the colonial origins of US academic geography.[9] First David Neft and then Michael Woldenberg joined the staff of the AGS as research assistants. Both were graduate students at Columbia University in New York City, David in the statistics department and Michael in geography. Their work at AGS expanded into doctoral dissertations which I need not say were superlative and now so well known that I need not expand upon them. I shall be eternally grateful for having had the opportunity to serve Columbia University as dissertation supervisor for these two magnificent scholars – I learned so much.

At that time, Columbia was the only one of the eight Ivy League universities to offer a graduate degree in geography. At the University of Pennsylvania in the PhD degree programme in economic theory (as I have indicated) one could offer also a (very) minor specialisation (application) from among ten fields, including economic geography. However, the student even had to design his own reading list to be approved. There was, of course, no undergraduate degree programme in geography there nor anywhere else in the Ivy League except at Dartmouth and Columbia. At Brown, Yale, Harvard, Cornell, and Princeton universities there were not even any courses at any level.

Ultimately our research led to the consideration of geography as general spatial systems theory (terrestrial scales), as part of the more ambitious attempts to expand upon the initial endeavours of the Social Physics Group which had resulted in a mechanical interpretation of various observed mathematical regularities of social phenomena. Although research in social mechanics continued, the scope was broadened to include the investigation of the various kinds of social energies and their interplays. The objective was to establish one social science, and to show that it and physical science 'are but mutually related isomorphic examples of one generalized logic'.[10]

We summarised this position as follows, recognising that the prewar notions of a liberal education for leadership no longer sufficed, nor did unalloyed expertise: some higher level of integration seemed necessary.

We stated that between various departments and divisions of a modern institute of learning there is only limited collaboration, except of the exterior 'administrative' sort. Even within a department advancing sub-specialisation is imposing ever higher barriers. Students at all levels find it impossible to examine most of the fields offered in the catalogue. To become educated nowadays one must be educated as a specialist. While this is a good beginning for a liberal education, truly liberal training ought to follow, providing bachelors of arts or engineering with a wide and sensitive ability to comprehend – and even a little to criticise – leading principles built up by generations of diverse, and today apparently unrelated, scholarship.

Academic leaders and faculties, although frequently deploring this situation, have made no consistent, enthusiastic and broadly based attempt to overcome it. It can be overcome only by team research orientated toward a general synthesis. At heart, scholars of today reject the possibility of achieving unification of knowledge, because whether they are physicists or humanists they have been reared in the faith of the extrovert philosophy which guided the gadget-making farm boy, Isaac Newton. He became history's first great specialist, and his apparently commonsense outlook has been popularised by the triumphant objective successes of natural science and science's startlingly useful technologies. The whole world is proud of these Newtonian successes – but are they enough for full advancement of human welfare?

Only one answer, so far as we know, has ever been suggested to the problem of intelligibly linking together leading concepts and principles which have been put forward with clumsy and unnecessary diversity in these many scholarly fields. This answer was indicated by Leibniz, who was Newton's contemporary and formidable rival in mathematics, theoretical physics and philosophy: it is to make effective Leibniz's search for 'isomorphism'. This means to exhibit each well organised discipline as possessing important item to item correspondence – concept to concept and process to process – with each of the others.

Needless to say, success was not immediately achieved! However, the search goes on. My files are full of unconsolidated findings to be re-examined at a later time.

As I suggested above, the detachment from the day-to-day workings of an academic geography department, the strong affiliations with other disciplines, and the non-participation for the most part in the professional organisations of geographers have made it difficult for me to perceive the discipline of geography with the empathy and understanding of an insider. In any event, Peter Gould has done just that – he has described in matchless prose the decades of the 1960s and 1970s as simultaneously the 'best of times' and the 'worst of times'.

As far as geographers were concerned the 'best of times' for me meant having interest expressed, and truly valid and by no means ambivalent or gentle but nonetheless constructive criticism offered, concerning my work by many outstanding geographers including William Garrison, and then Waldo Tobler, Michael Dacey, William Bunge, Peter Gould, Arnold Court and later still Terence Smith, Roger White, Bernard Marchand and Michael Goodchild.

The 'worst of time' for me meant crank letters, rigged meetings, editorial conspiracies, but perhaps most of all the general malaise of the vast number of geographers who though in general mildly antagonistic to the works of those scholars mentioned immediately above, were in reality shockingly indifferent to it.

It seemed to me as early as 1963 that as a discipline geography had achieved at least the semblance of cumulative intellectual growth, a self-correcting mode, and a lively commerce among a small but important group of scholars and researchers interested in (and capable of enlarging upon) the same important topics. I predicted continuing progress and stated with confidence that not only would we see the strengthening of academic geography in those places where it was already well established but also its imminent re-introduction as a discipline into the prestigious universities where it had been strongly represented in two earlier 'cycles' of geographic thought.[11] This has not yet happened, although individual scholars nurtured in geography have moved to positions in such universities in other connections.

In 1966 I had an important decision to make: should I attempt to continue the agreeable arrangements of the past decade, or should I accept the offer of a professorship at Harvard University? The Harvard offer had been standing for quite some time and I was now being urged to make a final decision concerning it. In the end I chose to accept it, largely because of the retirement of Professor Stewart from Princeton and his migration to Arizona and distressing and saddening news about the state of Dr Hitchcock's health.

The attraction to Harvard was twofold. In the first place, as Professor of Theoretical Geography in the Graduate School of Design I was to introduce concepts of macrogeography into the city and regional planning curriculum. In addition I was to carry out my research in (and later to direct) the Laboratory for Computer Graphics and Spatial Analysis. The research in the laboratory led to two sorts of findings. Many computer programmes achieving mapping and other graphical displays were accomplished. My greater interest centred, however, in the research results that led to the establishment of the *Harvard Papers in Theoretical Geography* series.

My graduate teaching consisted of one course entitled 'The Theory of the Region' and participation as one of four faculty members in another, 'Physical Geographical Systems'. The greatest satisfaction and challenge, however, resulted from being invited also to teach in the Harvard College undergraduate Freshman Seminar series. This famous programme had been instituted to accommodate those entering freshmen at Harvard who had sufficient advanced university standing in several subjects (as per examination test scores) to warrant their becoming involved immediately in small groups in an ongoing research context with senior faculty members. Needless to say geography was not one of those subjects in which the students had advanced standing. In fact none of them who chose to work with me had ever done a geography course during their secondary schooling. However, they did have that easy familiarity with place names and geographical configurations so characteristic of well read people generally.

Nevertheless 'Geography, Geometry, and Graphics' was the course topic. The review reports about the programme and the students' enthusiasm for it were so encouraging that Dean Franklin Ford (Faculty of Arts and Sciences, Harvard College) invited me to submit to him an initial statement and proposal for (re-)introducing geography as an undergraduate programme. A series of meetings followed; faculty members from other disciplines joined me; resources available and strategies required to achieve the required Arts and Science Faculty approval for recommendation to the Corporation were considered. Progress was being made when the outside world intruded heavily indeed upon us.

I have so far alluded only briefly to the general political, economic, and social circumstances as they had unfolded in the USA during the four decades. The events of the latter part of the 1960s leading to the complete though temporary breakdown of activities at Harvard in April 1969 cannot be ignored. The original Massachusetts Hall confrontation generated, with no prior organisational effort, spontaneous responses in literally every school, department, and programme in the University. I do not wish to pursue this topic at this time except to say that in the midst of the furor Dr Ford suffered a heart attack and subsequently resigned as Dean. The consideration of geography seemed of no consequence to me or anybody else during the long uncertain period that followed. And when considerations were taken up again much later with Dean Dunlop it was obvious that for the time being a chance had been irrevocably lost and that we would have to begin at the beginning. Now, in 1980, curriculum reform is again a major concern, and arguments can and should be made.

Dean Ford's kindly disposition toward the re-consideration of a geography programme had naturally not derived solely from the then current circumstances. It was clear that his interests encompassed all of geography and a well rounded programme was sought. He was, it seemed, intrigued by our discussion of the role of the discipline in the curriculum of colonial Harvard College and other American Colleges.[12] The history of cartography through to modern computer use on the one hand, and the in itself transforming and revolutionary nature of Waldo Tobler's mapping transformations on the other were matters looked on with favour. Another unshakeable conviction I retain from those times is of the deep and very favourable impression the work of Professor Clifford Darby had made upon the historian Dean Ford and his colleagues during his two earlier periods as Visiting Professor at Harvard.

Meanwhile in the Graduate School of Design the typical kinds of debates found in academic planning programmes everywhere at that time were taking place. The adversaries were arrayed in a fashion recognisable to anyone who had been paying attention to the revolution in geography and in regional science. The spatial analysts in the Laboratory for Computer Graphics along with Walter Isard (who then served on a part time basis in the Graduate School of Design) and his group of research associates argued one point of view against the others who can perhaps be best described as being in the 'architectural tradition' of city planning and for many of whom mathematical models in the social sciences were anathema. This represented for the most part honest intellectual endeavour and in that sense a wholesome undertaking. But it seemed not to be able to be separated from long standing personal disaffections. Relative newcomers were at first amused, then shocked, and finally totally disgusted by the circumstances that had become brutally nasty. Many of the events came into the public's knowledge because of press coverage of the various trials and tribulations. There is no need, nor do I have any wish, to discuss these matters at this time. Moreover they occurred after the time span dictated by the editors of this volume, and very recent re-organisation there offers some hope and perhaps a public policy educated 'not so élite' will achieve for the nation what the liberally educated élite could not.

Notes and References

1. J.G. Crowther, *Scientific Types* (London: Cresset Press, 1968).

2. P. Gould, 'Geography 1957–1977: the Augean period', *Annals of the Association of American Geographers*, vol. 69 (March 1979) no. 1, pp. 139–50.

3. J.Q. Stewart, *Coasts, Waves and Weather*.

4. W. Warntz, 'Toward a geography of price' (University of Pennsylvania).

5. Wilma B. Fairchild, 'Two eastern institutions', *Annals of the Association of American Geographers*, vol. 69 (March 1969) no. 1, pp. 33–40.

6. Expressed in his annual report of the council of the American Geographical Society (1961).

7. From among a number of important papers, see A.G. Wilson and M.L. Senior, 'Some relationships between entropy maximizing models, mathematical programming models, and their duals', *Journal of Regional Science*, vol. 14 (1974), pp. 207–15.

8. W. Tobler, 'Spatial interaction patterns', *Journal of Environmental Systems*, vol. 6 (1976–7), no. 4, pp. 271–301; M. F. Goodchild and M.Y.C. Kwan, 'Models of hierarchically dominated spatial interaction', *Environment and Planning* vol. 10 (1978), no. 11, pp. 1307–1317.

9. W. Warntz, *Geography, Geometry, and Graphics* (Princeton, 1963).

10. P. Gould, 'Geography 1957–1977'.

11. W. Warntz, *Geography Now and Then* (New York: American Geographical Society, 1964).

12. W. Warntz, *Geography Now and Then*.

Part III
Reflections

Unmasking Technocratic Geography

DAVID MERCER

> the specific purpose which the mind industry performs is essentially
> the same all over the world, no matter how the industry is operated:
> under state, public or private management, within a capitalist or a
> socialist economy.... The mind industry's main business and concern
> is not to sell its product: it is to 'sell' the existing order.[1]

The 'Future' of Geography

In a previously published debate with Peter Haggett speculating on
the 'future' of geography, I presented the argument that in order
fully to comprehend the development of professional geography we
need to do several things.[2] First and foremost, utilising the
common 'external influence, internal change' framework,[3] it is
necessary to grasp the idea that 'geography', like any discipline, is a
totally artificial construct that is produced in response to varying
time and place specific social, economic and political forces. Moreover, it is then packaged and marketed by a small coterie of profes-
sionals and their agents (e.g. publishers, government bureaucrats)
who stand to gain by the perpetuation of the notion that the long,
hard study of this particular subject area leads to the acquisition of
esoteric skills and special insights into the workings of the physical
and social landscapes. Such marketing of a discipline – whether it
be medicine, mathematics or geography – may take place in a
favourable climate of public opinion characterised by broad community agreement that a subject is indeed 'needed' or, alternatively
(as appears to be the case with geography in Australia at the present
time), it may represent a tardy response to what seems to be the
gradual 'withering away' of a particular academic area.

This is by no means an exceptional way of viewing this (or any) field of inquiry in the physical or human 'sciences', and countless analyses and counter-interpretations have now been presented focusing on the 'manufacture' and institutionalisation of most professional academic disciplines.[4] Indeed, the fairly recent establishment of specialist journals such as *Science and Public Policy*, *Social Studies of Science* and *Science of Science* is a clear indication that the study of the philosophy, politics, economics and sociology of what we might broadly call the 'scientific enterprise' is now a flourishing research field in its own right. This focus of course has its ancestry in Marx and Engels's 1845–6 writings[5] in which they uncompromisingly attacked Hegelian idealism and emphasised that 'world-building activity' has as much to do with the production of conceptions and ideas as with the fabrication of commodities for exchange. Marxist orientated interpretations of the growth and development of intellectual activity – such as are favoured by the present writer – generally see the latter as a fairly uncomplicated expression of the socioeconomic base of a specific society at any given time. Thus, whether we are talking about the social reformist British imperialist ideology underlying Mackinder's geography or the more recent applied research of contemporary corporate-orientated retail geographers, plant location analysts and the like, the story is the same: the prevailing economic and political situation both conditions and demands a particular kind of 'geography' (and economics and sociology etc.) to give it legitimacy. In other words, if a Halford Mackinder had not appeared at that time, another forceful individual of similar mould would almost certainly have been publicising and advocating the same kind of academic and political values.

Critics of this 'externalist' viewpoint,[6] on the other hand, argue that material conditions have little or no influence on changes in the nature or direction of scientific thought. Such dissenters, however, invariably base their criticisms on analyses of science in earlier centuries. The situation today is that perhaps the majority of scientists – including geographers – work towards applied or utilitarian goals that are *externally determined*. Writing almost 30 years ago in *The Organisation Man*, Whyte, for example,[7] indicated that even at that time in the USA there were some 600,000 people directly involved in scientific investigations but that a mere 4 per cent of the total national research expenditure went towards projects not directly linked with the accumulation of profits. He also calculated that only about 5,000 out of the entire research army had 'freely chosen' their areas of scientific inquiry. There are some interesting parallels here with intellectual activity in earlier times. Throughout the Middle Ages and the Renaissance creative artists were shackled to the much needed patronage of the church and the aristocracy, and it was only much later that a genuinely autonomous 'intellectual field' of painters, writers and philosophers emancipated itself from this external controlling authority. Today, in both the natural and social sciences one can discern signs of a reversal of this trend towards intellectual independence and a return to a kind of mediaeval dependency on state and corporate patronage.

In order to emerge in the first place, and then to continue surviving, all institutions and social systems must be *legitimated* at the level of consciousness. This process can occur either 'pretheoretically' (in the form of long established myths, beliefs etc.) or – increasingly in rich societies – at the 'theoretical' level through the continual affirmation of favoured economic, social and physical 'laws' or 'theories'. In traditional societies religion served as by far the most significant instrument of legitimation. Rationality was essentially 'practical', largely unconcerned with notions of 'control' or 'manipulation', but strongly governed by consensual norms relating to the goodness and correctness of the established social order.[10] As commercial relations expanded globally, the religious legitimation characteristic of the Middle Ages was of course steadily displaced by the substitution of 'means ends', 'technical' or 'instrumental' rationality. Traditional standards for assessing 'reliability', 'truth' and so on were gradually eroded by the emergence of an entirely new legitimating force based around the canons of 'science'.

In order to understand the persistence and strong influence of such 'authoritative' ideas, we need to look at the workings of forces other than those of a strictly defined 'rational' scientific community. Harding, for example,[11] poses the question: How are we to explain the 200-year survival and entrenchment of the highly restrictive Humean empiricist conception of "mind", when there is so much evidence that it is a wholly inadequate formulation? 'The answer for Harding is perfectly straightforward, and lies in the fact that the conceptualisation of 'mind' as basically formless and infinitely malleable provides a perfect ideological weapon for imperialism, for class society and for excluding a whole range of 'underclass' groups from playing any significant political role. The 'theory', in short, has a very important social and political function – 'treat people as if they are passive and need direction from others, and they will become or remain able to be manipulated and controlled'.[12] The popularity of 'Social Darwinism' can be explained in the same terms. Darwin's evolutionary ideas suffered quite severe distortion when they were enthusiastically appropriated and applied to human societies by such influential writers as Carlyle, Ruskin and, notably, Spencer. Spencer's ideas on social struggle, individual rights and the 'survival of the fittest' were rapidly incorporated into the ruling ideas of capitalist societies from the 1850s on, even though they were highly suspect. In time they became very influential in bourgeois social science, particularly in human geography, where they can be traced right through the Burgess model of urban residential structure to the more recent 'social area analyses' that have been labouriously carried out on most large capitalist cities. As with the Humean conception of mind, 'Social Darwinism' performed the important legitimating function of 'explaining' the existence and persistence of a weak underclass.

Social ideologues such as Spencer are not alone in ignoring or distorting the 'facts' of science for particular personal or political ends. Historically there are numerous examples of 'rational' scientists who chose to ignore conflicting or contradictory experimental data in order to develop their own intuitive, 'counter inductive', yet ultimately powerful theories. Both Copernicus and Galileo provide us with excellent examples of individualist intellectuals who pressed on with 'oddball' ideas in the face of apparently recalcitrant 'commonsense' evidence. Perhaps of more immediate relevance to the subject matter of the present discussion, we shall have occasion later to draw attention to similar yet much more recent fundamental challenges currently being mounted to orthodox conservative thinking in the area of 'urban modelling' by US and British feminist social scientists.

Aspirations to 'aristoscience'
While there has never really been much argument about the 'scientific' status of physical geography because of its strong links with related disciplines such as geology and botany, I take it as axiomatic that the years since 1950 have also witnessed a strong impetus to mould the social 'sciences' such as human geography along the methodological lines of physics, chemistry and biology.

Thompson[13] points out that in western societies – clearly
paralleling images of the gender division – there exists a quite
explicit prestige hierarchy ranging from the 'hard', 'pure', 'tough',
'rational', 'objective' disciplines of the physical sciences through to
the 'soft', 'emotional' and 'undisciplined' subjects such as
sociology, economics, psychology, history and human geography.
In a transparent reference to its status and prestige, Passmore
collectively describes the former as 'aristoscience'. It:

> is specialised, analytic and abstract. It concentrates on a limited
> set of natural processes and analyzes them abstractly into rela-
> tionships between elementary constituents, relations which, pre-
> ferably, are describable in purely mathematical terms.[14]

Clearly there has been a strong feeling within the so called 'social
sciences' for some time that in so far as they take on the
accoutrements of the 'hard' disciplines – notably quantification
and 'predictive' model building – they can move closer to the
hallowed halls of 'aristoscience' and thereby gain added status in
the eyes of technological society. With the rise to dominance of
homo economicus it is perhaps not surprising that within the
human sciences it was the discipline of economics that first made
the break with traditional legitimation by claiming that their
'science' made a clear separation between fact, theory and value.
Economists made a direct transplantation of the mechanistic
physical science world view into the workings of the economy so
that the motor force of 'individual self-interest', for example,
could be directly equated with the force of gravity, and so on.
There is little doubt that in some academic circles 'progress' in a
social science discipline is directly related to the extent to which that
discipline has become more 'scientific'. Recently a past President
of the American Sociological Association, Philip M. Hauser,
proudly declared on the occasion of the 75th anniversary of the
Association that not only was sociology actually '*progressing* [my
emphasis] rapidly towards being a science but that happily the
perception of sociology as a science in the popular mind had also
been accelerating'.[15] Predictably, for someone steeped in the US
technocratic tradition, Hauser was also at pains to point out what is
(to him) the important distinction between 'objective science' (e.g.
sociology) and social engineering.

Hauser's views are interesting, for in a moment we shall be

drawing attention to the link between favoured lines of academic development and professional self-interest. For the present, suffice it to say that not all students of human inquiry – including the present writer – are so happily disposed towards the sanctification of aristoscience. In their foreword to an important recent book Rowan and Reason, for example, charge that orthodox 'objective' social science research 'kills off everything it comes into contact with, so that what we are left with is dead knowledge'.[16] As we shall see, this is a not altogether unexpected outcome of an approach to intellectual activity which sees it, not as an exciting, vibrant enterprise, or even as one which is concerned with ascertaining the 'truth' but which, more often than not, is simply used as an ideological 'technical' weapon to legitimate the status quo.

Professionalism and institutional 'stake'
In writing of the distinction between 'science' and 'magic' the anthropologist Malinowski,[17] argued that 'science is open to all, a common good of the whole community; magic is occult, taught through mysterious initiations, handed on in a hereditary or at least in very exclusive filiation'. Science and scientists have been characterised in numerous stereotyped ways by the public at different times. 'Weapon', 'saviour', 'devil', 'priest' and 'plaything', for example, all readily spring to mind as relevant designations for particular periods, events or innovations. But arguably in the contemporary world of *in vitro* fertilisation, high technology computerisation, semi-private technical languages, systems theory and the rapid global and interstellar transmission of information, it is probably Malinowski's 'magic' that most cogently encapsulates the public's perception of science, including large areas of geography. Its language, techniques and rituals appear esoteric and élitist. Hence I also emphasised in the 1977 paper[18] that it is important to focus attention on the transmission of geographical knowledge and ideology through an analysis of the workings of *professionalisation* and *patronage*, both of which are so vital to the reproduction of consensus, mystification and the existing hierarchical power structure within the discipline. So strongly imbued are we with the bourgeois conception of science as being something that is accessible only to a highly trained minority that we tend to forget how relatively short lived is the 'cult of the expert'. In the 19th century, for example, in countries like Britain and the USA, science was very much more democratised, being carried out by a large army of enthusiastic amateurs.

Third, it was stressed that one's views of the past achievements and present and future state of a subject such as geography are very much a function of one's current and anticipated position – or 'stake' – in the institutional power structure (is one viewing the subject's role and evolution from 'above' or from 'below'? does one discern genuine 'progress' over the years or gradual intellectual 'impoverishment'?). This of course parallels the notion that there is no 'objective knowledge' or 'reality', as such, merely a series of more or less conflicting world views reflecting people's positions in society. The critical social scientist's task then is not to 'explain' but continually to seek to unmask both the contours of the world views themselves and the processes giving rise to these various subjective realities.

To this end, and finally, in the response to Haggett's 'Mid-Term Futures for Geography',[19] a full consideration of the place of the subject within the broader context of the practical and ideological function of tertiary education was urged. The reason for this emphasis lay in a belief – which I hold even more strongly now – that undergraduate students, postgraduates and full time academics in any given field are painstakingly initiated not only into certain methodological practices and theories relating to their discipline but that, much more importantly, they also tend to take on a particular set of fairly blinkered stereotyped attitudes and ways of looking at the world. Feyerabend notes that:

> From our very childhood we are subjected to a process of social-ization and enculturation compared with which the training of household pets, circus animals, police dogs is mere child's play.... So elementary education joins hands with higher education to produce individuals who are extremely limited, unfree in their perspective though not at all in their deter-mination to impose limitations on others under the name of knowledge.[20]

As in any hierarchical situation, the task of 'handing down' this knowledge, these values and beliefs, and of making sure that they are not transgressed, falls on the mediating 'gate keepers' or 'agenda setters' at the 'head' of the profession – principally the professors, journal editors, referees, research granting overseers and the like. On the grounds that 'critique' is a continual source of democratic and anti-authoritarian renewal, the article argued strongly for a much more 'interpretive' and 'critical' human geography than had generally been demonstrated by the vast majority of papers published in the well established professional journals up to that time. ('Criticism', of course, need not necessarily be destructive – as Macherey has pointed out, the term is ambiguous in that 'it implies, on the one hand, a gesture of refusal, a denunciation, a hostile judgement; and on the other hand it denotes (in its more fundamental sense) the positive knowledge of limits, the study of the conditions and possibilities of an activity';[21] even a cursory scrutiny of the writings of a sample of literary or social science critics will reveal that it is commonplace for the same writer to move back and forth between that Macherey calls 'criticism-as-condemnation' and the more positive 'criticism-as-explanation'.)

Scope of the discussion
The present, written in 1982, extends some of these arguments, partly through a personal 'retrospective' and 'prospective' interpretation of the 'quantitative revolution' which seduced the discipline in the early 1960s and which, I would argue, still maintains a strong ideological hold on geography today. The discussion centres on why I believe this hold continues and finally, following Feyerabend[22] and a long anarchist tradition, presents the case *against* the hegemony of so called 'scientific' or 'technocratic' geography and the case *for* 'self-managed' or 'democratised' knowledge.[23] As will become increasingly apparent, many of the ideas presented here sit fairly firmly within (and draw their inspiration from) a long and well established tradition, as old as science itself, which includes such diverse bedfellows as Plato, Goethe, Kierkegaard and Nietzsche, and more recently Marcuse, Roszak and C.S. Lewis, to name but a few. This tradition is sometimes called 'anti-science', though personally I do not go along with all that is implied by this rather emotive iconoclastic label (I would perhaps prefer *'responsible* science'). The essay is written from the standpoint of a libertarian socialist, favouring widespread decentralisation, participatory democracy and intermediate technology and who, like Horowitz finds himself increasingly disturbed by, and strongly opposed to, emerging fascist tendencies on both the 'left' and the 'right'.[24] It will also become clear in the discussion that I include certain features of contemporary technological change – especially as manifested by the rapid diffusion and application of high technology computerisation – as one highly significant aspect of an emergent 'technological' fascism.

Unlike previous discussions and critiques of quantification in geography (or indeed in any field) the present essay does not deal specifically with the nuts and bolts of particular statistical techniques, whether they are 'appropriate' or 'inappropriate' for certain problems, data etc. The canvas is much broader, situates the subject generally at the levels of culture and 'consciousness' and focuses more on what we might call the 'hidden agenda': on the causes and consequences of the emergence and gradual strengthening of scientism and a particular kind of scientistic cognitive style in intellectual activity over the last few decades: geography has been caught up in this. By 'scientism' I mean the culmination of the positivist tradition which holds unquestioningly that: (i) there exists only one 'true' scientific method; (ii) knowledge is neutral; and (iii) the standards of 'precision' operating in the physical sciences offer the only genuinely explanatory framework for the generation of scientific knowledge. Chomsky argues that this is the triad underpinning the 'menace of liberal scholarship',[25] and in a stimulating analysis Wilson uncompromisingly labels the world view stemming from these presuppositions 'The *American* ideology' on the grounds that its evolution would not 'have been possible at all had it not been for the emergence and coming of age of this "first new nation", with all that this has since come to mean for knowledge, process and development'.[26] Thus positivism and scientism are the main targets under attack here. In particular, the *lack of reflection* so characteristic of mainstream positivistic research is roundly criticised. The typical 'scientistic' researcher is trained to steer clear of any 'diversionary' critical consideration of his or her role, presuppositions, data, personal or group actions and historical situation. It is precisely this schooling in 'abstraction' and 'detachment' which feeds a world view in which there are no 'people', merely 'body counts' or 'unemployment statistics'. Isiah Berlin describes this cold utilitarian perspective as 'the calm moral arithmetic of cost effectiveness which liberates decent men from qualms, because they no longer think of the entities to which they apply their scientific computations as actual human beings'.[27]

I present the argument that 'science' and 'technology' are now intimately inter-related and that the onset of the so called 'quantitative revolution' in the subject in the 1960s set in motion a process leading to a serious (some would say healthy) cleavage within the profession between two opposing perspectives – on the one hand a *technocratic* orientation towards geography, and on the other, a *normative* or *prescriptive* slant, with humanistic roots. This is a widely recognised division within the intellectual community. The benchmark ideological publication of David Rockefeller's Trilateral Commission entitled *The Crisis of Democracy* pointed to the split between 'technocratic and policy oriented' and 'value oriented' intellectuals.[28] The report described the first group favourably as 'constructive and responsible' but had little time for those in the other camp, who the Commission saw as seeking to 'challenge authority' and 'delegitimate' established institutions. With Carroll, I charge that social and natural scientists alike – including many geographers seduced by the technocratic mode – are preoccupied with superficial 'technical' problems and are failing to address themselves to what should be the central moral and intellectual questions of our day: 'How to live, and what to do?'[29] This 'trivialisation' process can be linked to the educational *deskilling* that Baran and Sweezy have pointed out inevitably accompanies the development of monopoly capitalism (and, I would add, centralised state socialism).[30] As part of this process academics and students alike are subtly 'encouraged' to become 'relevant' and unquestioning functionaries and (within well defined limits) to *analyse* rather than to *synthesise*.

Intellectual labour is becoming increasingly fragmented and proletarianised as Taylorisation[31] moves steadfastly into the professional and white collar areas, including academia. With the installation of highly capital intensive computerised equipment in our factories and universities, employers inevitably seek to maximise their use by demanding higher and more efficient output from employees. In 1971, for example, the Rolls Royce company in Britain sought to impose the following conditions on its professional design staff in Bristol:

> The acceptance of shift work in order to exploit high capital equipment, the acceptance of work measurement techniques, the division of work into basic elements, and the setting of times for these elements, such time to be compared with actual performance.[32]

In other words, the formerly fairly autonomous but 'undisciplined' creative design staff were being instructed to become more 'machine like', more 'predictable' in their productivity and to adapt their rather unsystematic working habits to the dictates of a centralised totalitarian computer design system. This is by no means an isolated example of what is becoming the commonplace extension of this kind of technological fascism into the intellectual labour process. The software package, HARNESS, for example, is now being extensively used in building design by architects, thus devaluing the creative input. As computerisation extends its influence, Cooley insists that corporate mathematicians will be 'programmed' to have their work ready at a particular time just as assembly line workers – where they still exist – are currently programmed to the speed and dictates of their machines. Carrying the mechanical metaphor a little further, it is also interesting to note that there is now growing talk of assessing the 'peak performance' ages of researchers in various disciplines as a guide to evaluating their continued 'usefulness' or 'obsolescence' in the knowledge industry.

Knowledge for what, and for whom?
Before proceeding to a brief outline and discussion of some recent changes in the 'external' global situation having an impact on intellectual activity, some prefatory remarks are in order relating to the difference between the social and natural sciences and the *utilisation* of the fruits of academic labour. This is important because one of the main issues of concern to the present writer, as we shall see, is not so much what ideas or findings are 'discovered' and manufactured by workers in the knowledge industry, but the *use* to which those products are put i.e. knowledge for *what*, and for *whom*? And it is at this point that we must focus on a significant difference between the natural (or physical) sciences on the one hand and the social 'sciences' on the other, and at the same time highlight the ambiguity which exists in a subject like 'geography' which, in some senses, spans the two. While there are a growing number of students of methodology[33] who argue fairly convincingly that the differences between the social and non-social sciences are minimal, there is, I believe, one significant difference which deserves mention. In principle, at least, the outcomes of research in the natural sciences are value-free, or 'neutral', in that potentially they can be used for a variety of political and social purposes. Such products can be utilised either for the benefit of state or private capital and for the 'emancipation' or 'repression' of certain groups in society. This sometimes places the natural

scientist in a difficult situation, for it is not uncommon for the fruits of scientific labour to be used for purposes never intended by their producers. The social sciences, by contrast are somewhat different. Despite protestations to the contrary by many liberal practitioners, they invariably have an unequivocal social function. This is usually fairly transparent when an analysis is made, first of the initial *choice of problem* (the way this is defined etc.), and second – most importantly – of the *methodological stance* taken. The two are intimately related, for in the social sciences the chosen methodology is always an essential element in the *kind of knowledge* produced. And this, of course, is why methodological disputes are so vociferous between social scientists.

Apart from the fact that the 'findings' are frequently trivial in the extreme – a feature we have already noted above – by far the most important purpose of empirical positivistic social science is the perpetuation of the *status quo* through the continual underscoring of the 'rightness' and 'inevitability' of existing institutions, modes of production and ways of living. At one level, then, the most dominant (positivist–empiricist) form of social science practice can be viewed as a kind of propaganda device for legitimating existing policies. While it is perhaps unfair to single out one isolated piece of empirical research from the mountains of uncritical material that are produced daily by diligent social science labourers around the world, a recent paper in a well known American geographical journal – *The Geographical Review* – provides a perfect initial illustration of my main argument, and should immediately attune the reader to my viewpoint. The article is entitled 'Evacuation from a nuclear technological disaster',[34] and presents the findings of a questionnaire survey of the spatial behaviour of residents living in the vicinity of the Three Mile Island (TMI) nuclear plant in Pennsylvania after the 'accident' at that site on 28 Mar, 1979. The dispassionate, 'objective' style of reporting on the part of Zeigler and his colleagues lulls one into accepting that what happened at TMI was nothing more than a 'normal malfunction'. There is no questioning of such basic fundamentals as the morality of nuclear power, of the certain health dangers to the inhabitants (born and unborn) created by the disaster or of the diversionary tactics of the Nuclear Regulatory Commission in this incident. Instead, what we are presented with is a dehumanised analysis of evacuation behaviour in which the researchers are totally detached from their 'subjects' and which successfully plays down the very real human factors of 'flight', 'fear', 'danger' and 'ignorance'. Moreover, lest the reader is in any doubt as to the ideological purpose and 'real world' application of this carefully documented piece of positivistic research, the authors offer the justification that 'societies using nuclear power today *must accept* major accidents not only as a theoretical possibility of no practical consequence, but as a risk to include in actual planning'[35] [my emphasis]. This is precisely the kind of 'apologetic study masquerading as objectivity' that Chomsky is referring to when he speaks of the 'menace' of liberal scholarship.[36]

I should state that unlike some radical critics who reject the 'facts and figures' cult outright, my purpose here is not to dismiss statistics and quantification totally. Clearly, data collection and dissemination are immensely important activities in contemporary complex societies. My criticisms are rather levelled at an ideology which equates statistical methodology with 'science', which underplays the subjectivity involved at every stage in data categorisation, classification, collection and analysis, which mystifies the process of statistical manipulation and is opposed to the widest possible dissemination of information. I also find myself in strong opposition to a viewpoint which avers that anything which cannot easily be 'counted' is irrelevant. In short, my principal argument here is not so much with 'quantification' *per se*, but with the way in which the phenomenon has been allowed to develop, with the *kinds of data* that tend to be collected, with its intellectual totalitarianism and with the ruling political forces that have always been served by its growth and development.

The discussion proceeds in the following sequence. First, in the following section, what I consider to be certain crucial changes in the contours of the world international order are briefly outlined. These represent the recent culmination of forces that have been operative for some time and therefore I consider it important to spell them out briefly in order to provide a context for discussing related developments in intellectual thought and activity. The choice of phenomena for consideration is, inevitably, subjective and reflects my own somewhat less than sanguine view of world history and academic enterprise over the last few decades. Then follows a section in which I address the issue of 'technocracy', briefly outline the history of the concept and spell out some of the political and intellectual implications of the 'technocratic mode'. This leads logically into a section in which I focus on a critique of certain aspects of quantification which is, of course, one of the central pillars of the technocratic edifice. 'Quantification' can be taken to refer to a range of phenomena, including as it does 'mere counting, the development of classificatory dimensions and the systematic use of "social symptoms" as well as mathematical models and an axiomatic theory of measurement'.[37] Given that any discussion – including the present essay – involves some degree of *selection* and *classification*, a kind of 'quantification' is clearly involved in most academic activity. Needless to add, the sense in which I use the term here implies an overwhelming faith in (and reliance on) mathematics as the primary language of expression and explanation. In view of the fact that other critics of geographical practice have dealt at length with such glaringly obvious shortcomings as space fetishism,[38] I have chosen to concentrate on only two related and yet relatively neglected features of quantification as it has come to be used by geographers and others – its role in the legitimation and maintenance of the existing order, and the unquestioning attitude that is invariably adopted towards the manufacture of official statistics.

External Change

Both 'externally' – and therefore inevitably 'internally' within the institutions supporting the discipline of geography – a great deal has happened since. After the halcyon full employment days of the post-1945 'long boom' the capitalist world has plunged into a serious recession characterised by steadily climbing unemployment rates, skyrocketing energy costs and high inflation. This recession has reached into every corner of the political and economic fabric of society in all the rich industrial nations of the world, and is having a marked impact on such things as social harmony and political polarisation as well as on education, especially at the tertiary level.[39] As in previous recessions, we are witnessing a strong resurgence of the conservative technocratic critique of secondary and tertiary education which asserts that educational practices have moved too far out of step with the needs of industry and commerce. A speedy return to the teaching of fundamental statistical and accounting procedures in line with dominant business values is invariably recommended. Depending upon one's political persuasion, the present depression represents the final death throes of

a decaying capitalist system or simply the fifth phase in an upswing
of one of Kondratieff's 'long economic waves';[40] though interestingly, even generally 'optimistic' economists in the Rostow
mould are now sagely suggesting that it will not be at all easy to
break out of the current crisis situation until we develop a whole
new arsenal of ideas and concepts and, obviously, the collective will
to carry them through.[41] Favoured political strategies vary from the
currently popular hardline monetarism, or New Conservatism –
with all that that implies in terms of cutbacks to 'non-essential'
services – right through to calls for the public ownership of banks
and key industries.

In all western countries the state has responded by strengthening
its links with multinational and national private enterprise, extending its control apparata and – in the manner already alluded to
in the Trilateral Commission Report[42] – constantly seeking out
academics and institutions sympathetic to its monetarist policies.
This new evolving form of state organisation is now generally
referred to as 'liberal democratic corporatism', which Panitch
describes as 'a political structure within advanced capitalism which
integrates organized socioeconomic producer groups through a
system of representation and cooperative mutual interaction at the
leadership level and mobilization and social control at the mass
level'.[43] As we shall see, statistics-gathering operations and
quantification have become more and more significant as one
important aspect of the process of state and corporate legitimation
and mass social control. This also means that 'information' –
particularly statistical information – becomes a key weapon in
either upholding or attacking certain government and industrial
policies, and *control* of that information through various means
therefore becomes crucial in power politics.[44]

'Official' statistics provide one of the most fundamental sources
of information for professional geographical research, and as such
they will receive a fair measure of critical attention in the present
discussion. In view of their enormous cost (the bill for the 1980 US
census, for example, was $1 billion), considerable public relations'
energy is expended to convince the general public of the utility,
objectivity and credibility of such data. What tends to be forgotten,
however – not least by unquestioning quantitative geographers – is
that the outcomes of such massive statistical gathering operations
are not 'findings', as they are commonly described, but rather
imperfect *creations* or *products*:

statistics do not, in some mysterious way, emanate directly from
the social conditions they appear to describe... between the two
lie the assumptions, conceptions and priorities of the state and
the social order, a large, complex and imperfectly functioning
bureaucracy.[45]

Environmental and social crisis
Notwithstanding the placatory comments on the 'sturdiness' of the
planet by such conservative geographical notables as F. Kenneth
Hare,[46] technological man continues to plunder spaceship earth at
an ever accelerating rate in the continued drive for domination and
profit. March 1979 witnessed the TMI nuclear disaster; as perhaps
the most dramatic example of what is happening to all the global
biological systems, the world's rainforests are disappearing at the
rate of 30 ha a minute; and 1978 in the state of New York saw the
first revelations concerning the horrors of years of toxic chemical
dumping – 'the environmental sleeping giant of the decade'.[47]
Nature, in short, has become polluted, commercialised, and, above
all, *militarised* as the military-industrial apparata have grown and
expanded globally. One recent estimate, for example, puts the
volume of military-related consumption of natural resources in the
USA at over half the total world consumption for this purpose.[48]
   Enormous upheavals are also taking place in the global and
national organisation of capital. The employment pool is rapidly
drying up as industries continue to desert the older established
manufacturing regions such as Britain, Australia or the north-
eastern USA in favour of Third World countries or the Sunbelt of
the USA Allied with far reaching technological changes in computerisation, robotics and telecommunications, this is having the
effect of producing a large unemployed (and probably unemploy-
able) class, often strongly concentrated in certain problem centres
of multiple deprivation. Several commentators on these trends have
used the 'collapse of work' catchcry to argue that we are presently
caught up in a profound social and economic revolution which, for
many people, will result in an enforced radical re-appraisal of the
centrality of 'work' in their lives.[49] One effect of all this is that the
western world is currently being swept by a new wave of conservatism which clearly has enormous implications for research and
educational practices. We have already witnessed the emergence of
a whole variety of fundamentalist sects, ranging from the Moral

Majority in the USA to the followers of Jim Jones. One explanation for the resurgence of these 'therapeutic' cultic movements – reminiscent, in many ways, of Germany in the 1930s – is that the west is currently at a stage of deepening cultural and spiritual crisis. Following Freud's general theory of culture, Rieff asserts that all cultures impose strict restraints on what is 'allowable' and 'possible'.[50] At certain times of crisis, however – such as the liberal 1960s and early 1970s – these cultural interdicts are widely transgressed as people seek to undermine and break free from long standing 'sacred' norms. The logical outcome of this phase, Rieff insists (incidentally, echoing Trotsky) is the emergence – as now – of a strong, conservative, even violent cultural backlash.

So far I have talked mainly of capitalist countries, but *all* advanced industrial societies are now sharing a common crisis. By and large they are all committed to policies which stimulate economic growth. This in turn has the effect of producing serious social dislocations. The environment is adversely affected, communities and individuals are uprooted, made redundant and so on. This results in growing pressure for various social welfare and other ameliorative programmes. So there always exists a contradiction between *economic growth* on the one hand and its *effects* on the other. While economic growth demands a massive commitment of public finance, so too do the broad range of much needed social welfare programmes, including education. The state is in a sense torn both ways and so suffers a *legitimation crisis* of major proportions. One response to this of considerable relevance to the present essay is that the state becomes *'depoliticised'*. It accomplishes this 'by becoming an administrative state where rational, efficient problem-solving takes precedence over democratic debate and dissent'.[51] Official, centralised data gathering exercises, statistical analysis and presentation on an ever expanding scale are central features of this new bureaucratised state formation.

'Dis-Europeanisation' and arms build up

The years since 1975 have also presented further evidence favouring the global 'dis-Europeanisation thesis.[52] Starting with the defeat of Russia by the Japanese in 1904–5 and extending through the overthrow of US interests in Vietnam and Iran and the post-1945 re-emergence of Japan, we have witnessed a steady erosion of US hegemony. With characteristic arrogance this has prompted many western commentators to voice dismay at the 'irrationality' of a world view such as Islam (we shall have more to say about so called 'rationality' later, but at this point it is worth noting that I tend to favour E.P. Thompson's view that it denotes nothing more than 'the pursuit of self-interest, as attributed to a nation, class, political élite etc.'[53]. In response to this and the perceived Soviet threat, the US Reagan administration has committed millions of dollars to the MX missile programme and to the development of that ultimate triumph of technological man, the neutron bomb.

I regard the recent global build up of weapons of war and the expansion of world trade in military hardware as arguably the single most important feature of our age. Yet while intellectuals of the stature of E.P. Thompson[54] and Raymond Williams[55] fully acknowledge it and tackle all the manifold implications of this 'unthinkable' phenomenon head on, geographers by and large have tended totally to ignore it. Let us briefly look at some of the facts. First, while estimates are still somewhat hazy, it appears as though the total world arsenal of nuclear weapons has already passed the 50,000 mark.[56] Second, according to official UN data, total world military expenditures now average over \$400 billion per year, 50 per cent higher than education expenditures and 250 per cent higher than spending on health care.[57] The 'research, development, test and evaluation' (RDTE) budget for military purposes in the US in 1981 stood at \$16.5 billion. Annual growth rates in expenditure have been set at 3 per cent in Britain and 5 per cent in the US.[58] Third, while civilian international trade has been virtually stagnant for some time, all the indications are that the arms trade is the world's fastest growing business, with the total volume of transfers rising from \$3200 m in 1963 to almost \$10,000 m by 1975.[59] Approximately 75 per cent of this trade goes to Third World countries.

The significance of these details to the present discussion is twofold. First, there is an enormous and burgeoning research industry associated with the arms build up which both directly and indirectly impinges on the discipline of geography – directly through such areas as remote sensing, satellite imagery and the like,[61] and indirectly through the development and encouragement of a sympathetic research 'style' centred around computerised systems modelling. Second, clearly related to this is:

a correspondent social system – a distinct organization of labour, research and operation, with distinctive hierarchies of command, rules of secrecy, prior access to resources and skills...a distinctive organization of production, which, while militarist in character, employs and is supported by great numbers of civilians (civil servants, scientists, academics) who are subordinated to its discipline and rules.[61]

Like Rostow, Thompson is also at pains to point out that we desperately need wholly new categories in order to analyse the emerging realities of arms production, world dominance and dependence. 'Imperialism' and 'mode of production', for example, he regards as rather archaic concepts which fail to adequately explain the new ground rules for understanding what is currently happening between the USA, the USSR and the Third World.

Later we shall have occasion to speculate further on some of these emerging tendencies in the 'external' environment and their relevance to professional geography, but let us now turn our attention more closely to a consideration of the 'technocratic mode'.

The Technocratic Mode

The term 'technocracy' is now in wide usage and is generally taken to refer to a situation where traditional leaders – politicians, capitalists and so on – are replaced by a new class of 'rational' scientific experts with specialist technical skills and training. The concept and ideology has a fairly long ancestry. Veblen was writing about it at the turn of the century, and by the 1930s a new political party – 'Technocracy Inc.' – had been formed in the USA. The party's main aim was to replace the existing 'irrational' political leaders with thinking engineers and scientists who would 'produce and distribute an abundance for everyone...by factual, non-political methods'.[62] Various writers since that time – notably Galbraith, Ellul and Touraine – have argued that control of the contemporary state now resides in the 'technostructure' and that political leaders are gradually being transformed into mere figureheads. Technocratic, quantitatively orientated social science has always been encouraged and fostered in the corridors of power in the USA where it is associated with the names of such leading ideologues as Daniel Moynihan, H.J. Eysenck and B.F. Skinner. Moynihan, for example, speaks enthusiastically of the social sciences ultimately giving 'government an enlarged capacity to comprehend, predict and direct social events';[63] and for Eysenck the goal of psychology is not human emancipation but the 'prediction and control of behaviour'.[64] The technocratic mode has been especially influential within geography in the USA and Britain, as well as in many of the state socialist countries, where it is an integral part of what Gregory has termed the broader 'ideology of control'.[65] This has been intimately linked by Gregory and others with the popularity of 'systems thinking', mathematical modelling and, of course, computerisation on a greatly expanded scale (in this context, it is interesting to note that Imperial College, University of London – and no doubt many other institutions of higher learning around the world – boasts a Department of Computing and *Control* [my emphasis]; though of what, and by whom, is an open question!).

In capitalist societies science and technology are called upon to aid the accumulation of profit and to assist in the smooth functioning of the economy. In 'Marxist' countries the natural sciences perform a similar 'nature dominating' function to that in the west, while the purpose of the social sciences invariably also 'consists in unceasing confirmation of how things ought to be according to ideological doctrine, rather than in critical analysis of how things stand in reality.[66] From the 'expert's' point of view the technocratic mode is comfortable to operate within, buttressed as it is by the myth of objectivity:

> Their world is a positivist one where an independent subject, the expert, looks from above at a series of independent entities given to his observations and which he calls objective facts – a bird's eye worldview. His task is then to explain the connections between these facts. To do that he will produce (quantitative and/or descriptive) models which he will consider to be a reproduction of reality.[67]

At this juncture, in order to underscore the central point that this represents merely *one of a number of possible alternative moulds of understanding*, it is useful to introduce the work of Mitroff and Kilmann. Their timely contribution has been to develop a typology of 'basic styles of thinking about and doing science', and for their fundamental classificatory dimensions they focus on the acts of *thinking, sensing, intuition* and *feeling* highlighted by Jung.[68] On this basis – and risking the obvious charge of 'objectifying' the categories developed – the authors suggest the fourfold typology of 'ideal type' attitudes to science and research activity depicted in Figure 1. For our purposes the so called 'analytical scientist' fits fairly and squarely into the 'technocratic' mode under discussion here, while the 'particular humanist' occupies the opposite pole of values and attitudes towards the operation and place of science in society. The basic differences are summarised in Table 1.

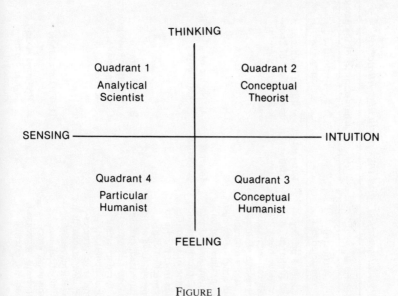

THINKING

Quadrant 1
Analytical
Scientist

Quadrant 2
Conceptual
Theorist

SENSING ——————————————— INTUITION

Quadrant 4
Particular
Humanist

Quadrant 3
Conceptual
Humanist

FEELING

FIGURE 1

One indication of the enormous success which the 'analytical scientific' viewpoint has achieved – especially in terms of promoting the 'special status' of science – can be gauged by the fact that the basic cleavage identified by Mitroff and Kilmann seems to parallel a similar deep seated binary societal split in all advanced industrial countries, whether capitalist or not. Investigations from places as far afield as Lille University's Epistemological Research Centre (CEREL)[69] and New Zealand[70] into the way in which individuals structure their worlds (their 'reality', as they see it) have consistently come up with the finding that 'ordinary people' invariably dichotomise society into 'them' and 'us'. 'They' are the 'ex-

TABLE 1 *Characteristics of the 'analytical scientist' and the 'particular humanist'*

	Characteristics of the analytical scientist		Characteristics of the particular humanist	
	Evaluative categories	Attributed characteristics	Evaluative categories	Attributed characteristics
External relations	Status of science as a special field of knowledge in relation to other fields	Occupies a privileged and a preferred position: value free, apolitical, cumulative, progressive, disinterested, clearly separable from other fields, clear lines of demarcation, autonomous, independent, strict hierarchical ordering of scientific fields from precise to less precise fields.	Status of science as a special field of knowledge in relation to other fields	Does not occupy a privileged and special position; may be subordinate to poetry, literature, art, music, and mysticism as older, 'superior' ways of knowing.
Internal properties	A. Nature of scientific knowledge	Impersonal, value free, disinterested, precise, reliable, accurate, valid, reductionistic, causal, apolitical, cumulative, progressive, clear standards for judgement, realistic, anti-mystical, unambiguous, exact.	A. Nature of scientific knowledge	Personal, value constituted, interested; partisan activity; poetic, political, action oriented; acausal, non-rational.
	B. Guarantors of scientific knowledge	Consensus, agreement, external reliability, external	B. Guarantors of scientific knowledge	Intense personal knowledge and experience.
			C. Ultimate aims of science	To help *this* person know himself or herself uniquely and to achieve his own self-determination.
			D. Preferred logic	The 'logic' of the unique and singular.
			E. Preferred sociological norms (ideology)	Counternorms to CUDOS.

	validity, rigour, controlled nature of inquiry, maintenance of distance between scientist and objects studied.	
C. Ultimate aims of science	Precise, unambiguous, theoretical and empirical knowledge for their own (disinterested) sake.	
D. Preferred logic	Aristotelean, strict classical logic, non-dialectical and indeterminate.	
E. Preferred sociological norms (ideology)	Classical norms of Communism, Universalism, Disinterestedness, Organised Scepticism (CUDOS).	
F. Preferred mode of inquiry	Controlled inquiry as embodied in the classic concept of the experiment.	The case study; the in-depth detailed study of a particular individual.
G. Properties of the scientist	Disinterested, unbiased, impersonal, precise, expert, specialist, sceptical, exact, methodical.	Interested, 'all too human', biased, poetic, committed to the postulates of an action oriented science.

SOURCE   I.I. Mitroff and R.H. Nilmann, *Methodological Approaches to Social Science* (San Francisco: Jossey–Bass, 1978).

perts and decision-makers of government and private enterprise; the ones who have the knowledge, the training, who are in charge and thus are responsible'.[71] Discourse analyses of 'average citizens' consistently uncover feelings of helplessness, of being dominated and threatened by obscure figures and events 'out there'. Moreover, detailed analyses of hours and hours of semi-structured discussions around the world based on the CEREL 'notional fields' format reveal that the metadiscourses invariably point to a world in which there is little or no possibility of change, no hope of anything different:

> Apart from a small feminine divergence and a slightly manifested fear of death, there is no crack in it, no opening, a well-oiled self-contained machinery repeating itself over and over again – the symptom of a totalitarian structure: no hope outside, no creation, no invention, no poesy.[72]

The politics of research and 'expertise'

Implicit in the argument presented here is the idea that the personal is 'political', that the distinction between 'private' and 'professional' concerns is false, and that the 'doing' of geography – whether in terms of teaching or research – is a 'political' act. The decision to follow a particular pedagogical line is 'political', as is the choice of research patronage, topics, techniques, strategies or the target groups for one's writing. One's very definition of geography is 'political' in that it can be defined very narrowly to exclude everything non-spatial (and usually, by extension, controversial) or it can be defined so broadly that, to all intents and purposes, it merges with other related disciplines and ceases to exist as an autonomous subject. Those with views towards the 'conservative' end of the political spectrum tend to go along with the highly fragmented institutionalised divisions of intellectual labour and to favour very precise and circumscribed definitions of what the subject is all about. As a rule they also make strong distinctions between the 'personal' and the 'professional', and argue that 'value neutrality' is both possible and desirable. Those at the opposite political pole, on the other hand, like the present writer, invariably emphasise that geography has 'no scientific existence, only an ideological purpose'[73] and that 'geographers' have a *responsibility* to make public statements voicing their opinions on a whole range of social concerns. We have already drawn attention in the previous section to professional geography's uninterrupted links with military concerns, in particular. Lacoste argues that since a concerted effort has been made to conceal and mystify the underlying political and military rationale of much geographical research and teaching.[74] Even if it *were* possible to be value free, or 'objective', in one's research and teaching, one would still have to concede the power of political bodies such as the University Grants Committee in deciding which universities or fields of intellectual endeavour should be allowed to flourish or die, and one would also have to concede the growing trend towards the politicisation and industrial-isation of areas of study such as geography through greatly expanded *external control*.

Increasingly, geographers are being co-opted by larger power institutions beyond the walls of the universities to carry out research legitimating this or that favoured course of action. Johnston and Robbins charge that the appropriation of research expertise in this way has had two main effects: (i) it has resulted in increasing conflict and confrontation between practitioners as they each follow their divergent ideological pathways; and (ii) – clearly related to the 'deskilling' noted earlier – it has accelerated the process of fragmentation within science. Subjects and problems become steadily broken down into smaller and smaller isolated packages. The 'cult of the expert' – proficient in one small area but feeling helpless to comment on anything outside that – inevitably results from this fracturing process.[75] The political consequences of this have been spelled out by Anders. He has suggested that one of the most glaringly characteristic features of the present era is that we live in the 'age of inability to fear'. He further argues that one important reason for this is:

> our *competence craze*; our conviction, nourished by the division of labor, that every problem belongs to *one* specific field of competence with which we are *not permitted* to meddle. Thus the atomic problem allegedly belongs to the competence field of the politicians and the military. Naturally the *'not being permitted'* to meddle immediately and automatically turns into a *'not having to'*, even into a *'not needing to'*.[76]

Anders's main concern is the build up of atomic weaponry, but precisely the same viewpoint could be applied to a whole range of pressing societal problems. In a similar vein, Arnoux emphasises the ultimately 'tranquillizing' effect of isolating out one specific 'problem', such as 'energy', from the broader context of industrialisation: 'Society tranquillizes us by drawing our attention to particular aspects such as energy, and isolating these from the other effects of the industrial system. By doing so it limits our awareness of the main question which is not confined to any particular aspect'.[77]

Reductionism and reification

Commoner also attacks scientific reductionism head on in his book *The Closing Circle*, and blames this particular aspect of science for the increasingly severe levels of environmental degradation being experienced all around the world.[78] If the 'problem' for Commoner is reductionism (which incidentally he feels can be corrected by using cybernetics to study complex ecosystem interactions), for Mumford, science started going seriously off course when Galileo's quantified, machine-like world view started gaining ground.[79] In Mumford's view 'this idea of nature discriminates against living things. All value, colour, life is sucked out of the world. The result is the devaluation of both nature and humanity; nature becomes just an instrument'. For these, and related reasons, I am no longer as certain as I was about the desirability of the split between 'physical' and 'human' geography. One prevalent view is that the two have nothing in common, that they have quite different intellectual roots, concerns and the like. But I am now sufficiently convinced by the arguments of such writers as Marcuse, Mumford and Commoner to believe that separating 'nature' and 'man' in this way is ecological suicide.

This fragmentation process also parallels the emergence of a kind of mass loss of identity or 'schizophrenia' in advanced abstract societies caused largely by the high degree of segmentation of institutional structures. Man finds himself increasingly caught up in what Zijderfeld calls a nightmare shifting 'institutional labyrinth' and reflects 'It is a miracle that he has not got even more lost than he has'.[80] Coping mechanisms somehow to come to terms with this loss of sense of totality and reality in both professional and private life vary considerably, but range through the entire spectrum from complete apathy and complacency to loud protest. The majority desperately try to build a kind of coherent and meaningful world picture out of the myriad of institutional fragments. For the intellectual, as we have seen, this invariably means focusing on a very narrow area of knowledge: 'he gets nervous outside his field of expertise where he senses an awful feeling of emptiness'.[81]

The ascendance of technocratic ideology has gradually alienated man from nature, man from man, and man from his cognitive and material artefacts. Some of the effects are immensely far reaching, yet subtle in their incremental impact and open to different interpretations. Cooley, for example, speaks quite openly of the computer *appropriating* intellectual creativity;[82] and on the subject of the profound yet uncharted moral territory surrounding the technological 'miracle' of *in vitro* fertilisation, White warns that 'when the developments take apart the character of the species and the human being and reconstruct these in another way, we are into something quite different'.[83] Certainly in their rhetoric, practitioners in all the social and physical sciences see their particular discipline as an instrument of human 'betterment', but in reality legitimation has been accompanied by the evil of *reification*, or:

> the apprehension of the products of human activity *as if* they were something else than human products – such as facts of nature, results of cosmic laws, or manifestations of divine will. Reification implies that man is capable of forgetting his own authorship of the human world, and further, that the dialectic between man, the producer, and his products is lost to consciousness. The reified world is, by definition, a dehumanised world.[84]

Before turning to a fuller consideration of the role of quantification it is probably only fair to point out at this juncture that the reification process is not always solely a characteristic of 'bourgeois' social and natural science. The positivism underlying the economic determinism of the later Marx, for example, certainly gave credence to a reified interpretation of history.

Critique of Quantification

For people born and raised in contemporary advanced capitalist societies it is difficult to appreciate alternative ways of viewing reality. Unlike today's prevailing scientistic mode of understanding, the pre-capitalist Aristotelian world view which held sway prior to the late 16th century did not treat the world as a kind of mechanical set of interacting 'facts' or 'objects' and had no notion of sharp disjunctions between separate 'things' or 'events'. Natural processes and events were tied together in a united, coherent cosmic framework and analysed in terms of their qualitative relationships, flows and 'purpose'. This is not to say that some 'counting' did not take place in earlier societies. Astronomy and geometry, for instance, have a very long ancestry. It seems likely that a census was carried out in Ancient Egypt almost 5,000 years ago, and William I's Domesday Book is another example of the 'tribute assessment' that was not uncommon well before the emergence of capitalism. But in periods when people were largely involved in producing goods for their own use, the level of quantification was extremely limited.

From the 16th century on, the rapid evolution and devolution of capitalism had the effect of placing a wholly new emphasis on the exchange value of commodities and hence on the *quantifiable* aspects of people, events, objects and so on. There is a fair measure of agreement that 'genuine' statistical inquiries – recognisable as such by today's standards – date back to 17th century Britain.[85] It is at this time that 'objectification' rises to dominance, that the easily quantifiable aspects of the world come to assume paramount significance and that the more 'subjective' features become subordinated and suppressed. While in the past qualitative judgments of the form 'more' or 'less' were deemed satisfactory, market transactions now demanded the institution of very precise measurements and accounting procedures. Statistical analyses of the 'labour force' and of 'the poor', represented early efforts to count, codify and ultimately control people in the production process.

It is impossible to over-estimate the extent to which the new quantitative world view completely re-orientated man's conception of knowledge, of himself, and of the world. As Whitehead put it in his famous philosophical critique:

The seventeenth century had finally produced a scheme of scientific thought framed by mathematicians, for the use of mathematicians. The great characteristic of the mathematical mind is its capacity for dealing with abstractions; and for eliciting from them clear-cut demonstrative trains of reasoning, *entirely satisfactory so long as it is those abstractions which you want to think about* [my emphasis].[87]

So complete was the process of elevating 'rational' intelligence and abstract thought above normal human passions and feelings that to criticise abstraction soon became synonymous with undermining the very idea of 'progress' itself. Profound questions relating to man's existential awareness or his moral nature could not be adequately accommodated within the closed system of quantitative, scientific analysis and so were deemed largely irrelevant. In the behavioural sciences, researchers such as Skinner laid the groundwork for mechanistic behaviourist geography and gradually reduced the dimensions of human experience to a series of quantifiable machine-like input/output parameters which had no place for such 'unmeasurable' (and therefore 'non-existent') characteristics as freedom or dignity.[88] As Marcuse so forcefully pointed out in *One Dimensional Man* a new 'official' reality became institutionalised and subverted 'the established universe of discourse in the name of its own truth'.[89]

Scientistic rationality and its social counterpart – technocentrism – rapidly became the intellectual arm of western imperialism. In the same way that the central concerns of scientism have always revolved around manipulation, control and prediction, domination, exploitation and above all *efficiency* were the allied concerns of imperialism. Efficiency, in its turn, became equated with rationality and practical and critical questions became reduced to technical ones. 'Exploitation' was foisted on 'subordinate' populations, both at home and abroad, in the name of 'development' and 'progress'. Traditional or commonsense thinking and discourse were downgraded and ridiculed, and monolithic instrumental rationality was quickly substituted. The so called 'authority' of science thereby became 'imperialism in the sphere of knowledge'.[90] The evolution of centralised, bureaucratised and 'efficient' societies, so clearly outlined by Weber,[91] gradually demanded the wider and wider extension of the need for predictable, regulated behaviour and allied classification schemes for codifying and structuring reality. This 'officially sanctioned' and 'taken for granted' world is – to use Bourdieu's terminology – the *doxa*.[93] it represents the universe of the undiscussed and the undisputed (see Figure 2), the 'accepted' world of 'official reality'. In all stratified societies the ruling groups develop concepts and languages for

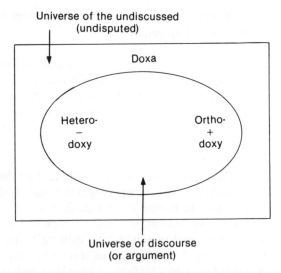

Universe of the undiscussed
(undisputed)

Doxa

Hetero-
−
doxy

Ortho-
+
doxy

Universe of discourse
(or argument)

SOURCE   P. Bourdieu, *Outline of a Theory of Practice* (Cambridge University Press, 1977).

FIGURE 2   *The universes of the undisputed and of discourse*

encapsulating *their* view of the world, and 'because any language that can command attention is an "authorized language", invested with the authority of a group, the things it designates are not simply expressed but also authorized and legitimated'.[93]

Legitimation of the status quo
One immediate criticism that can be levelled at quantification as it came to be developed in human geography and in the other social sciences is thus that the data techniques used tended (and indeed still tend) to provide tacit support for certain entrenched social inequalities and views about the world. At the same time the blinkered vision of 'statistical geography' helped to build a fairly impregnable framework of closed discourse which, in effect, prevented genuinely *alternative* world views from being aired. The sanctioned and legitimated reality which emerged − and which was invariably constructed from the building blocks of official government or corporate statistics − inevitably became part of the *doxa* of the ruling groups in both capitalist and state socialist societies: 'This is the way the world is'; 'This is the undisputed truth'; 'There is no point in discussing alternatives'. In summary − as has always been the case in the social sciences − a strong dialectical relationship became built up between the manufactured

'scientific' theories and their objects. Studies utilising official statistics in a spatial context had the effect of reifying and then *reinforcing* the existing situation. As Bhaskar has put it: 'accounts of social objects are not only value-impregnated, but *value-impregnating*'.[94]

Attention was drawn earlier to a empirical study of evacuation behaviour from the vicinity of the TMI nuclear reactor accident and the comment was made that inquiries of this type simply serve to legitimate highly controversial decisions in the area of energy policy. Precisely the same criticism can be levelled at literally hundreds of 'objective', unquestioning research projects in the social and natural sciences where the underlying *assumptions* of the project's definition and methodology remain unstated. The recent resurgence of 'electoral geography' provides another obvious target for this kind of criticism. Unlike data relating to a host of 'controversial' topics that are as yet untackled, electoral results are, of course, readily available, reasonably accurate and detailed. They are also published in a spatial form so that they are ideally suited to rapid manipulation and analysis by the psephologist's computer. It is precisely because studies of this type are so easy to carry out and so amenable to 'recipe' statistical treatment that they are deemed to be 'scientific', and frequently receive widespread publicity. At the same time, much more difficult, 'subversive', yet fundamental questions assessing the *real* significance of ritualistic elections, the extent to which they *really* make any difference to the power structure of liberal democracies etc. are rarely aired, least of all by political geographers seduced by the superficial attractions of 'hard' electoral data.

The availability and accessibility of information mirrors the power structure of hierarchical societies. In another context I have drawn up a table briefly illustrating some of the kinds of statistical information potentially available to research geographers, ranging along a continuum from 'freely available' information at one extreme to 'highly confidential' or 'suppressed' at the other (see Table 2).[95] My main point in that paper, and I reiterate it here, is that the vast majority of geographical research – as well as empirical research in the social sciences in general – has always tended to concentrate on the statistical manipulation of 'freely available' and relatively uncontroversial data rather than on more 'dangerous', difficult or 'subversive' issues. To this extent geographers have contributed – and indeed continue to contribute – to the reproduction of conservative ideology. The power

Table 2   *Categories of information*

	Examples
1. Freely available to the public	Aggregate census data. Some opinion polls. Dwelling, employment, mortality statistics etc. Industrial production statistics Social trends etc.
2. Available to special interest groups and/or individuals	Corporate plans and strategies e.g. planned factory closures. Rationalisation of transport network e.g. future freeway routes, rail closures etc. Future nuclear power station sites.
3. Suppressed or highly confidential	Precise estimates of resource reserves e.g. coal, oil, forestry etc. Data on deleterious effects of various industries, drugs, products etc. e.g. nuclear industry, 245-T, air pollution. Precise details of toxic waste dumps – size, locations, effects. Defence and military information. Land speculation. Foreign relations. Business deals. Personal property ownership, wealth and income data. Bribery payments.

Source   D.C. Mercer, 'Freedom of Information and applied geography' (n.d.).

structure of society remains unquestioned, research on the wealthy and the politically powerful is much less common than research on the powerless, the poor and so on. In a classic paper aimed at the anthropology profession Laura Nader forcefully put the case for 'studying up', or investigating the powerful rather than the traditionally over studied 'underclasses'.[96] Her arguments for an upward focus, I would suggest, are equally relevant in geography. First, she believes that her approach is infinitely more energising, exciting and illuminating than one which constantly focuses on hapless 'victims'; and second, she reasons that the cause of genuine democracy is better served if researchers concentrate much more on the difficult task of probing the workings of the real centres of power and prestige in society and then making that information widely available.

Some of the most trenchant recent criticisms of conservative empirical social science have come from feminists. The title of Acker's 1981 paper on British sociology of education (1960-79) – 'No woman's land' – would unquestionably be equally appropriate for the almost exclusively male dominated world of professional geography.[97] Earlier, when discussing Passmore's notion of 'aristoscience', the observation was made that the status hierarchy among the sciences appears to mirror images of the gender division in society. Thus positivist/empirical = hard, masculine, rational, while naturalistic/phenomenological = soft, feminine, emotional. Acker also argues strongly that the dichotomies so prevalent in the social sciences (e.g. rational/emotional; hard/soft; objective/subjective) parallel unconscious beliefs concerning the differences between men and women, and that their abandonment would have a liberating impact on the scope of the social sciences. Other feminists have begun to take a very close look at the well entrenched models of residential structure so favoured by urban social geographers, complete with their implicit distinctions between 'masculine cities and feminine suburbs'.[98] They are beginning openly to expose the conservative male assumptions so clearly shown when city space is viewed from a quite different perspective to that revealed by packaged factor analyses of census data. In particular, feminist urban researchers such as Markusen are developing challenging alternative analyses of cities based around the wholly neglected concept of the *patriarchal structuring* of urban space.[99] Given one of my central arguments here – namely that social theories always act as a powerful weapon for reinforcing or undermining particular views of 'reality' – this intellectual process is obviously of vital political significance to the feminist struggle for equality and less male dominated urban policies.

If one were to isolate the most characteristic feature of the typical 1960s urban geographer's view of the city, it would almost certainly highlight a focus on *urban hardware*. The city is seen as a mosaic of houses, roads, factories and so on, which are connected by a series of 'flows' of various kinds. Thus the 1960s' 'quantitative revolution' also witnessed a massive outpouring of descriptive spatial 'movement' studies ranging from journey to work through retail and social/recreational trip inquiries to residential migration. Invariably the movement habits identified were uncovered through household or site interviews or questionnaires, and were usually later 'explained' in terms of various subjectively weighted gravity model formulations which, in their turn, were deemed to demonstrate an understanding of the way cities 'function'. But again, as with social area analyses, the fundamental criticism has to be made that such inquiries – however mathematically sophisticated they may have appeared – simply *described the existing situation*. They served merely to reinforce the technocratic engineering view of the city as a *machine*, and were of extremely limited value in terms of coming to definitive conclusions about *what should be*. They were of next to no significance in answering the basic question: *To what extent are cities meeting basic human needs*?

Statistics as social products
Another related criticism associated with the particular form that quantification has come to assume in contemporary geographical practice has already been touched upon at various points in this discussion. This concerns the *reification* of data, or the assumption that the geographer's statistics are the 'same' as the reality they are seeking to portray. The metaphor of the camera is of value here. It is not uncommon for numerical facts to be presented as something analagous to statistical 'snapshots' of a specific society or region at a certain time. Indeed, the English 'social indicators' publication, *Facts in Focus* once highlighted this view of statistical reporting by featuring a camera aperture on the front cover. However, as everyone knows, the kind of photograph that is taken depends entirely on *who* is holding the camera, *what* they choose to focus it on, the manner in which they *process* the film, and the purpose for which the shot was taken. In short statistics are *social products*, manufactured by particular individuals or groups with certain assumptions about the world, and they are produced for certain fairly clearly defined purposes. Data relating to some subjects are deemed 'worthy' of collection, while others are considered taboo. These rather obvious points are all too often forgotten in the course of the typical unquestioning quantitative study made by practising

geographers. The data are invariably accepted as 'true' and 'beyond question'. Interviews and questionnaires provide much of the initial material and the scale of this form of statistical accounting in all rich countries is now quite staggering. Taking just one year – 1963 – Hartmann estimated that in continental Europe alone some 4–5 survey research interviews were carried out.[100] Considering the scale of such operations and the mountains of material created, it is surprising that the data 'production process' – the essential precursor to quantitative analysis – has not been looked at more closely.

Census surveys provide an interesting case, for the information collected and the definitions used in the course of different censuses vary considerably in line with the political climate of the time and in concert with changing attitudes to such things as privacy, sexism, racism and so on. At times of high unemployment census questions relating to the numbers out of work, for example, quite frequently are omitted from census schedules because it is considered that they would prove 'too embarrassing' to the government of the day. Similarly, challenged sexist assumptions that the 'head of the household' is a always male have also brought about changes to the precise wording of census questions – and hence to the final statistical 'product' – in several countries.

Both phenomenological and Marxist sociologists have for long been focusing research attention on the production of official statistics, but this work is rarely publicised in the geographical literature. More recently the Government Statisticians' Collective in Britain has carried this research forward by examining the subjectivity involved at the various stages of the 'cycle of statistics production' in government bureaucracies (see Figure 3).[101] At the outset, government policies and directives determine precisely which data shall be collected, in what form, and the manner in which the statistics shall be presented and used. What is more, at every stage there occur either overt or covert 'slides' or 'shifts' of various degrees of subtlety in the analysis, interpretation and presentation of the data.

We noted earlier that the recent rise to dominance of the techno-structure in advanced societies has paralleled the 'depoliticisation' of the state apparatus. Under the terms of the new political rhetoric, politicians and bureaucrats alike assume a posture of 'detachment' from the kind of society they have helped to produce, and constantly appeal (and make reference) to various 'objective'

188

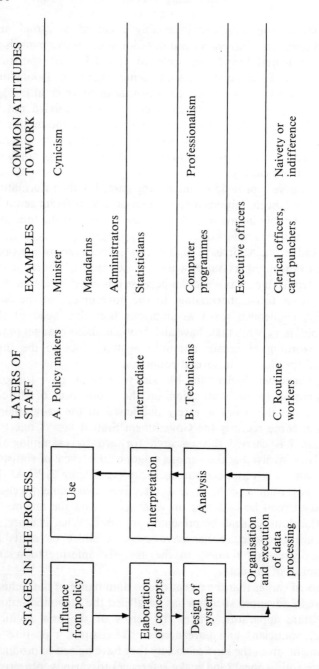

SOURCE *How official statistics are produced*, Government Statisticians' Collective.

FIGURE 3   *The cycle of statistics production in a typical government department*

indicators and measures to advise them what is happening 'out there'. Accordingly 'public opinion' and 'social indicators' research have both exploded in recent years to provide this much needed information. Many professional geographers have become involved in this burgeoning industry. Let us examine these two phenomena briefly, starting with 'public opinion' investigations. Under this general umbrella I would place many of the quantitative geographer's 'attitude' surveys, covering everything from studies of stated preferences for residential neighbourhoods, shopping centres and landscapes through to investigations of favoured city size, freeway routes, spatial layout and the like. Commenting on the hidden political dimension inherent in all such inquiries Bourdieu highlights three invariably unstated assumptions.[102] First, he reminds us that attitude surveys presuppose an agreement about *which questions are worth asking* – they assume a consensus about the initial definition of 'the problem'; second, they are based on the untested assumption that everyone can form (and does have) a clearcut opinion on one or more set questions; and third, it is accepted that all opinions are of the same weight and that all the researcher has to do is to simply 'collect' them and 'add them up.' Bourdieu concludes of such research that 'its most important function is perhaps to impose the illusion that a public opinion exists, and that it is simply the sum of a number of individual opinions'.[103]

A similar criticism can be aimed at social indicators research. The Radical Statistics Group (RSG) in Britain, for example, has pointed to a central contradiction in the development and use of social indicator measures.[104] At one level they are used simply as an ideological tool for promoting the capitalist notion of 'progress', as in the publication *Social Trends*. At a more fundamental level they are deliberately used to predict 'trouble spots' in the political and economic system and to head off potential obstacles to the continued accumulation of capital. Predictably 'as economic "progress" ground to a halt governments became more interested in indicators useful for more repressive forms of planning'.[105] Despite the fact that international agencies such as the OECD painstakingly present their particular set of social indicators as 'neutral' and 'objective' measures, there is considerable evidence that they are used in much the same way as public opinion and attitude surveys. Selected phenomena are measured in particular ways in order to set an agenda or framework for discussion and to 'impose a view of what is important for people'.[106] 'Quality of life' or 'social well-being', for example, are defined extremely narrowly in terms of easily measurable phenomena such as employment, earnings, education, health etc. This has the inevitable effect of limiting discussions of social well-being to such measures and diverting attention away from much more meaningful yet 'subversive' factors such as racism, sexism, and access to power and information. Defining 'quality of life' in the orthodox quantitative manner, then, permits 'endless but harmless debate within an imposed framework'.[107] And from the point of view of the established corporate and state power élites the outcome of such a process is highly satisfactory because it ensures that 'the future' will be much like the present and it also encourages a fatalistic attitude that 'things cannot possibly be changed.'

At the outset it was stated that the aim in this discussion was not to 'throw the baby out with the bathwater' and dismiss data gathering and statistical analysis completely, but that the purpose was to take issue with the *kinds* of statistics that are usually collected and to question the interests generally served by large-scale data collection procedures and the subsequent quantification exercises. A genuine participatory socialist agenda would be strongly opposed to massive centralised programmes of statistical collection and analysis serving the needs of capital, but would favour the accumulation and dissemination of material relating to genuine *social needs*. It would also encourage a process of agenda setting and problem identification 'from below' rather than 'from above', as at present. I will end this section with a quick 'geographical' example to illustrate these points. Geographers have recently demonstrated considerable interest in the construction of 'territorial social indicators' relating to health care. Travel distances to hospitals and doctors are computed in order simplistically to identify geographical regions of health care 'need'. I would argue that such an approach is misplaced because it fails to address itself to the logically prior, and much more important question: 'What causes people to be unhealthy in the first place?'. If populations are being *made* ill because they work in dangerous industries or because their air, water or food is contaminated with industrial chemicals it makes little sense to engage in social science investigations which inevitably will argue in favour of 'fixing people up' temporarily and then sending them straight back into the situation which created the problem in the first place! The real task is to change the kind of society which produces such unhealthy conditions.

Summary and Prospect

I have chosen in the latter part of this discussion to focus primary attention on only two main facets of what Rowan and Reason call 'quantophrenia' in human geography, namely: (i) its role in the reproduction of conservative ideology; and (ii) the related issue of the suppression of reflection on the basic processes of statistical production.[108] Both of these questions are clearly worthy of much fuller treatment (indeed, a recent paper by Jenks on the subjectivity involved in the 'objective' technique of computer mapping suggests that at least some geographers are finally becoming much more attuned to the second issue).[109] At the same time, other features of the dominant 'technocratic' mode in the social sciences as a whole have been mentioned briefly in passing. In particular, attention was drawn to what I regard as the negative aspects of *detachment*, *abstraction*, *reification* and *mystification* involved in the process of aping 'aristoscience'. The time has now come to pull together the various strands of my main argument and to make some brief concluding comments on both actual and favoured directions of change in the practice of human geography.

Notwithstanding the relatively recent emergence of various 'critical' Marxist and humanist perspectives in the discipline, I should state at the outset that I regard the dominant technocratic/ scientistic mode discussed here as still by far the most politically powerful ideological strand in contemporary Anglo-American human geography, in particular. What is more, I suspect that over the next few years this viewpoint will strengthen within our centres of higher education. Why do I say this? First – and most significantly – because over the years the scientific/industrial establishment has been remarkably successful in marketing its ideology and in convincing the public that it alone holds the key to enlightenment and 'progress'. Second, because we live in times of economic recession with a steadily declining employment pool, the call from increasingly competitive and conservative undergraduates and graduates for unquestioning skills orientated courses will inevitably grow. Third, often quite explicit pressure is being exerted on the universities and colleges from external business and government sources to become more 'relevant' and supportive of business values. Moreover, this influence coincides in its timing with the rise to power of 'sympathetic' academics totally steeped in the technocratic thinking of their formative research schooling years in the 1960s. And finally, as we have noted in the previous section, from the standpoint of the ruling political parties and corporate strategists the current economic and political crisis demands the production of masses of 'legitimating' studies and data to provide ideological support for conservative practices. Hence we are likely to see a continuation and consolidation of recent trends whereby research funding from the state and private enterprise is overwhelmingly directed towards 'Big Science' – towards 'respectable', yet totally uncritical, empirical studies in the 'objective' quantitative social science tradition. In times of serious 'legitimation crisis', as at the present, it becomes crucial for the state to exert strong influence over the kinds of official data that are collected, and also over the manner in which they are analysed and presented. Thus what we are witnessing today is simply the most recent manifestation of the use of quantification for social control purposes in the long historical line running from William Petty through such 19th-century 'moral statisticians' as Quetelet and LePlay to the ever expanding and vastly more sophisticated contemporary computerised bureaucratic data systems.

As Michell has so forcefully argued, there are currently 'two general world-views or cosmologies, one established in power, and the other, still in the process of formation, which is emerging to challenge it'.[110] This discussion has mainly been devoted to a consideration of what we might call the dominant 'orthodox' cosmology based around such notions as the expanding universe theory, the 'apes to spacemen' vision of historical progress, the central role of *struggle* and *competition* and, finally, the ultimate myth that an 'objective' world exists and can be somehow understood independently of our prior suppositions. The last few decades have witnessed a rapid global expansion of the dominant scientistic and quantitative world view or Great Myth – to such an extent that it now seems possible to speculate on the form of an emerging world system. It 'would no doubt be a duality of powers like two magnetic poles, each representing a rival economic theory, but both united by one basic view of the world, *and neither allowing any serious challenge to the cosmological consensus*'[111] [my emphasis]. Ironically, the rise to dominance of technocratic thinking and the quantitative mode has come at a time when traditional science is coming under consistent and mounting attack both from *within* the scientific fraternity and from 'outside'.[112] Strongly entrenched Darwinian ideas in both the cultural and biological spheres are now under serious challenge, and that stalwart of instrumental rationality – physics – is still reeling from the iconoclastic revelation that 'matter' is non-existent. There is a growing recognition that today's ruling ideas – whether grounded in capitalism or state socialism – show all the signs of being inimical to the very survival of all living systems.

In response, there are some encouraging indications of both a populist and professional worldwide counter movement which draws inspiration from Kropotkin rather than Darwin, from Schumacher rather than Adam Smith, which argues that *mutual aid* and *symbiosis* are the guiding principles of all natural systems and which prefers the more realistic concept of a steady state universe. While broadly in agreement with these principles, for reasons that I have already enumerated I am not quite as optimistic as Michell when he confidently asserts that 'the possibility of cosmological revolution and the dethroning of the Great Myth no longer seems a remote one'.[113] This 'alternative cosmology is not *totally* opposed to 'science' and 'scientific method' (including of course the centrality of quantification), but it does stand counterposed to much that passes for 'objective knowledge' in the contemporary world and to many of the supporting economic and political institutions.

Ultimately one's attitude to the issues discussed here is a function of one's idealised conception of society, of research and education. Hambye and others have argued that in terms of pedagogical implications we can recognise three broad societal 'models' based respectively on:

(a) the adaption of society to economic development
(b) the reform of society aiming at a reduction of social inequality without a radical change in the economic system
(c) a radical change in the relationship between society and the economic system.[114]

Models (a) and (b) both require a fairly similar hierarchical ordering of society, with differential access to information and rewards. Each also demands the collection of similar kinds of legitimating data and is usually characterised by mystification of the scientific and academic enterprise and by the presence of a docile and information starved electorate. The third, 'utopian', alternative favoured by the present writer, is quite different. It would foster and support a completely different educational and research enterprise, with the emphasis being on free access to information and learning, widespread political participation, and a commitment to a humane society in which each individual would be encouraged to fulfil his on her talents to the utmost. The achievements and status of Big Science and technocratic problem solving would be dramatically downplayed, and science as we know it would be relegated to its rightful position as simply one of a number of equally 'valid' modes of understanding. Thompson has stressed that in the contemporary world science is regarded as 'successful' to the extent that it has emancipated itself from personal or 'agent centred' knowledge – that unique set of attitudes, beliefs, skills, experiences etc. that we all continually draw upon in order to 'make sense' of our world in a kind of holistic way.[115] The significance and value of practical, local, agent-centred knowledge has been progressively eroded and ridiculed over the years as societies have become more centralised, 'rational' and technocratic. Yet in such phenomena as the alternative technology, conservation and anti-nuclear movements we can perhaps recognise the first stirrings of the resurrection to prominence of 'commonsense', democratised knowledge.

Within the professional geographical fraternity, as we have noted, the last few years have witnessed a small – though perhaps temporary – retreat from the more lunatic excesses of flat earth quantitative geography towards a growing recognition that reality is not in fact beautifully ordered but that it is characterised much more by *contradiction*, *tension* and *disharmony*. The daunting fourfold task for the critical geographer – whether 'Marxist' or humanist – is to continue the fight against the hegemony of naive, blinkered, technocratic thinking; continually to expound the consequences of the uncritical acceptance of such a world view; to encourage constant *reflection* on the research and teaching enterprise and, above all, to expose the supreme arrogance of Big Science. Let us give Feyerabend the last word:

> Knowledge...is not a series of self-consistent theories that converges towards an ideal view; it is not a gradual approach to truth. It is rather an ever-increasing ocean of mutually

compatible (and perhaps incommensurable) alternatives, each single theory, each fairy tale, each myth that is part of the collection forcing the others into greater articulation and all of them contributing, via this process of competition, to the development of consciousness. Nothing is ever settled, no view can ever be omitted from a comprehensive account.[116]

Notes and References

1. H. Enzensberger, 'The industrialisation of the mind', *Urban Review*, vol. 8 (1975) pp. 68–75.

2. D.C. Mercer, 'Conflict and consensus in human geography', *Monash Publications in Geography*, No. 17 (1977), Monash University, Melbourne.

3. J.M. Powell, 'The haunting of Soloman's house: geography and the limits of science', *Australian Geographer*, vol. 14 (1980) no. 2, pp. 327–41; O. Granö, 'External influence and internal change in the development of geography', in D.R. Stoddart (ed.), *Geography, Ideology and Social Concern* (Oxford: Basil Blackwell, 1981) pp. 17–36.

4. R. Pascoe, *The Manufacture of Australian History* (Melbourne: Oxford University Press, 1979); K. Knorr, *The Manufacture of Knowledge* (Oxford: Pergamon Press, 1980); H. Capel, 'Institutionalization of geography and strategies of change', in D.R. Stoddart (ed.), *Geography, Ideology and Social Concern,* pp. 37–69.

5. K. Marx and F. Engels, ed. C.J. Arthur, *The German Ideology* (London: Lawrence & Wishart, 1970).

6. A.R. Hall, 'Merton revisited, or science and society in the seventeenth century', *History of Science*, vol. 2 (1963) pp. 1–16.

7. W.H. Whyte, *The Organisation Man* (New York: Simon & Schuster, 1956).

8. P. Bourdieu, 'Intellectual field and creative project', in M.F.D. Young (ed.), *Knowledge and Control* (New York: Collier-Macmillan, 1971) pp. 161–88.

9. J.M. Powell, '"Professional" geography, into the eighties –?', *Australian Geographical Studies*, vol. 19 (1981) no. 2, pp. 228–30.

10. J. Habermas, *Toward a Rational Society* (Boston: Beacon Press, 1971).

11. S.G. Harding, 'The social function of the empiricist conception of mind', *Metaphilosophy*, vol. 10 (1979) no. 1, pp. 38–47.

12. S.G. Harding, 'The social function', p. 46.

13. J. Thompson, 'What's wrong with science?', *Arena* vol. 58 (1981) pp. 30–50.

14. J. Passmore, *Science and its Critics* (London: Duckworth, 1978).

15. P.M. Hauser, 'Sociology's progress toward science', *The American Sociologist*, vol. 16 (1981) no. 1, pp. 62–4.

16. J. Rowan and P. Reason, 'Foreword', in P. Reason and J. Rowan,

196   *Reflections*

Human Inquiry: A Sourcebook of New Paradigm Research (Chichester: J. Wiley, 1981) pp. xi–xxiv.

17. B. Malinowski, *Magic, Science and Religion* (Glencoe, Illinois: Free Press, 1948) p. 3.

18. D.C. Mercer, 'Conflict and consensus'.

19. P. Haggett, 'Mid-term futures for geography, *Monash Publications in Geography* No. 16 (1977).

20. P. Feyerabend, *Science in a Free Society* (London: New Left Books, 1978) pp. 174–5.

21. P. Machery, *A Theory of Literary Production* (London: Routledge & Kegan Paul, 1978) p. 3.

22. P. Feyerabend, *Against Method* (London: Verso, 1975); *Science in a Free Society*.

23. A. Roberts, *The Self-Managing Environment* (London: Allison & Busby, 1979).

24. I.L. Horowitz, 'Left-wing fascism: an infantile disorder', *Society* (May/Jun. 1981) pp. 19–24.

25. N. Chomsky, 'The menace of liberal scholarship', *New York Review of Books* (2 Jan. 1976) pp. 29–38.

26. H.T. Wilson, *The American Ideology* (London: Routledge & Kegan Paul, 1977).

27. I. Berlin, *Fathers and Children* (Oxford: Clarendon Press, 1972) p. 55.

28. The Trilateral Commission, *Crisis of Democracy* (New York: University Press, 1975).

29. J. Carroll, *Sceptical Sociology* (London: Routledge & Kegan Paul, 1980).

30. P.A. Baran and P.M. Sweezy, *Monopoly Capital* (Harmondsworth: Penguin, 1970). 10.

31. H. Braverman, *Labor and Monopoly Capital* (New York: Monthly Review Press, 1974).

32. M. Cooley, 'Contradictions of science and technology in the productive process', in S. and H. Rose (eds), *The Political Economy of Science* (London: Macmillan, 1976) pp. 72–95.

33. K. Knorr, 'Social and scientific method, or "What do we make of the distinction between the natural and the social sciences?"', in M. Brenner (ed.), *Social Method and Social Life* (London: Academic Press, 1981) pp. 27–52.

34. D.J. Zeigler, S.D. Brunn and J.H. Johnson, 'Evacuation from a nuclear technological disaster', *The Geographical Review*, vol. 71 (1981) no. 1, pp. 1–16.

35. D.J. Zeigler *et al.*, 'Evacuation from a nuclear technological disaster', p. 3.

36. N. Chomsky, 'The menace of liberal scholarship'.

37. P.F. Lazarsfeld, 'Notes on the history of quantification in sociology – trends, sources and problems', in H. Woolf (ed.), *Quantification. A History of the Meaning of Measurement in the Natural and Social Sciences* (Indianapolis: Bobbs-Merrill, 1961) pp. 147–203.

38. L. Busch, 'Carving up the social world: the impact of geographic

units on research results', *Sociological Focus,* vol. 11 (1978) no. 4, pp. 289–99.

39. M. Castells, *The Economic Crisis and American Society* (Princeton: Princeton University Press, 1980).

40. J. O'Connor, 'Accumulation crisis: the problem and its setting', *Contemporary Crises*, vol. 5 (1981) pp. 109–25.

41. W.W. Rostow, 'Power and economics', *Society* (May/June 1981) pp. 10–15.

42. *Crisis of Democracy.*

43. L. Panitch, 'The development of corporatism in liberal democracies', *Comparative Political Studies*, vol. 10 (1977) no. 1, pp. 61–90.

44. D.C. Mercer, 'Freedom of information and applied geography', mimeo, Department of Geography, Monash University.

45. Government Statisticians' Collective, 'How offical statistics are produced: views from the inside', in J. Irvine, I. Miles and J. Evans, *Demystifying Social Statistics* (London: Pluto Press, 1979) p. 130–51.

46. F.K. Hare, 'The planetary environment: fragile or sturdy?', *Geographic Journal*, vol. 146 (1980) no. 3, pp. 379–95.

47. C. Cookson, 'The spoiling of America', *New Scientist* (21 June 1979) pp. 1,015–17.

48. H. Hveem, 'Militarization of nature: conflict and control over strategic resources and some implications for peace policies', *Journal of Peace Research*, vol. 16 (1979) no. 1, pp. 1–26.

49. C. Jenkins and B. Sherman, *The Collapse of Work* (London: Eyre Methuen, 1979).

50. P. Rieff, *Fellow Teachers* (London: Faber & Faber, 1975).

51. F. Hearn, 'Adaptive narcissism and the crisis of legitimacy', *Contemporary Crises*, vol. 4 (1980) pp. 117–40.

52. M. Kaldor, *The Disintegrating West* (London: Allen Lane, 1978).

53. E.P. Thompson, 'Notes on exterminism, the last stage of civilization' *New Left Review*, vol. 121 (1980) pp. 3–31.

54. E.P. Thompson, 'Notes on exterminism'.

55. R. Williams, 'The politics of nuclear disarmament', *New Left Review*, vol. 124 (1980) pp. 25–42.

56. E.P. Thompson, 'Notes on exterminism'.

57. I.T. Frolov, 'The philosophy of global problems', *Soviet Law and Government*, vol. 19 (1980/81) no. 3, pp. 46–74.

58. E. Rothschild, 'The American arms boom', in E.P. Thompson and D. Smith (eds), *Protest and Survive* (Harmondsworth: Penguin, 1980) pp. 170–85.

59. U. Albrecht and M. Kaldor, 'Introduction', in M. Kaldor and A. Eide (eds), *The World Military Order* (London: Macmillan, 1979) pp. 1–16.

60. Y. Lacoste, 'An illustration of geographical warfare: bombing of the dikes of the Red River, North Vietnam', in R. Peet, *Radical Geography* (London: Methuen, 1978) pp. 244–61.

61. E.P. Thompson, 'Notes on exterminism', p. 7.

62. H. Elsner, *The Technocrats* (Syracuse: Syracuse University Press, 1967) p. 30.

63. A. Naess, 'The case against science', in C.I. Dessaur (ed.), *Science Between Culture and Counter-culture* (Nijmegen: Dekker & van de Vegt, 1975) pp. 25–48.

64. A. Naess, 'The case against science', p. 33.

65. D. Gregory, 'The ideology of control – systems theory and geography', *Tijdschrift voor Economische en Sociale Geografie*, vol. 71 (1980) no. 6, pp. 327–42.

66. C.I. Dessaur, 'For science – against science', in C.I. Dessaur (ed.) *Science Between Culture and Counter-culture*, pp. 1–24; G. Nonvad and I. Szelenyi, *The Intellectuals on the Road & Class Power* (New York: Harcourt Brace Jovanovich, 1979).

67. L. Arnoux, 'Energy and equity', unpublished paper presented at the ANZAAS conference in Brisbane (May 1981).

68. I.I. Mitroff and R.H. Kilmann, *Methodological Approaches to Social Science* (San Francisco: Jossey-Bass, 1978).

69. S. Latouche, *Introduction à l'Epistemologie de la Science Sociale* (Lille: CEREL, 1976)

70. L. Arnoux, 'Energy and equity'.

71. L. Arnoux, 'Energy and equity', p. 8.

72. L. Arnoux, 'Energy and equity', p. 5.

73. M.E. Eliot-Hurst, 'Geography, social science and society: towards a de-definition', *Australian Geographical Studies*, vol. 18 (1980) no. 1, pp. 3–21.

74. Y. Lacoste, 'An illustration of geographical warfare'.

75. R. Johnston and D. Robbins, 'The development of specialities in industrialised science', *The Sociological Review*, vol. 25 (1977) no. 1, pp. 87–108.

76. G. Anders, 'Commandments in the atomic age', in C. Mitcham and R. Mackey (eds), *Philosophy and Technology* (New York: The Free Press, 1972) pp. 130–5.

77. L. Arnoux, 'The consumption society – energy, environment and our future', in M. Diesendorf (ed.), *Energy and People* (Canberra: Society for Social Responsibility in Science, 1979) pp. 97–103.

78. B. Commoner, *The Closing Circle* (New York: Bantam, 1974).

79. L. Mumford, *Pentagon of Power: The Myth of the Machine* (New York: Harcourt Brace Jovanovich, 1964).

80. A.C. Zijderfeld, *The Abstract Society* (Harmondsworth: Penguin, 1974) p. 74.

81. A.C. Zijderfeld, *The Abstract Society*, p. 77.

82. M. Cooley, 'Contradictions of science and technology'.

83. D. White, '*In vitro*: towards the industralisation of birth', *Arena*, vol. 58, (1981) pp. 23–9.

84. P.L. Berger and T. Luckmann, *The Social Construction of Reality* (New York: Anchor Books, 1967) p. 89.

85. M.G. Kendall, 'Where shall the history of statistics begin?', in E.S. Pearson and M.G. Kendall (eds), *Studies in the History of Probability and Statistics* (London: Griffin, 1970) pp. 131–54.

86. See, for example, W. Petty, *Political Arithmetic* (1690).

87. A.N. Whitehead, *Science and the Modern World* (Cambridge University Press, 1925) p. 81.

88. B.F. Skinner, *Science and Human Behaviour* (London: Collier-Macmillan, 1953).

89. H. Marcuse, *One Dimensional Man* (London: Routledge & Kegan Paul, 1964) p. 14.

90. J. Thompson, 'What's wrong with science?'.

91. M. Weber, *The Theory of Social and Economic Organization* (London: Collier-Macmillan, 1953).

92. P. Bourdieu, *Outline of a Theory of Practice* (Cambridge University Press, 1977).

93. P. Bourdieu, *Outline of a Theory of Practice*, p. 170.

94. R. Bhaskar, 'Scientific explanation and human emancipation', *Radical Philosophy* (Autumn 1980) pp. 16–28.

95. D.C. Mercer, 'Freedom of information'.

96. L. Nader, 'Up the anthropologist – perspectives gained from studying up', in D. Hymes (ed.), *Reinventing Anthropology* (New York: Random House, 1969) pp. 284–311.

97. S. Acker, 'No woman's land: British sociology of education, 1960–1979', *The Sociological Review*, vol. 29 (1981), pp. 77–102.

98. S. Saegert, 'Masculine cities and feminine suburbs: polarized ideas, contradictory realities', *Signs: Journal of Women in Culture and Society*, vol. 5 (1980) no. 3, pp. S.96–S.111.

99. A.R. Markusen, 'City spatial structure, women's household work, and national urban policy', *Signs: Journal of Women in Culture* and *Society*, vol. 5 (1980) no. 3, pp. S.23–S.44.

100. H. Hartmann, *Empirische Sozialforschung* (München: Juenta, 1970).

101. 'How official statistics are produced'.

102. L. Bourdieu, 'Public opinion does not exist', in A. Mattelart and S. Siegelaub (eds), *Communication and Class Struggle* I (New York: International General, 1979) pp. 124–30.

103. L. Bourdieu, 'Public opinion', p. 125.

104. Radical Statistics Group, *Social Indicators: For Individual Well-Being or Social Control?* (London: RSG, 1979).

105. Radical Statistics Group, *Social Indicators*, p. 2.

106. Radical Statistics Group, *Social Indicators*, p. 5.

107. Radical Statistics Group, *Social Indicators*, p. 5.

108. J. Rowan and P. Reason, 'Foreword'.

109. G.F. Jenks, 'Lines, computers and human frailties', *Annals of the Association of American Geographers*, vol. 71 (1981) no. 1, pp. 1–10.

110. J. Michell, 'The ideal world-view', in S. Kumar (ed.), *The Schumacher Lectures* (London: Blond & Briggs, 1980) pp. 95–120.

111. J. Michell, 'The ideal world-view', p. 104.

112. H. Nowotny and H. Rose, *Countermovements in the Sciences* (Dordrecht: D. Reidel, 1979).

113. J. Michell, 'The ideal world-view', p. 119.

114. C. Hambye, 'Three models of society and their pedagogical implications', in D. Berstecher *et al., A University of the Future* (The Hague: Martinus Nijhoff, 1974) pp. 154–70.

115. J. Thompson 'What's wrong with science?'.

116. P. Feyerabend, *Against Method*, p. 30.

One Man's Quantitative Geography: Frameworks, Evaluations, Uses and Prospects

ALAN G. WILSON

Introduction

It is now commonplace to recognise that there are many 'quantitative geographies'. Many of us are prisoners of particular skills. This is useful for the field as a whole since it at least guarantees that a wide range of methods is applied in any particular context; it is not necessarily an efficient way of discovering the most effective methods but the test of time, in the long run, sorts this out.

The multiplicity of quantitative geographies raises two kinds of questions for an evaluative essay. First, of all the possibilities, which types offer most? Secondly, how do these methods stand against post-revolution competition? I can attempt to answer the first set of questions only in relation to my own experience: in making my own choices in research design, I have voted with my feet! I start, therefore, by outlining the frameworks which are the props of my own choices and add to this my own contribution to research autobiography. I respond to the second set of questions by offering an outline of radical critiques and an assessment of prospects.

At the outset, however, one or two general observations will set the context. I believe that, in the long run, mathematical methods offer more than statistical methods and so I will concentrate on the former. However, this is not to argue against the value of statistics in the presentation and interpretation of data and in the fitting and evaluation of mathematical models. I also share with many others the view that the characterisation of the (once!) 'new' geography as 'quantitative' is misleading: the more important feature was increasing ambition in relation to the development of theory. That this theory has since been criticised by radical geographers as at best inadequate and at worst trivial is a separate issue and one to which I will return later.

In the next section, I make some observations on frameworks and illustrate my idea of quantitative geography with examples from my own research experience. This, needless to say, contains much of the same kind of elements of chance described by many others; but also, I hope, some more consistent threads representing conscious choice. I then attempt to evaluate this kind of contribution to mathematical modelling within the context of quantitative geography. In the following section, I outline more radical criticisms of the quantitative movement, and respond to these with proposals for ongoing research in the final section.

Frameworks: Systems and Methods

By coming into geography from the outside, I avoided much involvement with the 'what is geography?' question and was able, rather luxuriously, to work from my own ideas of first principles. The frameworks I describe here are, of course, offered with the benefit of much hindsight and I suppose must now be considered to constitute my own answer to what have been vexed questions for geography as a discipline. Most of what I say will relate to urban and regional geography, but I believe that the frameworks are more widely applicable within the discipline.

I begin by distinguishing two main dimensions of geographical research: (i) system definition and theory, and (ii) methods of analysis and theory building. With respect to the first, 'system' is used in the spirit of 'system of interest' rather than to carry all the connotations of 'systems theory', though the idea that there is much inter-dependence in geographical systems which cannot be neglected has always been an important one. I discuss each dimension in turn.

I believe that it is important to take seriously what Graham Chapman has called 'entitation':[1] defining the main elements of each system of interest in a straightforward way. In geography, these elements are people, organisations (and their products, services and roles, land, transport networks and so on). These are the stuff of traditional geography. Starting in this way has two immediate advantages. First, it provides a grounding for theoretical development in what we can 'see' (even if more complicated concepts have to be added later). This means that complicated-looking theories and models have to stand up to the test of being relatable back to these primary entities. This is a good way of avoiding 'mystification'. Secondly, it relates geography directly to other disciplines. The entities, sub-systems and systems thus defined are shared with other disciplines. Geographical study – distinguished by a concern with location or whatever – will always overlap, at this basic level, research in other disciplines. Indeed, I believe that a prime focus on substantive systems nearly always makes effective research on systems of interest to geographers multidisciplinary – or, at its best, supra-disciplinary. We should not be afraid to engage in research on this basis.

This starting point then forces us to choose how we will describe a system of interest for a particular piece of research: the scale (or level of resolution), the way space is represented, the extent to which we are partial or more comprehensive in our approach. For example, we might choose to work on industries rather than firms (a mesoscale), with space divided into discrete units (zones rather than continuous) and to seek to represent the inter-dependence of members of a set of industries (rather than a single industry in a 'fixed' environment of other industries). An advantage of being explicit about these decisions is that it permits some sorting out of alternative theories about the same system: often they are not directly competing; they are theories grounded in alternative representations of the system.

And then the most important step of all: the development of theories about how the system works, what processes govern it, why its structure is as it is.

At this stage (in this unreasonably neat account of how we progress!), we need to formalise our theoretical ideas, to articulate them by building working models. So we seek appropriate methods to do this. Quantitative methods are then to be seen as a subset of all possible methods; and no more than that. For certain kinds of theoretical problems, they are more effective than the alternatives.

Theoretical development and methodological development obviously proceed in a related way. At any one time, there is a set of existing (alternative) theories, formalised by using the set of currently available methods. A research problem will be rooted in the system of interest. Existing theory is inadequate, or wrong, or not deep enough. There are, therefore, theoretical problems. Sometimes theoretical advances are achievable for which methods are then immediately available. Often, the theoretical problems demand the generation of new methods.

The map of geographical theory (and methodology) forms a complex whole. I now believe (with the benefit of a lot of hindsight!) that it may be possible to define a kind of theoretical problem at a higher level of generality: can we define system *types*, and define method *types* and learn how to map one on to the other? I think we are now at a stage where we can begin, albeit highly imperfectly, this enterprise[2]. Weaver's characterisation of system (or problem) types as 'simple', 'of disorganised complexity' and 'of organised complexity' and his associated methods offers a beginning.[3] I will return to this programme as part of my review of prospects below. Meanwhile, I hope the argument can be illustrated if I insert at this stage an element of research autobiography.

A Research Autobiography

My sphere of interest has always been the city (or systems of cities, or regions containing cities). My motivation has always been the visible problems of cities. Ultimately, I wanted the work I was doing and was responsible for to contribute to city planning, but I began with, and still have, the belief that this could be achieved only if there was a much improved analytical basis to our understanding of what went on in cities. It also seemed that relatively few people worked on this analytical basis and that it was therefore a useful contribution to the division of labour to decide to do so.

My background was in mathematics and theoretical physics, and this did not offer much directly in terms of theory or concepts with which to approach cities. My first contacts in the social sciences were mostly with economists and I acquired some of their notions, in particular the theory of consumer behaviour and the concepts of welfare economics. But my background did offer methods, and this attracted me to a field which was beginning to develop at the time (and had been developing very slowly for a considerable time): the mathematical modelling of urban phenomena. I was working in a research group whose brief was cost-benefit analysis in the transport sector, and much of initial attention was focused on spatial

interaction. My planning interests determined that whatever
models I or my colleagues developed should be tested against data
and used predictively. This is the broad background against which
a set of research design decisions was made.

With hindsight, it is possible to identify a number of general
principles which I could claim had motivated many of these decisions, and it is probably useful to present these first as a further
element of crucial background. They can be summarised under
four headings:

1. *Comprehensiveness and generality of approach.* This meant
recognising the inter-dependence of many elements of cities and in
that sense being 'comprehensive' (this includes an early decision to
attempt to build a comprehensive urban model in order to answer
transport questions). It also implied seeking generality, in that the
model should be applicable – with appropriate changes in
exogenous variables and parameters – to a wide range of cities.

2. *Eclecticism of method.* This implies seeking whatever
combination of methods from those available, including those
from other disciplines, seem to bear on a particular problem. This
seems so self-evident a principle as to be hardly worth stating, but
in practice in many fields at any particular time there is often an
adherence to a particular 'fashion'.

3. *Integration of concepts and methods.* This notion is a
corollary of the previous one. When different methods, or even
theories and concepts, are applied to the same system of interest,
then a simple-minded view of knowledge implies that tests should
be carried out to decide which approach or theory or model is the
'true' one. I would argue that it is likely that no single one is 'true',
that most have something to contribute to our knowledge, and that
a fruitful approach to research (often, but not always) is to try to
force them together. This has sometimes lead to new models;
sometimes to apparently very different models being recognised as
essentially the same or similar.

4. *Maximum use of concepts, theory or methods.* When a
discovery is made, it is usually in a particular context (or at least, it
is usually in a context which is much more restricted than that to
which it could be applied in principle). This means that a fruitful
line of research is to apply ideas 'as far as they will go'.

In the account that follows, I have emphasised the research
products which, in retrospect, I find interesting. It should be

emphasised as another general background point that in all cases, none of these products have arisen out of research projects which were *designed to generate them*. They have all come as byproducts from other, 'bread and butter' research programmes.

In my first social science research project in 1964, I had some responsibility for looking at models of transport flows – then mostly known as gravity models because of their history in analogy with Newton's famous law. However, even then, what is now referred to as a doubly constrained spatial interaction model existed, as did the singly constrained one. Cruder examples of each were evident as components of Lowry's model which was also published at that time.[4] By coincidence, I had studied statistical mechanics as a subject in some depth as a student. I regarded it as something which was aesthetically very pleasing and enjoyable, but essentially as a piece of 19th-century applied mathematics which I was not likely to have any use for (and I still think that I had retained an in-depth knowledge of the subject longer than many others because we had a 'bad' lecturer who made 'mistakes' in the notes he offered us; this meant that the only way to build a set of correct notes was through assiduous use of the classical texts like Tolman and ter Haar,[5] and to compare these with the lectures – (a good model for effective teaching?)). Somehow it occurred to me that it might be possible to treat people in cities, in some mathematical sense, like particles in gases were treated in statistical mechanics.[6] But people, unlike most 'real' particles, were distinguishable, which meant that I had to rewrite most of my old 'quantum' lecture notes in classical form, and they also had to be distinguished by type. The only example of multiple types of gases I could think of in statistical mechanics was the mixing of chemicals in the law of mass action. That was where I started. I treated people in a similar way, using grand canonical ensembles and distinguishing them by origin and destination as 'types' and by origin–destination pairs as 'states'. Eventually, the appropriate result emerged clumsily, and then I found I could do it more neatly using microcanonical ensembles if I did not worry too much about the 'particle–person–type' definitions. Thus emerged the entropy maximising spatial interaction model.[7]

As often happens in cases which turn out to be 'interesting and significant' (and the model acquired these properties only after a couple of years or more), similar research was done in a number of parts of the world independently. The statistical mechanics analogy was used by authors in Norway, Japan and Australia for example, and the model was shown to be derivable from a mathematical programming formulation by John Murchland in England. Most people, however, stopped at the transport model and application. I enjoyed applying the fourth principle outlined above, and applied it in a wide range of spatial interaction situations (shopping, residential location and so on) as well as to regional input-output modelling.

It was also possible, eventually to take a general look at the range of spatial interaction models which could be generated and to classify them – initially as unconstrained, singly constrained and doubly constrained, later to include various 'hybrids' which were important in planning with several different types of constraints. From this evolved the notion of a spatial interaction 'model building kit' which may, in the end, have turned out to be more important than the notion of the entropy maximising base, since it allowed many people who were not interested in the under lying theory to build models which were more appropriate to the situation they were modelling.

The entropy maximising idea also planted a number of other general thoughts. One was the notion of the importance of *constraint equations* in modelling: somehow ensuring that certain (*consistency*) relations you know must be satisfied are built into the models. A second was the notion of *accounting equations* – in effect a more general statement of the first idea: that an important element of model building style is to 'follow' elements 'through the system'. In the case of entropy models the 'following' is from origin to destination, and these elements of the constraint equations are spatial accounts – but it was also an important idea for other kinds of accounts. Third, the approach offered a way of dealing with *dynamics* – with interpreting parameters (and in particular the distance–decay parameter) through the other kind of constraint equation in such a way that its change over time could be predicted. This seemed to offer a way of escaping from the not very plausible assumption that certain parameters remained constant over time. Fourth, and at a more general theoretical level, there was the idea that phenomena at a *mesoscale* of resolution had an existence and could be modelled, since entropy maximising, by definition, was about this. Such an approach was in marked contrast to much economic analysis where the resolution level seemed to have to be macro or micro – the whole system, or individuals.

These ideas take me to 1970 (and indeed some of the more general notions came later). From that time, at Leeds, I was involved with a team of people who tried to put the 'building a comprehensive model of a city' idea into practice, and both of the following lines of research to be discussed arose out of research design questions initially generated by the broader project. They arose in particular from two elements of the project and were developed in parallel, one in work with a graduate student, Martyn Senior, and the other in collaboration with a colleague, Philip Rees. They developed from attempts to build respectively the residential location and the spatial demographic components of the model. They were pursued in parallel, as noted, but will be discussed in the sequence just mentioned because the residential location work connects more directly to the entropy maximising work just discussed and shows how the latter came to be extended in a crucial way.[8]

The residential location work illustrates the 'forcing things together' principle. There existed models of residential location based both on spatial interaction theory and on economic theory – the latter operationalised as a linear programming problem in the Herbert–Stevens model. They appeared to be completely distinct approaches to the same problem. As part of our overall research programme, we agreed to implement both models empirically to see what we could learn. During the programme, our attention was also drawn to Suzanne Evans's formal proof of the suspected idea that the transportation problem of linear programming was a limiting case of the doubly constrained spatial interaction model.[9] The limit was reached when the distance–decay parameter in the latter became infinite. Martyn Senior and I were able to show that the same principle could be applied to any entropy maximising model, to generate a limiting case mathematical programming model (not necessarily linear) and vice versa. We also deduced some results about the dual variables in the limit.[10] So this was an application of the 'generality' principle and the 'taking things as far as they will go principle. In particular, this had the major consequence that the benefits of the 'apparently better' theoretical basis and interpretation of the economic programming models could be combined with the 'better fit to data' properties of the entropy maximising models. This idea had since had a wide range of applications.

The new lines of research in spatial demographic analysis arose out of what Philip Rees and I thought was a purely routine attempt to build the then conventional model for our study region – West Yorkshire and the local authorities within it – as part of our comprehensive model building project. A difficulty emerged early on: the model had to be supplied with birth and death rates. The latter, for example, were to be measured as numbers of deaths divided by some base year population. The problem was in matching the base year population to the number of deaths measured during a time period. Whichever way we thought of doing it – at least using the obvious ways – there were problems. If the initial population was used, then some of those people would have migrated during the period, while others would have migrated in whose deaths would be included in the observed total for the region. It turned out, on closer investigation, that the accounting basis of the model we were trying to build was inadequate. Our eyes were then opened to this question, and it was possible, with some labour, to build an entirely new model on principles which did not have the difficulty of the original.[11] This model made data demands which could not be met, and this lead to a new research problem: how to build good approximations into the model to estimate 'missing' data. This is a good example of how new questions can arise out of apparently routine research, and also how important it is *for ongoing theory* to carry out empirical work. The results of the overall empirical programme, which had involved a large number of contributors, were written up in a book.[12]

One recurring theme in much of the research I have been involved with has been the singly constrained spatial interaction model, especially in its guise as a 'shopping' model: a representation of consumer flows to shopping centres. Because it is singly constrained, it also functions as a location model, in this case predicting the spatial distribution of revenue attracted to centres by the summing of the consumer cash flows. The actual size of the shopping centre at each location is fed exogenously into the model. This of itself directly suggests a new research problem which I began to work on with another graduate student, Jose Coelho. It turned out that from another theoretical derivation of the spatial interaction model – using random utility theory and the work of a colleague, Huw Williams (and perhaps noting in passing the influence of the proximity of other particular research workers) – it was possible to obtain an exact formula for the total consumer surplus derived from a particular distribution of shopping centre sizes. This then suggested the following problem: find the distribution of centre sizes which maximises consumer surplus subject to a set of constraints which say that consumers flow according to the spatial interaction sub-model. Since this sub-model can itself be represented as a mathematical programme, we had one programme 'inside' another. We showed how to combine these with a so called 'embedding' theorem, and hence proposed a method for finding the optimum size and distribution of shopping centres.[13] Again this theorem, worked out in the context of a very specific example, has turned out to have wide ranging applications. It also formed a part of the foundation of the next and broader stage of research development, again using the shopping model as a 'laboratory' but with much more important consequences: the investigation of urban dynamics.

The attention of urban modellers had been drawn to issues of dynamics by the publication in 1969 of Jay Forrester's *Urban Dynamics*.[14] This work was outside all the traditions (of nearly 10 years' standing!) of the field and was easy to criticise because of its inadequacies at many particular points. However, it did show that there were new issues to be tackled. In a sense what stopped immediate development of Forrester's methods – using systems of simultaneous difference equations – was lack of time series data. This is still the situation today, and more recent theoretical developments (almost for the first time in urban modelling) are taking place against a context of an inability to test them adequately immediately.

My own ideas about urban dynamics stemmed from two sources, one methodological the other substantive system oriented (indeed involving the shopping model again). The first was the emergence of catastrophe theory in the early 1970s and the acceleration of interest following the publication of Thom's book, *Structural Stability and Morphogenesis*, in English in 1975.[15] It was argued that it offered a general methodology for dynamic modelling and could be applied in a number of disciplines. My own early 'theoretical experiments' were in the transport field – but this was really an exercise so that I could learn something of the method. At about the same time, I also realised that any interesting question of dynamics – in relation to the shopping model as a paradigmic example – related not so much to consumers' behaviour, but to suppliers' behaviour. As noted earlier, we had previously taken such 'size and location' variables as given until we formulated the embedding problem and generated (static) optima. In some discussions with Britton Harris of the University of Pennsylvania, it emerged that a geometrical technique could be used to gain more insight into the nature of these optima, which were also understood as a certain kind of equilibria, and that they could appear or disappear suddenly, in a zone, at some critical parameter value.[16] This was exactly the feature which had aroused most interest in catastrophe theory, and it was possible to interpret the results in terms of the fold and higher order catastrophes. However, it should be emphasised that what had happened was this: we had not applied catastrophe theory directly, but the existence of that theory had made us alert to the possible existence of types of phenomena we had not previously thought to investigate.

The work just described can be thought of as an extension of comparative statics: parameters change and the equilibrium changes; the extension is that the change in equilibrium state, for a small and smooth change in one or more parameters, may be discrete and large. But the next stage in the argument was obviously to seek to *model* change using either differential or difference equations. I had previously tried to write down a suitable set of differential equations for modelling the evolution of shopping centre sizes. It now started to become clear that there was another situation where bifurcation phenomena could be important: at a critical parameter value, the nature of the *solution* might change. The earlier analysis could be incorporated as a special case: the appearance or disappearance of stable equilibrium values for particular zones in the differential equation system. It turned out that there were indeed other possible forms of transition – from stable equilibrium to periodic solutions if the equations were represented in difference equation form, and the nature of this phenomenon was obtained from a study of Robert May's work in ecology – again illustrating the potential methodological contribution of other disciplines.[17]

The shopping centre work was a 'typical' example in that the same kinds of methods could in principle be applied to other urban sub-models. The long term programme for building a comprehensive and general model of cities was moving into another phase. Potentially, this work offers a detailed model of the evolution of urban spatial structure, the overall features of which are deterministic, but within which stochastic features enable a great variety of possible patterns to be generated.

It is useful to conclude with two general observations which arise out of this account. First, it is interesting to stand back and to compare this route for tackling a particular general problem with the more traditional one in geography: central place theory, which had been applied at both inter-urban and intra-urban scales. This theory had been largely a static one, and had been unsatisfactory in its account of dynamics or system evolution. The difference between the two approaches can, with hindsight, be seen to be one of choice of *system representation*. In central place theory, space is treated largely in a continuous way, while in the spatial interaction and activity (SIA) models space is treated as a set of discrete units. The different mathematical representation in the second case is then more amenable to an adequate treatment of dynamical topics.[18]

Second, it is clear that my own research programme, as described above, has moved away from direct involvement in planning in the sense that the most recent work (because insufficient empirical work has been done) cannot be handed to planners as a tool –the earlier work on spatial interaction and location models, on spatial demography and on optimum location methods had all had very direct application. What is clear, however, is that it offers the possibility of a new perspective for planning which may, in the end, be of greater importance than the detail of any particular model. This is best explained from the basis of a brief description of the typical use of models in planning in the past.

Usually, models are used in planning as the basis for making *conditional forecasts*. These are predictions on the basis of assumed values of exogenous variables or parameters, some of which will represent a particular plan. Thus, models can be used to assess the impact of a plan. The shorter the time horizon, the more effective this procedure is likely to be. Otherwise, the predictions of the model are likely to be overtaken by unforeseen events, like oil price rises. The new dynamic perspective, however, offers a concern not entirely with forecasting (ironically?!) but with stability and criticality, with what Holling has called 'resilience'.[19] How stable are urban structures to parameter change? Do we want to 'encourage' change in particular parameters to attempt to achieve evolution to a new structure? And so on. But to achieve this perspective, the planner needs to have a working dynamical model system as part of his armoury.

Models in Quantitative Geography: An Evaluation

Much of the criticism of 'quantitative geography' has come from people who have chosen, often interestingly, to focus on alternative methods and perspectives – for example, Marxian approaches. Much of this work will have relevance in relation to mathematical modelling and I will take up this issue in the next section. Much of the criticism, however, is directed at the work of the 1950s and 1960s (a lot of this style of work is still taught and still appears in the journals); many of the critics do not have a picture of the steady, indeed often dramatic, progress which has been made since the 1950s and particularly are the post decade. The volume is intimidating. I recently started to compile a bibliography to write a review chapter on spatial interaction models and associated network equilibrium models. A first trawl produced over 500 references (all of them 'geographical', but not all by geographers). This story could be repeated in relation to many sub-systems and methods. My first plea, therefore, is that judgements should be made in relation to the full range of achievement.

This is not to argue, however, that a 'satisfactory' position has been reached. As in many fields of research, progress uncovers deeper and harder problems and we now stand on the threshold of some of these. Here, I begin with the broadest of sketches of the progress which has been made, and then assess prospects in relation to these harder problems in the next section. I use my own field of urban and regional geography as the basis of illustration.

Most of our modelling problems are, in Weaver's sense, complex.[20] Much more progress has been made with so called 'disorganised' systems (or with systems which can be treated in this way to a fair degree of approximation). There are reasonably effective spatial demographic models and inter-regional economic input-output models (though neither has yet been applied on a very substantial scale). Models describing the location of person activities and spatial interaction exist in a variety of forms – there will usually be at least a reasonable starting point for any problem formulated in this area. The location of economic activity – a problem of *organised* complexity because of the degree of interdependence between units – has proved a more difficult modelling problem, though some progress has been made in relation to the location of public facilities using both mathematical programming methods and various kinds of dynamic analysis.

In some of these cases, it would help if the models and methods were used more systematically in historical geography, since relating the models to different (or longer) time periods would throw up new theoretical problems and force new insights. I have also argued that there is a case for the resurgence of regional geography in the sense of working with linked sets of models on whole regional systems instead of, as is more usually the case, on sub-systems (though this is easier said than done because of the scale of effort involved).

In general terms, I am arguing that there are grounds for optimism. However, a full evaluation requires both more tests and empirical work on the one hand, and a systematic comparison of alternative models (using something like the 'frameworks' discussed above) on the other. These are both tasks involving monumental efforts which are difficult to mount. More importantly, perhaps, the prospects for future development of the field have to be measured against a range of more radical critiques, and it is to thse that I now turn.

Radical critiques

We can take 'radical', following Raymond Williams, to mean something concerned with 'vigorous and fundamental change' and a radical critique to be therefore directed to such an end. It is useful to identify three kinds of radical perspective. The first is a 'conventional' argument that something is wrong with the new model based planning technology: 'quantitative geography' has failed to produce an analytical basis for planning, it has failed to be useful. The second is based on the idea that there has been a major shift of goals – either in the minds of planners or more broadly in society. Concerns with equity and with the quality of the environment are offered (by Hall, for example) as illustrations.[21] Third, it can be argued that a broadly Marxist perspective offers more opportunities for radical change, both in analytical and in political sense.

We can identify a number of inter-related broad issues which can be tackled from these various perspectives. First, there is the argument that urban modellers have failed to focus on the main processes of urban development, and in particular have neglected to study the influence of some of the most significant agents participating in those processes. Second, it is argued that urban analysts have not focused sufficiently effectively on topics which are central to planning. Third, an inadequate account is offered of the political processes within which planning systems are embedded. Fourth, and finally, there is the more serious charge referred to earlier that the 'new methods' have actually exacerbated urban problems. There is a slightly weaker but nonetheless damaging version of this (analogous to wilful neglect): by focusing on less important topics, planners have somehow 'allowed' certain urban problems to develop and to get worse. We consider these issues in turn and illustrate them with examples, first from the conventional and second from a Marxist viewpoint. The arguments of those who argue that perspectives have shifted will be largely picked up under the 'conventional' heading.

As an example of the kinds of agents neglected by urban modellers, consider the financial institutions which are part of the urban development process. Property has been an important form of investment for both individuals and institutions – it can be argued that the peculiarities of the property market, and the acquiescence of local authorities and government departments in a process which allowed developers to make 'abnormal' profits, have generated much of the present form of city centres. And it can also be shown that building societies, for example, through their 'red lining' policies (developed they would argue in relation to their own concept of security of investment) have inhibited private investment in inner city residential areas. The issue is: Are these kinds of determinants more important than those represented in urban models? To which we can add: Would an analysis of these kinds of agents show that the predictions of urban models are analytically unsound?

It is in relation to the second issue that we can pick up various forms of 'alternative society' perspectives. It may be argued from such a viewpoint that the methods of spatial planning are all right in the terms of their original conception, but that the basis has now shifted. The new viewpoints vary from the essentially physical and ecological concerns with resource availability and environmental quality, to a broader concern with the 'quality of life', which embraces environmental goals but is also concerned with equity topics. And yet somehow there is an apparent tendency for the concern with equity which comes from this direction to be 'above' conventional politics. It is also mixed up with a not very clearly articulated view that there is an alternative lifestyle which is 'superior'. This can be 'taken' and adopted by those who can afford it – Californian dropouts or Highland crofter immigrants, for example – but which is also perhaps assumed without clear justification as a goal for all. The complication is that an active majority do not accept the alternative: even this brief argument shows that the 'alternative' perspectives vary enormously.

There is also an important critique of modern analytical planning methods which has a more conventional basis, and may be all the more powerful for that. This is the argument that the methods are not focussed on those aspects of urban systems which should be most important for planning. Harvey, for example, in the 'liberal' part of his book *Social Justice and the City* argues for a stronger focus on 'real income'.[22] This is to be interpreted as including measures of accessibility to different kinds of opportunities and of the effects of various external factors as well as money income.

The third issue was that model-based urban planners operate with an ineffective picture of the political processes of which they are a part and also fail to take account of the political influence on what they see to be 'professional' matters. There are many variants of this. Planners are sometimes accused of seeking 'value-free' solutions to problems when the political context makes this impossible (and indeed undesirable). Or they are sometimes accused of imposing their own values on a population which may not share them. The central issue, however, is concerned with 'power'. It is obviously important to know more about power structures in relation to decisions about urban development. This then relates very closely to the first issue: Is it a consequence of existing power structures and relations that the form of urban development is determined largely by factors other than those represented in urban models? What are the implications of this for planning?

The fourth issue was, essentially: Is there any evidence that the applications of new planning methods have made problems worse? Probably no one is arguing that, if this has happened, it has been deliberately engineered. So the nature of the charge is: Are the new methods so bad in some respects (through the models not reflecting the main processes of change) that their application will actually lead to problems becoming worse? We proceed by looking at two examples: the application of transport models, and the acceptance of the 'suburbanisation' solution for urban development.

A crude way of posing the question in relation to transport models and their application in the major conurbation studies is: Did the studies create or support the urban motorway system and associated infrastructure, and if so (and with hindsight) was this unreasonable? It can fairly easily be argued that the models were used in an inadequate framework of cost benefit analysis. For example, some goals were not adequately represented – the impact on environmental quality, for instance. Indeed, in the early days before cost–benefit analysis, it can be argued that the main goal was the relief of congestion and that road building has not in fact solved this problem (though the question as to whether we are better off with congested motorways than no motorways at all is an interesting one). It can also be argued that, through a crude belief in the consumer surplus concept, the weights of the cost–benefit process were wrong: that what happened in the studies were that the 'relief of congestion' goals of the middle classes commuting to centre cities were met, while insufficient recognition was given to the accessibility problems (through urban form and through the run down of the public transport systems) of those without cars. It could now be argued that this recognition could have been achieved only by giving more unit weight to the costs (in 'real income' terms) of the non-car owners. But this is not an argument against models so much as one for improvements in the surrounding planning processes. It can also be argued that the models have been significantly wrong: that predicted responses are likely to be wrong no matter how good the statistical fits in the base year if some of the underpinning relations are absent or wrong. This research needs to be incorporated in our view of 'best practice' with models.

There is a stronger argument still from a Marxist perspective. This anticipates some of the discussion below, but is conveniently taken here while the example is in front of us. It can be argued that, because of some of the inherent tendencies in capitalist societies – such as the declining rate of profit – there is always pressure from capital for more rapid circulation. The state 'supports' capital in this by appropriate forms of transport development; and transport modellers 'support' the state by using their models simply to extrapolate the *status quo*. It is also sometimes argued that a lively motor industry is essential to a capitalist economy, and that this is another reason why the state, in supporting capital, supports more road building; and that transport planners have gone along with this because they have not recognised the underlying causes.

The second example referred to suburbanisation in its typical western form, and the questions to be put are: Was there an alternative? And if so: Have planners missed it through inadequate methodology? The question arises from two or possibly three angles. It is often argued that suburban life has all sorts of problems associated with it and that there is, potentially, a 'better' quality of life. This usually involves a return to 'communities' and is perceived by a usually intellectual' subset of the middle class who see themselves and the 'good life' as metropolitan (possibly with country cottage added) rather than suburban. It is part, in other words, of the second groups of attacks. It is not clear whether a majority of present suburban residents would share this view. A second angle is from the planning side: that there should be alternatives, and that they can be designed. Unfortunately (if we forgive some oversimplification) it is this school which has generated, for example, high rise developments in many locations. The successful alternative is not, therefore, visible. The third angle on this question again involves our anticipating the Marxist viewpoint. There, one form of argument runs: The present form of western cities is a characteristic outcome of the nature of the capitalist mode of production in the late 20th century. There are, therefore, alternatives to be had, but only by understanding at a deeper level than hitherto the causes of suburban development, and probably only by transforming the form of the mode of production in some substantial way. There is also a related argument, to which we shall return, about the extent to which those who live in the suburbs and report pleasure from the experience can be believed in relation to their 'consciousness' of the 'choices' they actually make. In summary, if this is a charge against planners it turns on first, failure to understand the nature of suburbanisation; second, design failure to imagine alternative futures which are acceptable; or third, failure to recognise that alternatives are doomed because of the inherent lack of influence of planners on the main dimensions of capitalist development. As in the transport case, because insufficient depth of understanding is available planners resort to models which are, in effect, trend projections and therefore by their nature 'support' the *status quo*.

Although elements of the Marxist radical critique have crept into the argument above, most of it could have been conducted without the benefits of Marxist analysis. The next task is therefore to explore what can be added to the argument from a Marxist perspective. We will then be in a position, in the next section, to respond to the critique as offered by both conventional and Marxist viewpoints, and at that stage we will attempt to assess how much of the criticism to accept, the extent to which it matters, and the impact it ought to have on our future approaches to spatial planning methods – both in practice and in research.

The Marxist approach is, in fact, a broad spectrum of possible approaches. They perhaps share some common characteristics, or modes of approach to analysis. What they offer (or claim to offer) relative to the conventional approach is alternative underpinning theory and, in some cases at least, deeper theory. Here we attempt to sketch some of the main ideas which may be found in such approaches. In different Marxist approaches, different points will be emphasised. Here a selection we note related as we go to the four issues already discussed in more conventional terms above.

The first focus of a Marxist analysis is likely to be the concept of a 'mode of production' and the notion that it has a distinctive dynamic which follows from the existence of a set of social relations necessarily engendered by it. A product of this kind of analysis of capitalism leads to the notion of class struggle and conflict as being one of the main agents of change and development. Capital has to respond to these conflicts and the crises which arise as a consequence of, for example, the (predicted) falling rate of profit. There are a number of very interesting questions about the precise nature and distinctiveness of a mode of production and in particular about the nature of the transformations from one to another. It can be argued, for example, that Marx's own predictions of the transformation of capitalism to socialism have not worked out; but also that late 20th century capitalism is very different from the 19th-century version – and that it may even constitute a new mode.

Ironically, it seems to me – brought up in a different tradition – that these arguments smack of systems theory: the emphasis on the need to specify social relations between the components of the system of interest, and that the dynamic behaviour of the system follows from an analysis of these relations. Indeed, it can now be argued that Marx, in focusing on the transformations between different modes of production, anticipated (in essence) bifurcation theory! But more of that in another context below.

There are some consequences of this approach for urban analysis, and the best known example of its application in this way is in David Harvey's *Social Justice and the City*.[23] In the terms of this discussion, its main immediate contribution relates to the notion of focusing on the main agents of the system, and the argument that urban modellers have failed to do this. It also has a number of other implications which are picked up in later Marxist themes below.

A second kind of theme is concerned with the theory of the state. The Maxist argument is that a deeper understanding is needed, a deeper level theory, in order to comprehend what planning is and how (or whether) it can be effective. Most Marxist theorists see the state as necessary to resolve conflicts between classes and to serve a number of other functions, but all essentially in support of capital. At a fundamental level, it is argued that the state is needed to support the reproduction of labour and the circulation of capital, for example. At the very least, it is argued that the role of the state is something more complicated than that of referee or arbitrator on behalf of the people as a whole. Scott has argued strongly, for instance, that planning practice must be seen in the light of an analysis of partisan role of the state.[24] So this kind of argument has a major bearing on the third of our themes above which was concerned with political processes: a deeper understanding of the role of the state is needed so that the possibilities of planning can be better understood.

A third theme in Marxist analysis is concerned with change in a more direct way: to add to the kind of theory which can be sketched about the nature of modes of production and the state and to begin to make predictions about the forms of change. Traditional Marxist theory is often associated with the idea that the determinants of change lie in the economic base of society, and not in the superstructure (of which 'planning' would be a part). Marxist theorists from Engels onwards have qualified this crude 'economism' and have argued that, while this may be the prime determinant, changes in the superstructure can be important and can, in some circumstances, bring about transformation. But whatever the outcome of that particular argument, there is a consequence of this style of analysis which has to be taken on board by modellers. That is: the way a society develops depends on relative power – whether in the representatives of capital in both the economic base and the superstructure, or (as is more likely in the greater complexity of late 20th-century capitalism) in a complex of classes and sub-classes. These ideas can be useful theoretical developments (though an aggregate version of them may add up to something like traditional Marxism).

How does this bear on our earlier issues? First, it can be argued that if the power bases of a society are not understood, then planning in the name of problem solving is more likely in the event to be in support of the most powerful groups; or at least will fail to obtain and distribute resources in such a way that the problems of the less powerful groups are likely to be alleviated. This is almost certainly very near what has happened in the last 20 years. So if we return to the question about why the new methods have not resolved any of the obvious problems, then the answer probably is more to do with the nature of power balances than of techniques. It is possible, in these circumstances, that the new techniques have been used, unconsciously, to support the *status quo*, to reinforce it.

A fourth theme involves the possibility of alternative forms of society. Marx has always been seen as offering a particular alternative vision together with the argument that a socialist or communist state will necessarily follow from the crises of a capitalist one. Closer analysis, as authors like Miliband and Williams have shown, indicate that this is not the case.[25] Further, when transformations have taken place, as in Eastern Europe, they have been to a form of state capitalism rather than to 'socialism' in any true sense. What this exposes is the need for hard thinking (and ultimately practice) about the question of what a truly 'socialist' state would actually look like. There is a need to invent new kinds of institutions.

Two more themes should be mentioned briefly. First, Marx was very concerned with the alienating effects of the capitalist mode of production and saw the need to return to human scales in some way. Miliband argued that there was a sense in which this kind of mission seemed more important to him than socialism, and that this may be one of the reasons why there is relatively little political argument in Marx.[26] This also links closely to a difficult, and in some ways dangerous, notion of 'consciousness' (which was mentioned earlier in the discussion on the suburbs). It is possible to argue that the alienated worker is not 'conscious' of his position and the alternatives. This is important, because there may be many respects in which this is true for all of us. It is dangerous because it is a very difficult thing to test and because it can then be used by a small minority to act politically 'on behalf of' an alienated majority without popular support. This is a knot which is difficult to untie.

The implications for planning are clear, but as difficult to apply as in any other part of politics.

The second subsidiary theme relates to method. Harvey, for example, argues that Marx's most important contribution is his use of the dialectical method because this facilitates the resolution of the contradictions which continually face the urban analyst. This seems to me the least important feature of Marx's work. It seems a reasonable conjecture that Marx, working in the 19th-century, used the available tools of his research and, working in Germany, was influenced by Hegelian philosophy. If he had started work in Vienna in the 1930s and completed his work in the United States in the 1960s, it would not seem at all surprising to me if he had started out as a logical positivist and then added to this position from the tools of systems analysis! He could have produced essentially the same results in a different language.

A final remark is a preliminary to more formal responses: I am sure there is an immense amount to learn from a broadly Marxist perspective and the rest of this discussion is written in this spirit. It also seems to be the case that many Marxist critics of planning methods use a particular technique which is worth a comment: they label those methods by particular characteristics – positivist, functionalist, instrumentalist and so on. Unfortunately, they often misunderstand the methods they are criticising in this respect, and in some cases – 'positivist' being a notorious example – they misunderstand the label they are attaching, unsolicited, to other people's work. The technique can broadly be described as having a close affinity with that of setting up an Aunt Sally and knocking it down. We will try not to proceed in the same way!

Responses, Prospects: Towards a Research Programme

It is perhaps as well to begin with the defensive part of a response, and to get it out of the way. Some of the criticism of the new methods has been directed against mathematical modelling as such. This is mistaken. Whatever the underlying base of theory, mathematical techniques are likely to be needed to handle the complexity which exists. They will also be needed within planning frameworks to guarantee that the most efficient solutions are found for achieving whatever goals are sought. Anything inefficient means that resources are being squandered. It can also be argued that some of the Marxists' attacks are mistaken, usually because of errors of interpretation arising from the use of different languages in different camps. It is nearly always a mistake to make an argument turn on language (and assume that one's own is the 'correct' one) since there are often alternatives and the important thing is to discover what the real points of substance are. An example of this is the Marxist critique of the new planning technology as positivist and 'value-free'. 'Positivism' to me, for example, is a branch of philosophy concerned with the nature of verification and falsifiability. Its main use is to eliminate meaningless metaphysical statements. This does not imply that it cannot be concerned with 'value'. It can be argued that values are determined by experience, and such experience is very much a matter for real empirical investigation. So the critique here is based on misunderstanding.

In the main, however, the defensive part of the response is a very mild one. By way of summarising the other side, we can return to the main heads of the critique and note the extent to which it has to be accepted. First, it is likely that some 'main agents' have been neglected. Second, insufficient attention has been paid to measuring planning sensitive notions like 'real income'. Third, insufficient attention has been paid to the political processes of which planning is a part. Fourth, it may well be that because of combinations of errors arising out of the first three heads, some problems have been made worse. So much has to be done to rectify deficiencies. We tackle this first by summarising the prospects for urban modelling in particular, and then by discussing some of the issues in more detail as a framework for ongoing research.

The first point to argue strongly is that there are many well defined planning problems for which mathematical modelling and associated planning techniques are eminently suitable. These would include, for example, the spatial planning of major public services e.g. the health and education services, both of which are currently subject to (different) demographic pressures at a time when public resources are not easily available for appropriate reorganisation. And yet something will have to be done. Second, many of the models are open to substantial improvement. If theories can be well stated about the influences of new agents, then these can be included. If the new information does not lend itself to mathematical form, then new 'hybrid' models and theories will have to be developed for analysis and for use in planning. Third, it can be argued that modellers are at the point of major breakthrough in their understanding of the broad mechanisms of evolution of urban structure. This is particularly important in relation to many past criticisms, because much has been made of the fact that most operational models are not 'dynamic' (in contrast supposedly, say, to a Marxist approach). The new 'evolutionary' models are explicitly dynamic. They can be constructured now using new techniques from applied mathematics which have become only recently available. It should then be said that one consequence of these advances is that it makes it more clear than ever how difficult 'prediction' is. This does mean that the traditional mode of use of models in planning may shift from a concern with forecasting to one which focuses on the analysis of stability and resilience.

What does all this add up to in terms of research priorities? First, it should be possible to mount a number of effective demonstration projects in the well defined areas where the new planning technology can make obvious contributions. It would be particularly helpful if this could be combined with another programme of central government-led research on the linking of research products with planning practice, and on the creation of environments within planning agencies which were capable of using the new technology most effectively. This can be summarised as 'good demonstrations' plus 'best practice research'.

Second, effort could be put into an assessment of detailed criticisms of models (with much more detail than has been possible in this broad discussion) with a view to exploring how the results of such investigations can be incorporated into models or alternative hybrid instruments of analysis. This would involve dealing with currently missing main 'agents', 'processes' which are not built in, power structures, the effective processes for the distribution and redistribution of 'real income' and so on. In many of these cases, the differences between traditional approaches and new ones turn not so much on whether there are algebraic equations or not, but on the interpretation of key terms, and decisions about which are 'driving terms' and so on.[27]

Third, a programme of fundamental research should be encouraged which builds on current breakthroughs in the understanding of the evolution of urban spatial structure.

Fourth, urban modellers should be more explicitly connected to the existing research programme on the theory of the state and the associated political processes. Modelling and this kind of research into politics should not be seen as separate and polarised fields.

A general comment can usefully be made which affects a number of the above research proposals. Urban analysts should be prepared to take on the radical critique in its own terms. There are a number of reasons for this. First, because it is important that major critiques be responded to; second, many radical practitioners are not going to operate in the language of modelling, and it is probably easier for modellers to attempt the reverse process; third, syntheses are nearly always fruitful.

With these proposals and with this comment in mind, we can now identify a fifth area of research, and one of the most important. This could be called 'issues' research. It involves a direct attack on issues and possible policies. Sometimes, the new planning technology will be relevant to this; but often, as Harvey points out in a telling passage, we *do know* what the problems are without carrying out any more factor analyses or model runs.[28] We have seen as part of the above argument that the reason why progress has not been made in many cases is essentially political and not technical. In a programme of 'issues' research, this could be pointed out forcefully. Here perhaps lies the answer to civil servants, and occasionally politicians, who are continually seeking research which is relevant to short run policy issues. Often, they seek this because they are not prepared to face the deep political nature of the problems under discussion. We can use the fruits of our present knowledge to make clear what the options are and the nature of the political choices which are involved. If and when major changes of direction are made, or resources rather than lip service are made available, then the planning technology will often be available to proceed in an efficient manner.

Notes and References

1. G.J. Chapman, *Human and Environmental System* (London: Academic Press, 1977).
2. I try to sketch this argument in A.G. Wilson, *Geography and the Environment: Systems Analytical Methods* (Chichester: John Wiley, 1981). Here, and in most of the subsequent discussion, I cite my own work or that of Leeds' colleagues. This is for economy only, and because the approach is autobiographical. The bibliographies in the works cited contain a much wider range of references, and should provide a broader access to the literature.

3. W. Weaver, 'A quarter century in the natural sciences', Annual Report of the Rockefeller Foundation, New York (1958) pp. 7–122.

4. I.S. Lowry, *A Model of Metropolis* (Santa Monica: RAND Corporation, 1964).

5. R.C. Tolman, *The Principles of Statistical Mechanics* (Oxford University Press, 1938).

6. The original 'spark', I think, was the notion that balancing factors looked rather like partition functions in statistical mechanics.

7 . A.G. Wilson, *Entropy in Urban and Regional Modelling* (London: Pion, 1970).

8. A.G. Wilson, 'A family of spatial interaction models', *Environment and Planning*, vol. 3 (1971) pp. 1–32.

9. S. Evans, 'A relationship between the gravity model for trip distribution and the transportation problem in linear programming', *Transportation Research*, vol. 7 (1973) pp. 39–61.

10. A.G. Wilson and M. Senior, 'Some relationships between entropy maximising models, mathematical programming models and their duals', *Journal of Regional Science*, vol. 14 (1974) pp. 207–15.

11. P.H. Rees and A.G. Wilson, *Spatial Population Analysis* (London: Edward Arnold, 1976).

12. A.G. Wilson, P.H. Rees and C.M. Leigh (eds), *Models of Cities and Regions* (Chichester: John Wiley, 1977). The structure of this parallels my earlier attempt to chart the urban and regional modelling field, in A.G. Wilson, *Urban and Regional Models in Geography and Planning* (Chichester: John Wiley, 1974).

13. The original shopping model structural equilibrium problem is described in J.D. Coelho and A.G. Wilson, 'The optimum size and location of shopping centres', *Regional Studies*, vol. 10 (1976) pp. 413–21; the embedding theorem is in J.D. Coelho, H.C.W.L. Williams and A.G. Wilson, 'Entropy maximising submodels within overall mathematical programming frameworks: a correction', *Geographical Analysis*, vol. 10 (1978) pp. 195–210. This was part of a much broader set of concerns with the role of optimisation methods in urban and regional modelling, which are collected together in A.G. Wilson, J.D. Coelho, S.M. Macgill and H.C.W.L. Williams, *Optimisation in Locational and Transport Analysis* (Chichester: John Wiley, 1981).

14. J. Forrester, *Urban Dynamics* (MIT Press, 1969).

15. R. Thom, *Structural Stability and Morphogenesis* (MIT Press, 1973).

16. B. Harris and A.G. Wilson, 'Equilibrium values and dynamics of attractiveness terms in production-constrained spatial-interaction models', *Environment and Planning A*, vol. 10 (1978) pp. 371–88.

17. R.M. May, *Stability and Complexity in Model Ecosystems* (Princeton University Press, 1973).

18. Much of my own work on different aspects of dynamics, including new approaches to central place theory, is described in A.G. Wilson, *Catastrophe Theory and Bifurcation: Applications to Urban and Regional Systems* (London: Croom Helm, 1981).

19. C.S. Holling, *Resilience and Stability of Ecological Systems*, IIASA Research Report (1973).

20. W. Weaver, 'A quarter century in the natural sciences'.

21. P. Hall, *Urban and Regional Planning* (Harmondsworth: Penguin, 1974).

22. D. Harvey, *Social Justice and the City* (London: Edward Arnold, 1973).

23. D. Harvey, *Social Justice and the City*.

24. A.J. Scott, *The Urban Land Nexus and the State* (London: Pion, 1980).

25. R. Miliband, *The State in Capitalist Society* (London: Quartet, 1969); and *Marxism and Politics* (Oxford University Press, 1977).

26. R. Miliband, *The State in Capitalist Society*.

27. For example, Leontief *v.* Sraffa; Keynes *v.* Freidman.

28. D. Harvey, *Social Justice and the City*.

Index

absolute space 6
Aberystwyth (University College
  of Wales) 110, 111
Acker, S. 185
Adams, J. 45
Adorno, T. 108
Alexandersson, G. 101
alienation 74, 179, 220
Allen, R. G. D. 41
Alonso, W. 93
American Geographical Society
  142, 143, 144
American Sociological Association
  157
analysis of variance 128
Anders, G. 177
*Annals of the Association of
  American Geographers* 43,
  62, 64, 84
Antioch College 91, 96
Antipode 130
Association of American
  Geographers 46, 62, 91,
  114, 130
anthropology 29, 36, 60, 67, 70,
  92, 158
architecture 106, 149
Area 114
areal differentiation 6, 28, 37,
  122
Arnoux, L. 178
'aristoscience' 156-8, 185, 191
astronomy 180
astrophysics 143, 144
attitude surveys 189

Banton, M. 108
Baran, P. 162
Barnes, B. 13, 14, 15, 16, 17
Bedford 108
behavioural approach 48, 99,
  114
behavioural geography 181

behavioural psychology 84
behavioural revolution 47
behavioural sciences 181
Benjamin, B. 111
Berkeley 90-5, 97, 100, 101,
  103 n7
Berkeley School 99
Berlin, I. 161
Berry, B. J. L. 10, 43, 50, 58,
  60, 61, 62, 63, 66, 93, 96,
  109, 113, 122, 126
Bhaskar, R. 183
bifurcation theory 218
biogeography 32
biographical approach 21
Blalock, H. 44
Bleicher, J. 18, 19
Bogardus, E. S. 108
Bogue, D. 105
Bourdieu, P. 182-2, 189
Bowen, E. G. 109
Boyce, R. 58
Buchanan, K. 46
Bunge, W. 41, 46, 58, 59, 62,
  146
Burgess, E. W. 42, 45, 47,
  106-7, 156
Bracey, H. E. 41
Bristol *see* University of
  Cambridge
Brown, L. 127
Burton, I. 6

Canberra 27, 30, 32
capitalism 78, 156, 162, 166-7,
  169, 173, 179, 180, 189, 193,
  216, 217, 218, 220
Carlson, A. 58
Carlyle, T. 156
Carroll, J. 162
Carter, H. 110
cartography 60, 63, 105, 119,
  126, 149